Mr. Chandler...

Gorgeous—

I admire the path
you have chosen..—
I accept your
ability to choose.—
I wonder if
you see the end.?,?,)
and I consider
maybe you see it clearly—
Let me know!!
I am interested
in the end - Millenium—
- May it come slowly

LIFE IN THE
SLOW LANE

LIFE IN THE SLOW LANE

Observations on
Art, Architecture, Manners and
Other Such Spectator Sports

RUSSELL LYNES

Cornelia & Michael Bessie Books
An Imprint of HarperCollins*Publishers*

"The Culturettes" was first published in *Art in America,* January 1970, in Russell Lynes's column, "The State of Taste."

"U" and "Non-U" was first published as the Introduction to *Noblesse Oblige* by Nancy Mitford, Harper & Brothers, 1956.

"Things" was first published in *Horizon,* 1969, vol. 11, no. 1, by American Heritage, a division of Forbes, Inc.

"Thurber's Bread and Butter" was originally published under the title "The Man Who Made *The New Yorker*" © 1959 by The New York Times Company, reprinted by permission.

"E. B. White, My Meat" was originally published under the title "The Divided Life of Stuart Little's Father" © 1984 by The New York Times Company, reprinted by permission.

"The Art of Accepting" courtesy *Vogue* © 1952 (renewed 1980) by The Condé Nast Publications, Inc.

"Shaping Popular Tastes" reprinted from *The Phenomenon of Change,* Lisa Taylor, ed. Cooper-Hewitt Museum, The National Museum of Design, Smithsonian Institution. © 1984, The Smithsonian Institution.

FIRST EDITION

Designed by Helene Berinsky

Library of Congress Cataloging-in-Publication Data

Lynes, Russell, 1910–
    Life in the slow lane : observations on art, architecture, manners
  and other such spectator sports/Russell Lynes. — 1st ed.
      p.   cm.
    "Cornelia and Michael Bessie books."
    ISBN 0-06-039122-7
    1. United States—Civilization—1970–   2. Lynes, Russell, 1910–.
      I. Title.
  E169.12.L96   1991
  973.92–dc20   90–55544

91 92 93 94 95 MV/HC 10 9 8 7 6 5 4 3 2 1

For
Elodie and Robert Osborn

Contents

III

IV

Preface

The earliest of the essays in this casual book date from the early 1950s, but most of them were written and published in the 1970s and 1980s. By all odds the greatest number appeared in *Architectural Digest* for which I wrote a column called "Russell Lynes Observes." It went on for thirteen years (1974–1987), some 127 essays in all. All these pieces (well, almost all) have to do with the visual arts in one way or another, most particularly with the uneasy, often friendly, interplay of art and society, between artists and patrons, architects and clients, and also between art institutions and what they think of condescendingly as "the public"—you, that is, and me. This is not art history or sociology (which too often is the science of making the obvious unreadable) or criticism; it is reflections on people and places and things and ideas, written primarily for fun and, of course, for money. (Dr. Johnson said: "No man but a blockhead ever writes except for money.") The reader will not find any solemn pronouncements in these pages, which is not to say that my intentions are not infrequently serious. I hope the reader will be amused as well as informed and in some cases persuaded as well as provoked.

Some years ago (twenty-four to be precise) I put together a volume of essays, also mostly about the uneasy place of the arts in our culture. They were published as *Confessions of a Dilettante*. This book could be called *Volume Two* of those *Confessions*. I am a professional and professed dilettante and proud of it. There are millions of us— we are baseball fans and collectors of medieval ivories, tracers of lost comic books (early ones) and incunabula. We are "in it" and "with it," as they say, for the pleasure and gratification of searching and finding and enjoying. Join us.

I have divided the essays in this book into four somewhat arbitrary groups, each with a hint of cohesiveness. The table of contents

xi

is essentially a picnic menu from which to make random choices according to taste. The date and place of original publication is at the end of each piece. In some cases where additional identification seems to be needed it is with the title.

I wish to thank the publishers who have given me permission to reprint these essays and most particularly to thank the editors who invited me to write them.

North Egremont
April 1990

$$\overline{I}$$

Life in the Slow Lane

*S*ome years ago a magazine no longer published but then widely read and respected asked me to write a piece about the "rat race." I did and was paid for it, but it languished in the editor's "hold" file for a long time and then disappeared without a trace. My thesis, evidently not agreeable to the editor, was that each of us makes his own rat race, that it is not an inevitability imposed by the nature of society, and that those who are caught in it are there essentially because they choose to be.

There was one anecdote in my manuscript that I remember with pleasure but that the editor accused me of making up. I did not, but someone else may have. I had found a very small, tucked away item in a New York newspaper about a rat that had been placed in a sort of squirrel cage as a way to measure its endurance or stubbornness or perhaps its wit. Instead of running in the cylindrical innards of the cage as any self-respecting squirrel would have done, the rat simply amused itself by spinning the wheel with one of its paws and not running at all. That's my kind of rat, I thought.

I live in a city that I regard as *the* city and that is referred to with boring frequency as "a nice place to visit but I wouldn't want to live there." It is New York, of course, and as every New Yorker knows, for all its drawbacks (and when we have drawbacks we settle for nothing less than the spectacular) it is a nice place to live and an exhausting place to visit.

But then, like most New Yorkers, native or by adoption, I live in the slow lane and leave the rat race to others. Also, like most New Yorkers who love the place, I come from "somewhere else." (My wife is one of those rare New Yorkers who was actually born in Manhattan—on East Twentieth Street to be precise.)

I am one of what is called the "general public," the epithet applied to millions of us who go quietly about our daily business and who do not qualify for being conveniently pigeonholed by municipal, cultural, commercial, or religious pigeonholers. Life in the fast lane, I am given to understand, is not only glamorous but hectic, fiercely competitive, and traveled by men and women whose primary ambition is to be conspicuous. Being conspicuous means being at the "right" place at the "right" time with the "right" people and, with luck, getting your name and, even better, your face in the paper for being there. (It can, of course, mean being in the wrong place at the wrong time with the wrong people, but that is a different sort of fast lane and, generally speaking, as some insiders have recently discovered, to be avoided.)

But we members of the general public live in New York because it is invigorating sometimes; relaxing many times; occasionally exhausting but worth it; sometimes unbearably hot; sometimes, with the wind off our surrounding waters, cuttingly cold. For some newcomers it can be and often is extremely lonely and unconcerned, though usually not for long. New Yorkers are not automatic gladhanders; they are more like New Englanders in that respect than like Texans. They believe in privacy, others' as well as their own, and this sometimes seems unfriendly. More particularly, it is a matter of minding one's own business, which New Yorkers soon learn if they weren't brought up with it. To the young who come to town to make their careers, it can be bewilderingly frantic and grueling. It is a place that takes getting used to—an acquired taste, like bran muffins, and like bran muffins it can be both nourishing and good for the system. Unlike bran muffins it can also be dangerous or debilitating.

Like many great cities, New York is a collection of quiet villages that orbit around centers of intense activity. I live in one of those villages and have for forty-odd years. It is known as Yorkville and has been since it was a hamlet far to the north of what was New York in the 1790s. It came to be called the German section of town, and before the Second World War was notorious for its pro-Nazi sympathies, parades, and rallies. When I moved into the district in the 1940s, German was heard on Eighty-sixth Street, the district's main shopping boulevard, almost as frequently as English. This hasn't been true for years, and with the speakers of German have gone what was once a unique, for New York, congregation of excellent German restaurants and cafes. Eighty-sixth Street is now chain store and discount to a large degree, and has for me lost whatever charm it had. It is not hard to avoid.

One reason it's easy to stay away is that we don't need Eighty-sixth Street. Essentially ours is a village of small shops ("mom and pop" businesses, as New Yorkers say) and services—upholsterers, framers, locksmiths, butchers, and fishmongers who go to the markets at Fulton Street long before the sun is up. Within a half-mile radius of our house—set among remodeled brownstones and tenements, many of them built in the 1880s and 1890s, and an increasing number of faceless and characterless high-rises—are Italian, French, Indian, Greek, Czech, and Chinese (but not Hispanic; these are in other city villages or "quarters") restaurants of a quality that would command four stars in most American cities and that we take for granted. Many of them are superior in quality of cooking and service to more famous restaurants at more conspicuous addresses. It's nice to know they're there, but we use them rarely. By and large the "slow lane" prefers to dine at home. It does not feel impelled to go out to be "seen."

Those of us who live in the urban slow lane are walkers, not runners (or joggers), and I am pleased to note a sharp decline in the number of running suits topped with anguished faces that I encounter on my daily walks. I prefer walking in the city to walking in the country, where I spend part of my time (country walking is for hikers), because even though I follow the same general routes to achieve my minimum of a mile, they are always filled with surprises, discoveries, disappearances (New York is constantly tearing itself down), and private faces that, as the poet Auden said, "are wiser and nicer than public faces in private places."

My friends tell me that I should give up the lined yellow pads and portable typewriters I have been using for years and "get with it, buy a word processor." They say, "It will save you a lot of time." They don't say time for what. To rack my brains? To write more essays? More books? The fact of the matter is that I am in no hurry. I am not competing with anyone, not even with myself. I have things I want to get done one of these days, to be sure, but I enjoy my pace. I understand it and, as much as I am likely to, I understand myself. I have developed a tempo, a technique, and an acquired taste for living in the slow lane, and I see no earthly reason to live anywhere else.

Architectural Digest, 1987

On Collecting

A book arrived on my desk a few days ago that weighs five pounds, and I have turned over its five hundred illustrated pages with a mixture of pleasure, awe, skepticism, and near disbelief. It is a book of what in careless use of the language some have come to call "collectibles." These objects are of the expensive variety that one might, by the same token, be tempted to call "beautifuls." The title of the book is *Christie's Review of the Season 1979*.

It is not my intention to comment about what passed through Christie's auction rooms in London and New York on their ways from one collection to another upon the exchange, in many cases, of surprising amounts of money, but it suggests some speculation about the nature of one of man's most ancient self-indulgences. There are, I believe, just three reasons for collecting—and always have been. To name them is to say the obvious: they are love, greed, and ambition. And they rarely occur in pure and undiluted form.

First, about love: Some years ago I was lecturing at the Grand Rapids Art Museum, where there was an exhibition devoted to regional artists—artists, that is, who lived in that part of the country. I was asked by an attractive young couple—obviously a young couple on their way up—if they should purchase a landscape they had selected out of many other artworks in the exhibition.

"Do you love it?" I asked. "Is it something you think you are going to regret deeply if you don't buy?"

This was not at all what they wanted to hear from me. They wanted my opinion about whether it was "good" or "bad." There are plenty of art counselors who tell people whether they should be in love with an object—agents who make "marriages between art and innocents." I am not one of them.

Many collectors fall in and out of love with the objects they give their hearts to. They are the real collectors. They can't help themselves; they don't want to. In this sense, a boy can be in love with a beautiful pebble he found in a stream, or with a perfect shell from a beach, and he wouldn't part with it to his best friend. I have known a few collectors of drawings and photographs and paintings (fewer of furniture and bibelots) who in this respect have never "grown up." They have perfect confidence in their taste, but the candid among them admit that their taste changes, develops, rejects. Only real collectors will confess they can be wrong.

I was once in the house of such a collector, whom I scarcely knew, and I admired a small painting of a Venetian scene hung in his hallway. "It's a Guardi, isn't it?" I said, feeling rather smug. "I thought so when I bought it," he replied, "but now I don't think it's good enough to be a Guardi."

A collector's love is rarely pure and incorruptible. Those who dig a last nickel out of their jeans, as a boy will to buy a baseball card, are few among collectors, but there are some. They are interested in quality, not rarity, and while they like to share their treasure and their enthusiasm with others, their pleasure and satisfaction is in the object—not in the envy or admiration of their friends.

There is a distinction to be drawn between true collectors and accumulators. Collectors are discriminating; accumulators act at random. The Collyer brothers, who died among the tons of newspaper and trash with which they filled every cubic foot of their house so that they could scarcely move, were a classic example of accumulators, but there are many of us whose houses are filled with all manner of things that we "can't bear to throw away." I except pure accumulators from this discussion, but not accumulators who fall in love with collecting, who are obsessed by it, consumed by it—by the process, the hunt, the chase, the capture. It is the process as much as the quarry that fascinates them. They are the victims of the "collecting bug"—a not uncommon and very often incurable disease.

And greed? It inserts itself quietly, and sometimes it is the sole motive for collecting. Greed is the easiest of all motives to understand, and it has nothing to do with the arts, fine or decorative; it has only to do with trade, with investment, with making a buck. It is as old as the market for art. In ancient Athens, for example, Aristotle warned young collectors to beware of fake antiquities that were flooding the market. There is a rush of such greedy collecting at the moment—as the prices in the Christie's book seem to attest—

toward art as a substitute for bullion or precious gems. Perhaps greed is too strong a word for what in many cases is just caution, and in others is just good old dog-eat-dog free enterprise operating at its most unhindered. Nowhere is it freer than in the art market.

Ambition is more interesting than greed, and always has been. The ambitious collector, the one who searches for objects he hopes to love, is quite different from the collector whose ambition is to improve his social status by the arts with which he surrounds himself. It is this kind of ambition that characterizes a host and hoard of collectors—including the young couple in Grand Rapids.

One of the most ancient of reasons for collecting art is the desire to endow the collector with an aura of culture. According to Francis Henry Taylor, in his book *The Taste of Angels,* Alexander the Great, when he founded new cities, was "eager to acquire the reputation for a culture which hitherto they had not possessed," so he became "a collector of antiquities." Later, in the nineteenth century, the Industrial Revolution created a new kind of wealth not based on land, and, in an attempt to acquire a status equivalent to that of the landed gentry, the new tycoons bought "ancestors" to hang on their walls. But "ancestors" are not as important as "old masters" when it comes to status today. Old masters exude culture and wealth simultaneously, just as collectors of what is brand new and fashionable display adventurousness along with wealth. It all depends on the style by which a collector wants to adorn his ambitions, and whom he wants to impress. Such collectors depend heavily on the advice of "experts"—those marriage brokers of taste— and on dealers. Collecting for social status is probably the most prevalent of all motives for acquiring works of art; perhaps it always has been.

But, in the final analysis, all collecting is for love—love of what is collected, love of the process of collecting, love of secure wealth, and, finally, love of self. But let's not kid ourselves. There is something of all these kinds of love in all of us who admit that we are collectors.

Architectural Digest, 1980

The Museum in My Head

*L*ike many people with an interest in art, I carry an imaginary
museum around in my head. I change exhibitions frequently,
not in any orderly way, adding new pieces and putting old ones in
storage. I throw away very little, so that the place, if it can be called
that, is cluttered. One of the pleasant attributes of an imaginary
gallery is that it can be any size, and there is no maintenance or
upkeep and no worry about conservation. Nothing costs anything.
If the pictures I put in it sometimes gain in value and sometimes
decline, it is a matter of taste (call it whim, if you please)—my
taste—and any arguments about it are between my taste today and
my taste of yesterday.

It is almost impossible not to put what is in my museum in
categories—landscapes, genre, nudes, portraits or nonrepresenta-
tional, religious, mythical, still life, and decorative paintings. Though
I have some sculpture and some *objets de vertu* and a great many
drawings, that is about it, except for a very few photographs and
prints. My museum doesn't tend toward "multiples" of any sort. It
is a matter of playing favorites; I am under no pressure to put or
keep something in my museum because some critic, or generations
of connoisseurs and dilettantes, have declared it to be a masterpiece. One generation's masterpiece can obviously be the next generation's colossal bore, which does not change the nature of the
object in the least. Some acknowledged masterpieces, I suspect, have
always been bores, and have been treasured because some prophet
or prelate or politician or princess said, "This is a masterpiece, and
you shall admire it whether you want to or not."

I have been taking inventory recently, and some paintings have
turned up that I have not thought of for a long while. Some of
them are very agreeable surprises (when did that handsome Mars-
den Hartley *Black Duck* first turn up?), and a few I once thought

9

highly of—probably because I was taught that they were important, like the *Mona Lisa*—have lost their charms for me.

In making my inventory, I found out several things about my taste that probably apply in some degree and in various ways to everybody's taste. It is not just the inherent quality of a work of art that puts it in my museum. Indeed, I'm not sure I know what the "inherent quality" of a work of art is. Does anyone? Sometimes it is love at first sight. Pow! That happened to me many years ago in the Prado in Madrid when I wandered into a room of El Grecos, which, in my ignorance, I did not know were there. I was stunned, but I would have been more stunned if I had not already, in the Metropolitan Museum in New York, made friends with the Grecos that were part of the Havemeyer Collection—an acquisition made by the Metropolitan at a time when I first began to look seriously at pictures. The *View of Toledo* by El Greco is in my private museum—a friend of my youth, whose charm does not pale. So is that other Met Greco, the crusty old cardinal with the "full-view" spectacles that were reinvented in the twentieth century.

So surprise has something to do with my acquisitions, and so does frequent association that develops into sound friendship. Presumably, even such silly considerations as tired feet, a good lunch, a congenial companion, a sultry day, have an effect on how one reacts on first being confronted with a work of art. I have added to my museum very few objects that I have seen only once. By the time I have truly acquired them as parts of my permanent collection, I have come to know them well, and often under a variety of circumstances. They are the ones I find myself drifting toward, like the little Antonello da Messina of Saint Jerome seated in his study in the company of peaceable beasts and birds, with a view through his window of a placid Italian landscape. He is in the National Gallery in London, which houses a great many pictures in my collection: Piero della Francesca's *Nativity,* for instance, and the van Eyck portrait of Mr. and Mrs. Arnolfini—a marriage certificate, of sorts. The artist is witness to a ceremony that, in fifteenth-century Flanders, could be performed by a couple without benefit of clergy, a plighting of troth by holding hands in the presence of another person. It is both a double portrait and a genre picture. If the occasion were less solemn, it might be a "conversation piece." I have a conversation piece in my collection, painted by Gainsborough when he was a young man: a perky and elegantly dressed young couple under a tree in their private park.

There are no murals in my collection, no paintings that are permanently fixed to walls, no details, for example, out of the Giottos in Padua or the Pieros in Arezzo. They belong in public places, places of worship, not in my private "cabinet." But since someone removed Piero's *The Resurrection* from its wall and set it up by itself in Borgo San Sepolcro, I do not hesitate to adopt it. It is the most awe-inspiring picture of the Renaissance. For sheer power it is rivaled only by Tintoretto's *Crucifixion*, in the Scuola di San Rocco in Venice, but that canvas is fixed to the vast wall for which it was painted, and I have no place in my head big enough to accommodate it, much less comprehend it.

Very few paintings in my gallery are large ones. Titian's *Sacred and Profane Love* from the Borghese in Rome is fairly large; so is Rembrandt's *Portrait of a Lady with an Ostrich Feather Fan* in the National Gallery in Washington (I met it first when it was still in the Widener house, in Elkins Park, Pennsylvania) and his *Saul and David* in The Hague. But his red-chalk drawing of Cleopatra, which I "acquired" from Christie's for nothing last summer, several weeks before the J. Paul Getty Museum in Malibu bid it in for $573,000, is just a sheet of paper, about the size of this page. I prefer smallish landscapes to vast ones, Corot's *Port de la Rochelle* at Yale, for example, to Church's *Icebergs* in Dallas, which I would not have on my imaginary premises. Monet's crisp *La Terrasse à Sainte-Adresse* is at home in my gallery, though his amorphous lily ponds are not. Indeed, nothing is in the museum in my head because it *ought* to be, and I am as ruthless about deaccessioning what I've grown tired of, or found to be false, as I was enthusiastic about adding it to my collection in the first place. Accountability is not one of my museum's problems.

Architectural Digest, 1982

Museum Without Problems

S ome years ago I was in the British Museum to look for the first time at the freshly cleaned, newly installed Elgin Marbles. I was interested to see two elegant gentlemen with proprietary airs, several times my age, also inspecting them. They were Andrew Mellon, formerly our secretary of the treasury, and Lord Duveen of Millbank. Mr. Mellon was a client of Lord Duveen (art dealers, unlike other storekeepers, have clients, not customers), who had, in a patriotic gesture, paid for the restoration and installation of the sculptures from the frieze of the Parthenon. Like me, Mr. Mellon at that time had a museum in his head, though I did not know it. His was (and is) the National Gallery of Art in Washington, of which he was the founder.

The more I read about the anxieties of great museums in these times of inflation and diminishing subsidies, the greater is my satisfaction in the museum in my head. It is free from the meddling of politicians and pressure groups, and its only budget is for traveling expenses, which is one way I add to its collection, and for books and magazines. If I feel detached from the sufferings of the great museums, the good people who are trying to maintain them have my warmest sympathy and, to the extent I am able, my support. But they have got themselves in a bind at least partly of their own making. I commiserate with curators and directors for the pressures on them to bait their traps with the honey of blockbusters and cutely contrived exhibitions, because trustees, as well as politicians, care profoundly about how many people come through their doors—no matter how little satisfaction those people may take out. It is the turnstiles at the entrance of the supermarkets of art that matter, not the checkout counters. This is a dilemma my imaginary museum is spared.

Having taken a smug and somewhat lofty stance about public

museums, I admit the private museum I carry in my head is a conceit in both senses of the word—an indulgence of vanity, and a metaphor.

The museum in my head, while it contains my favorite works of art, leaves out all sorts of things about museums that I do not find congenial. Though I admit their usefulness to many others, I do not have to put up with them. There are no long and wordy labels that tell me what I ought to think. There are no electronic gadgets to tell me what I am looking at and give me no opportunity to talk back. There are no long corridors to make my feet ache in anticipation. There are no docents lecturing to huddles of ladies in hats or schoolchildren pinching each other. There are no couples reading diligently out of catalogues, with their eyes long on the printed page and short on the object in question. There are no supercilious aesthetes, who give the impression that no matter what they are looking at they have seen better examples elsewhere. I do not begrudge these people their pleasures in museums; to me, people-watching is an essential ingredient in any museum—except my own.

My museum is not arranged by schools or periods, and I constantly move things around. When there happen to be pictures side by side in my imaginary gallery, they are there for my pleasure, not to prove a point. If I put a Goya portrait next to a Manet, for example, it is not to demonstrate the former's influence on the latter, though the coincidence is likely to tell me things I had not known before about both painters. Occasionally I put Goya's *La Maja desnuda* (a favorite) next to Boucher's delicious *La Femme couchée* and the *Rokeby Venus* by Velázquez, because of what they say about how the unclothed female looked to three different periods and about their fashions in femininity. Usually they are in separate galleries in my head; together they are enough to swamp the id. Manet's *Olympia* does not belong with them, of course. Manet's nude courtesan attended by a servant is a parody of a Titian, an aesthetic shocker to some and a social outrage to others, much as Marcel Duchamp's *Nude Descending a Staircase* was a social and aesthetic outrage a couple of generations later. Both the Manet and the Duchamp are in my museum, and are sometimes juxtaposed.

There are a great many pictures that are by no stretch of the imagination masterpieces but are quite at home in my museum. Without dwelling on what is a rather tricky distinction, there is "good corn" and "bad corn" in paintings, as there is in theater. There is almost always an element of sentimentality in corn, and it is likely to surface at some time or other in the work of any artist with humor. One of the great pieces of corn is Ingres's little *Odalisque and the Slave*, an exquisitely painted bit of romantic nonsense in the Fogg Art Museum at Harvard. And who, on occasion, could be cornier than Picasso? The Tate Gallery in London, which is the home of dozens of Victorian narrative pictures, is a veritable cornfield of bathos—much of it beautifully painted. My favorite is a series of four pictures by Augustus Egg called *Past and Present*. They depict the ravages brought on a respectable family by a wife's indiscretion. Very different is Bronzino's *Venus, Cupid, Folly, and Time*, as loony a bit of ingenious composition and slick paintings as has ever been crowded into one canvas. I also happily make room for the antithesis of such conceits—genre pictures: Brueghel's *Peasant Wedding*, Winslow Homer's *Long Branch, New Jersey*, Renoir's *The Luncheon of the Boating Party*.

I will match the museum in my head against Mr. Mellon's National Gallery any time; not, to be sure, for range, but for quality in some respects and variety in others. On the other hand, if it weren't for great museums like Mr. Mellon's, I would have no museum at all.

Architectural Digest, 1982

Going Places Again

*I*t is a sentimental fallacy that attempting to recapture the past is inevitably a disappointment. "Don't go back there," we often hear (and say to ourselves). "It won't be as good the second time. In fact, it won't be at all the way you remember it."

Sometimes this is true; yet often it keeps us from pleasures we might enjoy more in the revival than in the remembering. Usually the experiences we think we can recapture have more to do with places than with people. (I'm not much for reunions; they are less likely to be reminders of times past than of time inexorably passing.) While places change, they are likely to change more slowly than people—physically, that is—even in this age of rampant "development." It is never possible to recapture the circumstances in which they were first encountered; it is, however, possible to rediscover them with a different excitement enriched by experience and spiced with anticipation.

The pleasure of travel, where I'm concerned, is as much in drawing comparisons as in making discoveries. The first time I saw the cathedral in Santiago de Compostela in the northwest corner of Spain, with its bold facade and soaring towers, I was in my early twenties. In the forty-odd years that intervened between then and seeing it again, I had learned a little about looking at architecture, though I do not think that was what made the second look so breathtaking. Part of my pleasure was unquestionably sentimental; part came from the false reassurance of apparent permanence. The facade, which was all I remembered, had not changed, although the plaza it faced had been tidied up. But this time I knew enough to understand that this was a "modern" facade. Behind it was a structure started in the eleventh century and remodeled and enlarged over the next five hundred years. The magnificent facade was a "false front" put on in 1738, and I couldn't help but think

15

how the eighteenth-century equivalents (if there were any in Compostela) of today's landmark preservationists would have howled at putting an elaborate Baroque front on what was basically a Romanesque building. Outrage! Desecration! But how splendid!

It would not be difficult for me or any other traveler to speak of places that were disappointing when revisited and others whose delights were not apparent the first time. Some of this disappointment, on the one hand, and delight, on the other, can be explained by the distinction between "sight-seeing" and "going places." A sight is a one-shot visual experience; a place is a social and, for many travelers, a religious experience. The Grand Canyon is a sight, as are the Swiss Alps, the Golden Gate Bridge, and the Taj Mahal, a building I would have liked to have seen more than I want to go see it. An almost inevitable attraction of a sight is its site. A place does not depend on an especially spectacular site, but this often increases its charm and fixes it permanently in the mind.

By and large I am a placegoer, not a sightseer, though there are sights I cherish in recollection. This is partly, I think, because I can take something to a place, some knowledge, some hope of learning (of having my senses sharpened), and a basketful of experiences to be used, as pedants say, for comparative purposes. I cannot take, as some experts can, anything to a sight but the willingness and expectation to have my eyes bedazzled by the spectacle. I don't dispute the pleasure of that sort of experience or the vividness of its images, which can stay in the mind's eye for years, but I confess that I am less moved by nature's spectacles than by what comes from the hand and mind of man, such as bridges, cultivated landscapes, temples, and tombs—sights though they may be.

Places do not happen all at once. They are not created by fiat the way temples and palaces are likely to be, but by slow hit-or-miss accretion. They are the residue of the needs and whims and aspirations, the failures and accomplishments, of layers of generations. I think of ruins as places, not as sights. They are narratives to which the final chapters have been written, as cities are narratives with their plots still unfolding.

There are places I go back to with increasing pleasure and others I have been to once and hope someday to visit again for long enough to befriend and understand them. I want to see again the medieval medina in Fez that bustles with commerce and ancient crafts and smells of roasting lamb and mint. I want to walk again through the wild anemones in the ruins of Olympia and look down on the orchards of blossoming almond trees from the Temple of Apollo at Delphi. I want to feel again the power and serenity of the vast mosque of Hagia Sophia in Istanbul, the greatest interior space I have ever experienced. I want to take the ferry across the Bosporus from Europe to Asia again, just because it seems such an unlikely way to get from one continent to another. To me these are places because they are alive still, whatever their age, though to many travelers they are merely sights to have seen, checked off, perpetuated by postcards, used as the backgrounds of snapshots or slides to establish a personal possession of culture.

The places I like most to go back to are those where I've done my duty long since by seeing the sights, places like Paris, where I can sit in the Tuileries gardens and watch the mothers knitting and gossiping while their children scamper about. The Louvre is at my back, and it can stay there. If there is a painting or several paintings that I am especially fond of (and there are), they will still be there when I'm in the mood to pay them a call. Venice is another such place. The Basilica in the Piazza San Marco isn't going to go away if I choose to have a cappuccino in the Piazza San Stefano and read a detective story. Even life in a jewel box, which Venice is, doesn't have to be spent weighing the carats or fingering the pearls, though it is refreshing to know they are there and no one is going to make off with them. I've seen many of them, but there are many that I have yet to see.

There are places I don't want to go back to, like the Costa del Sol in Spain—now a high-rise paradise for sunbathers—and Acapulco, which was a beautiful fishing village when I saw it. Florence is on my marginal list, a city without charm for me, a sight not a place. I wish someone would bring the paintings and sculpture to me. One of the pitfalls of travel is being a captive of conventional taste; another is the way the eyes glaze over from too much exposure to scenery and works of art; another is tired feet. These I regard as the penalties of sight-seeing. Going places has a very different tempo, and while there may be penalties (travel is never without its aggravations), there are generous civilized rewards—a sip at a time, not a gulp.

Architectural Digest, 1986

Perils of the Platform

*S*ome years ago, about thirty, I was on a platform (in this case, at a speaker's table) with two famous men, Alben W. Barkley, known as "the Veep" (he had been Truman's vice-president), and the legendary comedian Fred Allen. The occasion was a Book and Author Lunch in the ballroom of the Astor Hotel in New York, at which Irita Van Doren, the editor of *Herald Tribune Books*, presided. The reason we were gathered there was the coincidence of our each having recently published a book.

Before this luncheon, where there were a great many ladies in hats and almost no men, Fred Allen and I chatted in a small room off the ballroom while the photographers concentrated on the Veep. I knew Allen because in those days (and maybe now, for all I know) when a writer (or a nonwriter) had a book published, he or she was likely to turn up frequently on the same TV and radio shows with others who had committed the same indiscretion.

As we came into the ballroom, Allen took one look and said to me, "I've got the wrong speech"—the wrong speech, that is, for the audience as he appraised it. Allen was not only a very gifted man, he was also a very amiable one, and he was troubled. He was also very adroit at adjusting to the unexpected, and he spent much of lunch crossing out and scribbling on the manuscript of his talk. As is the custom on such occasions, the least conspicuous speaker starts things off—so, of course, I was first, Allen second, and the Veep, who had recently been reelected to the Senate, was last. He had served in it for years before becoming the vice-president but was now officially the junior senator from Kentucky.

When I was introduced by Mrs. Van Doren, I proclaimed solemnly, "It is a great honor to speak on the same program with the Senior Comedian and the Junior Senator." (Mild laughter.) Fred

Allen immediately got to his feet and said, "I demand equal time." (Loud laughter.) I was brief, Allen was predictably funny (his tinkered-with speech worked splendidly), and the Veep, seasoned politician that he was, went on so long that Mrs. Van Doren, who was sitting in a chair next to him, finally tugged gently at his coattails hoping her signal would make him subside. It did and he did.

The lecture platform has a long and honorable place in American cultural history and, it appears, an indestructible future. People in droves have been willing to sit and listen to lectures on almost every conceivable subject from the pharaohs to Picasso since lyceums were regenerated in the 1820s by a Connecticut educator named Josiah Holbrook. He wrote an article promoting the idea of informal education for adults by the establishment of organized series of lectures. It was a suggestion that took on a soaring life, and within five years it had become the American Lyceum and was going full tilt in more than a hundred cities. It was a windfall both for the purses and the egos of writers of all sorts. Ralph Waldo Emerson was in great demand and greatly honored by lyceums; so were James Russell Lowell, Mark Twain, and such visitors from England as Charles Dickens, William Makepeace Thackeray, and Matthew Arnold.

There were not many forms of public entertainment then, especially in rural areas, so listening to moral oratory and indulging in intellectual uplift was for many a welcome diversion. Toward the end of the nineteenth century the tent Chautauquas, which traveled to small towns and cities and stayed about a week, brought famous musicians, actors, and authors to audiences that otherwise had no chance to glimpse the glamorous world beyond their narrow horizons. The movies killed Chautauquas, for obvious reasons; they also crippled a lot of other sorts of live entertainment, and television threatens (but not seriously) to finish the job.

When a lyceum or Chautauqua lecturer found he had a speech that worked, he stuck with it, as lecturers do today. The champion of them all was the Reverend Russell Herman Conwell. His canned lecture was called "Acres of Diamonds"—a plea, peppered with anecdotes, for the well-to-do to support the education of the less fortunate. Conwell gave it more than six thousand times, without losing his verve, mostly for Chautauqua audiences. It made him a fortune, which he spent, it is said, giving "ten thousand young men" a chance at higher education, and he founded Temple University with what was left.

Lecture bureaus have replaced the lyceum and the Chautauqua as providers of speakers for ladies' clubs and of verbal frosting at social and business conventions. I know very little about them. I have never been "on the circuit"—I have limited my lecturing to museums and colleges and universities, dozens of them, and to symposia on some aspect of something I know a little something about.

The platform, however one gets to it, is a perilous and unpredictable place. There are gremlins that persecute lecturers. They put slides in the projector upside down and out of order; they swipe the light from the lectern; they hide the glass of water or put it out of reach. They make the microphone squeal. They laugh at the wrong times. They mix up the pages of the manuscript. They turn up the lights before the last slide and start clapping before the lecture is over. They are not always there, but their threat certainly is.

Any lecturer will confess that what worked well for one audience bombed for another seemingly identical one. One lecture of mine, for example, obviously pleased students and faculty at the University of Southern California and was a catastrophe at the University of Oklahoma. There is no telling . . .

Or perhaps there is. By and large lecture audiences are predominantly female, for reasons of tradition and perhaps of temperament or tolerance or time. Out of the lyceum movement came a burgeoning of ladies' literary societies and cultural uplift clubs that consumed lecturers like peanuts. I am told they still do, and I wish them well. It is a tradition worth preserving.

In the purveying of ideas and information and opinion, the live human being is preferable to the canned electronic personality, just as live music has virtues that recorded music cannot have. Well, perhaps not always. For audiences there's one drawback with lecturers: he or she cannot be silenced by the flick of a switch. There is a nice story that gives this another dimension. It goes like this:

A visiting English author of impeccable literary credentials, and who commanded large fees, had had a few drinks before he was to give his lecture. He was elaborately introduced to the audience by the man who was presiding at that occasion, and he was greeted with great applause suitable to his eminence. So he got up and gave, without a hesitation or flaw, a brilliant lecture and then sat down. It was greeted, like the introduction, with vigorous applause. He got up and started all over again.

Architectural Digest, 1987

Sources of Light

While I was looking for something else the other day in my bookshelves, my eye fell on a small volume called just *Art*. It is a book that once meant discovery to me and to many others of my generation. I had not looked at it in years. It was published in 1914 in London and written by Clive Bell, one of the Bloomsbury set. Pasted in the front by a previous owner is a letter from Bell dated June 10, 1915, addressed merely "Dear Sir." "Thank you," Bell wrote, with a very fine pen, "for your too flattering note," and went on to say what other art criticism he had published. In the back of the volume are pasted two reviews from London papers, one of *Art* and the other of a later book by Bell called *Since Cézanne*. I must have bought the book in a secondhand shop in the 1930s. The price on the inside front cover, in pencil, is $1.50.

Can you conceive of anyone today having the gall to write and publish a book called merely *Art*, any more than a writer would call a book just *Politics* or *Science* or *Love?* Any such book would have a qualifying subtitle at least, explaining what aspect of art, or art of what period or kind or place. Bell had no such reservations. He took the entire landscape of art as his battlefield, and the banner under which he marched bore the strange device "Significant Form."

One critic, whose words are pasted into the back of the book, thought Bell's declaration that "significant form is the one quality common to all works of visual art"—and the only important quality—was arrant nonsense. Not so to those of us who were wrestling with the challenges of abstract art in the 1930s. All that mattered, Bell said, were lines and colors and the forms they created; subject matter was totally insignificant—it merely got in the way of the "aesthetic experience." We took to it, I suppose, because it gave us a pat answer to those Philistines who thought Cézanne was a lunatic, and Picasso and Matisse were pulling the public's leg. What

22

did it matter that some pictures could be hung with equal effect right side up or upside down? It was only significant form that counted.

Right or wrong, Bell's *Art* was an invigorating book by a compelling writer. Finding it prompted me to look for other books that had been important to some of my generation in the shaping of our tastes and in upsetting the comfortable artistic clichés (or so we thought them) that governed our parents' taste.

Vision and Design (1921), a collection of essays by Roger Fry, a friend of Bell, was one of them. Fry was not only a connoisseur of Renaissance art, but an early champion of Cézanne, Picasso, and Matisse—he coined the name *Postimpressionists* for the first group show of their work in London in 1910. He said of them, "They do not seek to imitate form, but to create form; not to imitate life, but to find an equivalent for life." He was also one of the early rediscoverers and champions of El Greco, whose work angered most Edwardian artists and critics. But it was to an essay called "Art and Socialism" that I found myself turning. I remembered it as a comment on the relation of artists to society, which had suggested a field of inquiry that I have been ploughing ever since.

Bernard Berenson, Fry's contemporary, whose word on attributions was considered something akin to divine law, was an acute and persuasive writer. According to his *Florentine Painters of the Renaissance* (1896), modern painting started with Giotto, who endowed it with what Berenson called "tactile values." For the first time, he said, the painter imposed the illusion of three dimensions on his figures in such a way that the eye not only saw but *felt* their solidity. "Tactile values" was more than a neat phrase; it was a lens to look with.

Neither Bell nor Fry nor Berenson told us what to like or how to feel; they gave us ways of looking. It took a while to get over thinking that what a painting was *about,* other than about the art of painting, was unimportant, but that temporary blindness to subject matter was useful. Those who have been brought up with the Abstract Expressionists take for granted what we had to adjust our sights to.

I went on through the day taking down books that had long ago been important to me, books that had not so much shaped my taste as sharpened my appetite. They were books that had suggested to me ways of considering the man-made world, the imposition of the artist's hand on nature and on materials. They were Geoffrey Scott's irreverent *Architecture of Humanism* (1914); Henry-Russell Hitchcock, Jr.'s solid and adventurous *Modern Architecture* (1929); Heinrich Wolfflin's *Principles of Art History* (in English, 1932). I took down Lewis Mumford's *Sticks and Stones* (1924) and *Brown Decades* (1931), which rediscovered nineteenth-century American architecture, then despised by many—me among them—and, finally, John A. Kouwenhoven's *Made in America* (1948), the antithesis of Bell's *Art*, and a far more important and revealing book.

I do not necessarily recommend this as a reading list. For these books to be as important to you as they were—and are—to me, you would perhaps have to have been my age in 1930. But then, perhaps not.

Architectural Digest, 1982

Look It Up!

*L*ooking things up is not so much a habit with me as a cheerful obsession. "I can resist everything except temptation," Oscar Wilde wrote (I came on this today in Bartlett's *Familiar Quotations* while looking up something else), and the gratification of such temptations is never, in my house, more than a few feet or a few yards away. I do not pretend to have a commanding collection of look-it-up books, but those I have are among my best and most frequently consulted friends. They never talk back or shame me for my ignorance, nor snicker at my secret shortcomings. Like good Victorian children, they speak only when spoken to.

Reference books are sometimes pompous, sometimes silly—especially books of quotations—and sometimes stuffy. They are often wise and witty and poetic, but they are never, the ones I use, long-winded. They are more likely to be epigrammatic than prosy ("What is an Epigram? A dwarfish whole,/Its body brevity, and wit its soul."—Coleridge), but whatever they are, I need and use them, and I like to share them with my friends.

The most essential of all reference books are, of course, dictionaries. To be sure, they are all trees and no woods, and once in them it can be hard to find a way out. They sometimes lead a searcher on a chase from a word to a synonym to a variation, and so on back to where he started, not much the wiser. Sometimes in the course of looking up a word, the words above or below open the eyes to visions never before suspected, and a new chase is on. Dictionaries are cradles of serendipity.

Preferences in dictionaries reflect temperaments. I am not, as some are, a reader of dictionaries. I do not pore over them, though I sometimes get lost among the trees with pleasure. I play favorites, and I have a rather large field to choose from. I would be denying an old friend if I failed to praise the battered copy of *Webster's Col-*

legiate Dictionary that has been next to my typewriter for more than forty years. But on my desk is the new *American Heritage Dictionary*, which I like for its clear type and illustrations and its enlightenment on questions of current usage. Of the big unabridged dictionaries, I rely on both the *Random House* (1966), which contains an atlas, and *Webster's Third New International* (1961). The emperor of dictionaries is the *Oxford English Dictionary (OED)*, which in its many volumes traces the changing uses and meanings of words, with quotations and dates showing how they have evolved over the centuries. I splurged a decade ago and bought the two-volume edition, "reproduced micro-graphically." You can't find anything without a magnifying glass, but everything is there. It is more than an artifact; it is an entire civilization.

Some years ago I was fortunate enough to chat with Somerset Maugham at a friend's house about the writer's craft—and what a craftsman he was! "The other day I wrote down a word," he said, "and then I wondered if, indeed, there was such a word. So, I looked in the *OED*. It was there, with just one mention of its use— mine. Now what kind of a dictionary is that?"

I am not a slave to my thesaurus, but Roget sometimes plucks me from a mire of indecision and sets me on a new path; a single unexpected word can start a fruitful train of thought. I have two kinds of thesauruses—the traditional one and one arranged as a dictionary. I find the updated but traditionally arranged volume much more to my taste. Peter Mark Roget, whose fame rests on this *Thesaurus of English Words and Phrases*, first published in 1852, gave most people a better but obscure reason to thank him. He was a physician, and it was he who recognized that an image remains in the eye briefly after it has been seen. He called it "the persistence of vision with regard to moving objects." It is this principle at work that makes movies possible.

There exists, though I have not seen it, a *Thesaurus of Quotations*, which might be fun, but I have half a dozen books of quotations, which I find more seductive than useful. They are rather like literary cocktail parties where authors preen themselves and show off their wit. The one I keep on my desk is Bartlett's, though I have an old friend that is fuller and cornier, Stevenson's *Home Book of Quotations*. In a few "modern" ones I find myself reacting much as Maugham did to the *OED*.

My life without encyclopedias would, considering my trade, be impossible. The more concise they are, the better. I use the *Columbia-Viking Desk Encyclopedia* a dozen times a week. It is a convenient, bare-bones version of the excellent one-volume *Columbia Encyclopedia* (about 2,500 pages). My only big encyclopedia is the eleventh edition of the *Britannica*, published in twenty-nine volumes in 1910–1911. A friend bought it at a country auction years ago for five dollars and gave it to me. I use it rarely, but when I do, it is with pleasure. I do not yearn for the new *Britannica*. I've consulted it in libraries and found its organization confused and confusing. I have compact encyclopedias of the decorative arts and architecture, which I find handy; atlases, which in our changing world seem ephemeral, though *The Times Atlas of the World* is a monumental wonder; and dictionaries of art history, and music (I haven't one I like); of film and so on.

I save my favorite for last. It is *Reader's Encyclopedia*, originally edited by William Rose Benét, the editor-poet-critic, in 1948 and revised in 1965. It answers more of my family's questions than any book in the house. It is a literary encyclopedia: who wrote what, when, where, and to what end, with summaries of plots and the cross-referenced names of characters, authors, and titles. (Who, for instance, was Phineas Finn or Fabian or Mrs. Jarley? What was Maat or La Pléiade or the original Ship of Fools?) It is the book I give as a present more often and more successfully than any other.

In his famous *Dictionary* (1755), Dr. Johnson (see Bartlett's) defined an essay as "a loose sally of the mind; an irregular undigested piece; not a regular and orderly composition."

What I have written, and you have just read, is an essay.

Architectural Digest, 1984

On Good Behavior

*T*here is a truism about manners that can be stated didactically: Each generation believes that the manners of the generation that follows it have gone to hell in a hand basket.

Some years ago when my son was about ten, his grandmother was visiting us; when she came into the living room, he stayed where he was sprawled. "On your feet!" I said. "Don't you stand when a lady comes into the room?" He looked surprised, got up, and quietly said, "You never told me that." I probably hadn't. It was a gesture so automatic in my upbringing that I took it for granted as something any gentleman (which by my definition meant any male beyond the age of six) did by instinct. If it was a lesson to my son, it was a rebuke to me. It told me that I had not only been remiss but old-fashioned to boot. That was nearly forty years ago.

We live in a time, as no one needs to be reminded, of informality—in clothes, in houses, in how we eat, and in the language of conversation—and our style has its own characteristic manners. Manners change (some would say disintegrate) slowly, and our changes have been speeded up by the imposition of technology on our ways of living, of traveling and amusing ourselves—indeed, of getting through the day from radio alarm to lights out.

Technology, it might be said, by providing machines to do what used to be done by hand (mostly by servants or, where I come from, "help"), has complicated our lives in as many ways as it has simplified and enriched them. I am not suggesting that we turn the electric clock back or discard digital watches (which are harder to read than dials with hands), but in committing ourselves to machine control we have sacrificed many of the pleasures of self-control—of manners, if you wish. For example, when you drop a quarter in the exact change receptacle at a tollbooth, a machine lights up with "Thank you"; your dashboard talks to you ("Who asked your opinion?" I want to know), and soon I expect so will your bathtub ("Turn me off, dear, I'm about to run over"). Maybe yours does already.

Everyone today is "dear" or "darling" or "old man" or "fella" or "pal" on immediate acquaintance, and nobody has a last name ("Fred, this is Russ"). I am Russ to people who don't know me, to the chairman of the board (never mind which board) just as to the plumber who calls to say that he can't come today to stop the flood in the cellar after all, maybe tomorrow. (George M. Cohan, the great song-and-dance man of the 1920s, used to say, "I don't care what they call me so long as they mention my name." He didn't mean "George.")

Now and then someone I have just met, avoiding false coziness, calls me "Mr. Lynes." I am as astonished as I am pleased, but it's my age and white hair that evokes it. I think of a story told by Dame May Whitty, the distinguished actress, who was in a London shop and was being waited on by an uppity salesgirl (there are two words that have vanished) who was offhand and rude. Dame May, piqued, said, "I suppose you know who I am," and the clerk replied, "Certainly." To which the actress said, "I suppose you think you're as good as I am," and the girl said, "Of course." "Then why," Dame May said, "can't you be civil to your equals?"

Civility is, of course, the root and branch of manners (etiquette is something else), and the nature of civility, or what is considered civil, changes as styles of living change, but not necessarily at the same rate. Manners are essentially the expression of goodwill as much as they are "the custom of the country," to use Edith Wharton's words. Occasionally in New York I have seen a boy stand to give an elderly lady or a young woman with a baby a seat on a bus. I haven't seen it often. Once, when I got up in a subway to give a woman of my vintage a seat, a girl grabbed it before the woman could get there. The man I was sitting next to said, "It takes all kinds."

Manners, or lack of them, apply equally to all kinds, and that, I am sure, has always been true—no worse or better today than a century or ten centuries ago, though as customs and costumes have changed so have styles of manners. We think of ourselves as members of a classless society or as a middle-class society, and by contrast with many societies we are justified in so believing. We believe, or profess to, that ours is a society of equal opportunity, and

if that is not a fact, it is at least a hope and a goal. It has not always
been thus, and this brings me to the distinction between etiquette
and manners, or to put it another way, between form and substance.

Changes in style bring changes in the external forms of manners, not changes in their content. A formal style, for example, brings
with it rigid rules of etiquette, an external code that has little or
nothing to do with manners themselves. Etiquette, I believe, was
invented to keep people from making fools of themselves or, more
exactly, to provide them with a shield against embarrassment.

In the early nineteenth century, when Andrew Jackson was
elected president and "the ruffians," as they were called by the old
families, took over in Washington, the first age of the common man
was ushered in. To guide the newly important, more than one
hundred books on etiquette and how to avoid social pitfalls—how
to hold a fork, how to make polite conversation, how to dress for
every occasion, and how to master the intricate uses of calling cards—
were published between 1830 and 1860 and sold hundreds of
thousands of copies. They were not condescending, but they made
no bones about what was proper and what was oafish. In a sense,
they were guides to what we now call "upward mobility" of a sort
that yuppies might read with profit.

Etiquette may give style to manners, though it cannot improve
them. It can conceal natural bad manners behind a shield of forms,
and there is something to be said for that. The forms of manners
vary greatly both with time and with place. There are regional styles
just as there are generational styles, formal styles and casual styles.
Good manners are based on goodwill, as good behavior is based on
consideration for others. Style, which has little or nothing to do
with the quality of manners, has much to do with the conventions
that make life livable and pleasant. In this, manners and style are
indivisible.

Architectural Digest, 1986

The Art of Accepting

*I*f you will look in any book of quotations (I have just looked in three), you will find page after page of solemn or witty aphorisms on the art of giving. The only advice you will find on receiving (except that it is less blessed then giving) is that you must beware of the Greeks when they come bearing gifts. Other than the observation that a piece of strategy such as the Trojan horse can give a nation a bad name that lasts for centuries, there is little meaning for us in Virgil's aphorism. You will look in vain in the books of quotations for any counsel about how to accept a compliment, or a bunch of flowers, or an invitation for a weekend. You will not even find any advice about how to accept an insult. The art of accepting appears to be an art without a literature.

That is, without a formal literature. For the journeyman accepter on his daily rounds, the basic forms of acceptance have been written down in books of etiquette, but I think we scarcely need to concern ourselves here with anything so elementary as routine social amenities. I should like, rather, to come to the rescue of the compilers of future books of quotations, and provide them (and you) with a few aphorisms of my own about how the subtle practitioner of the art of accepting can move from social indebtedness to social indebtedness and leave behind him a trail of grateful and satisfied givers.

First let me define in a general way the art of accepting as I see it. If you cannot accept my first aphorism, you need go no further. The guiding principle of what I have to say is this: *The art of acceptance is the art of making someone who has done you a small favor wish that he might have done you a greater one.*

•This may, at first glance, seem to be a very materialistic approach to anything so gentle as one of the arts of human relations. I certainly do not mean it to be. It is merely realistic, for it is an

31

inescapable truth that a person who pays a compliment always hopes to be warmed by the light of pleasure in the eyes of the person who receives it. There is also some truth in an ancient observation (I could not find it in the books of quotations) that you make more friends by letting other people do you favors than by doing favors for others. It is not unnatural for anyone to prefer to have someone in his debt to being in debt himself.

But let us proceed from such generalities to more specific aspects of the art of accepting, and let us start with the most primitive level as it is practiced by very small children. Art, that is self-conscious art, operates very little at this level, but what art there is has a primitive clarity that not only has a special charm of its own but elements that one also finds at the most sophisticated levels.

Let me illustrate what I mean with an example from my own experience. When my son was about three, a friend who was visiting us in the country for the weekend went to a nearby town on Saturday morning and returned with a small, neatly wrapped package that he presented to the little boy, cautioning him to remove the wrappings without upsetting it. With some help from me, my son took off the paper and discovered a little carton which contained a goldfish. He uttered the most piercing squeal of pure pleasure I have ever heard. But this was not all he did to show his gratitude. The minute our backs were turned, he plunged his little hand into the box, grabbed the fish and tried to cuddle it. The fish had no choice but to capitulate and die.

I consider this an almost perfect example of primitive acceptance, and it leads me directly to another aphorism. It is this: *A truly appreciative child will break, lose, spoil, or fondle to death any really successful gift within a matter of minutes.*

I know of some adults to whom this generality also applies, but as this is a discussion of art and not neurosis, let us move on to adult problems that are adult. Some of these problems closely parallel that which I have mentioned, for there are many gifts that require that they be consumed or otherwise disposed of as soon as possible. Take, for instance, the guest who arrives for the weekend with an especially good or an especially bad bottle of wine. Even if you are a hostess who prides herself on a distinguished wine cellar, it behooves you to serve the wine at the next suitable meal. If it is bad, you have, at least, the satisfaction of seeing your guest take his own medicine, but good or bad you must convince your friend that there is no occasion on which it is more important to drink it than when he is your guest. Just remember that to the artful accepter, *a bad wine needs no beating about the bush.*

Sometimes gifts that are apparently imperishable can be deceptive. My wife once received a present of some very diaphanous monogrammed silk underwear from a friend who had brought it to her from Paris. It was so very fragile, so exquisitely pleated, that she put it away in tissue paper to save for a very special occasion. Several years later she came on it in the back of a bureau drawer and decided, bless her, that she might as well put it to use. As she took it from its wrapping, it fell apart in ribbons in her hands. Where it had been pleated, the silk had broken. "I guess," she said, "that *for a present there is no time like the present.*"

Any investigation of the art of accepting quickly leads away from the relatively simple matter of accepting presents into more subtle, if not more agreeable, questions of how to receive gracefully any number of other things that life thrusts upon one. It immediately becomes apparent that there are two quite distinct kinds of accepting that require quite different attitudes and manners of behavior on the part of the receiver. The first is the active kind such as that which we have been discussing—the acceptance of presents, compliments, invitations, and propositions. The other is the *passive* kind, which requires more than an agile tongue and a quick smile; it requires patience and fortitude. I refer to the accepting of life as it is and the facts as they are.

But before we undertake to explore the art of passive acceptance, I should like to dwell for a few moments more on the active aspects and to suggest some further rules that you might wish to observe.

Consider the problem of flattery, for example. Flattery is intended to please, of course, but not just to give pleasure for its own sake. Behind it usually lies some ulterior, if not necessarily dastardly, motive. It is sometimes used to extract favors from people; sometimes it is used merely for the purpose of turning people's heads and so inviting them to make fools of themselves. Some susceptible men and women never learn to distinguish between a compliment and flattery, and they go all soft in the middle with pleasure over what may be an outrageous appeal to their vanity. There are several ways of receiving flattery, and they depend on whether you want it, or not, which, in turn, depends on whether you like the

person who is giving it or not. If you like it, then pay for it in kind
. . . with flattery. If you don't like it, dismiss it with the laughter
it deserves.

This leads me to still another aphorism. It is this: *Never accept
flattery as though it were a compliment, and never treat a compliment as
though it were merely flattery.*

The art of accepting an insult is something quite else. Since an
insult is more likely than not to upset the adrenal glands, and the
adrenal glands often make people make fools of themselves, and
since I do not pretend to be a glandular specialist, I wish to treat
the insult very lightly (a good thing to do with insults anyway).
Children customarily retort to any insult with "You're another."
There is currently in use among teenagers in New York a phrase
that is intended to ram an insult down the insulter's throat; I like
it because it has the pure ring of the local dialect. It is, "I take that
from whence it comes."

No two insults call for quite the same treatment, but I offer you
this as a generality: *The only graceful way to accept an insult is to ignore
it; if you can't ignore it, top it; if you can't top it, laugh at it; if you
can't laugh at it, it's probably deserved.*

Let us turn now to passive acceptance. It is, as I have said, the
acceptance of such inevitabilities as your age, your physical and
intellectual limitations, and your husband's income. None of these
are proper subjects of conversation; they are all in the realm of
grin-and-bear-it, and the less you inflict them on other people, the
more artful you are as an accepter and the more palatable you are
to your friends. If you cannot avoid talking about them, *it is always
well to accept your own shortcomings with candor but to regard those of
your friends with polite incredulity.*

Passive acceptance is, however, unbecoming in the young, who
should always be at war with their limitations, always trying to
extend their horizons, always determined to scramble to the top-
most branches of the trees. It is not in the least unbecoming in
those who have grown up and who have recognized, identified,
and made peace with their limitations and their capabilities. To ease
your tension over those circumstances you cannot avoid, I offer
you this triple bromide: *Always accept defeat as though it were defeat
and success as though it were success, but never take either for granted;
neither is permanent.* I have never understood why it is that people
are naturally more tolerant of those who accept defeat badly than

of those whose success goes to their head. It is the successful who are likely to die young and despairing; the defeated have some place to go.

Curiously enough, the very same people who are artful about accepting their limitations and their successes are more likely than not to be the very ones who are artful about accepting gifts, and compliments, and other forms of pleasantness and good will. That is, I think, because personal dignity and sincerity are not merely qualities that one can trot out to meet an occasion but are either fundamental to a person's being or not of it at all.

I have now completed my efforts to provide the literatureless art of accepting with a brief literature. It occurs to me (as it should have occurred to me in the first place) that the probable reason why accepting is unsung as an art is that no one has as yet devised a more artful formula for accepting any gesture of generosity or thoughtfulness than the simple phrase "Thank you." There are pleasant embellishments that can be used with it. There are certainly a thousand tones of voice in which to say it. But if the art of accepting is, as I have suggested, the art of gratifying those who would be generous to you, "Thank you" has no peer.

Thank you.

Vogue, 1952

"U" and "Non-U"

*I*n 1956 Harper & Brothers published the American edition of *Noblesse Oblige: An Inquiry into the Identifiable Characteristics of the English Aristocracy*, edited by Nancy Mitford. It was better known as the *U and Non-U Book*. In addition to an essay by Miss (The Hon.) Mitford, it included essays by Alan S. C. Ross, Evelyn Waugh, "Strix," Christopher Sykes, and a poem by John Betjeman, not yet Poet Laureate. Cass Canfield, who then presided over Harper, asked me to write an introduction for this edition to explain the entertaining furor the book has provoked in England and to put it in an American context. This is that

INTRODUCTION

"Nothing stirs us to such a frenzy of shame-faced excitement," Philip Toynbee wrote in the London *Observer* last February, "as a public issue which involves class distinctions. Miss Nancy Mitford's article 'The English-Aristocracy' was published in *Encounter* only four months ago, but the terms 'U' (upper-class speech) and 'Non-U' are already part of the current literary vocabulary."

There were just a few paragraphs in Miss Mitford's article that started the frenzy. Ostensibly her essay was an attempt by one of the most gifted comic writers of our day to characterize, justify, and define her peers. Miss Mitford is the daughter of a baron and therefore a "Hon."[1] In order to demonstrate, as she said, that "the upper middle class[2] does not merge imperceptibly into the middle class" she used the researches of Professor Alan S. C. Ross of Birmingham University[3] into the differences of speech that distinguish the mem-

---

1. The title "Honourable" is pronounced " 'onorable." "Hon" is pronounced as it is spelled.

2. The use of a hyphen between "upper" and "middle" is evidently non-U.

3. Professor Ross is a U scholar in a non-U university.

bers of one social class in England from another. Professor Ross, in whose mind there seems to be little doubt that upper-middle-class usage is superior to middle-class usage, first published his findings in a Finnish philological journal where, presumably, they didn't cause the flutter of a single Finn.

The flutter in the Hon-coop[4] as a result of Miss Mitford's quotations from Professor Ross's learned findings was, however, exceedingly noisy and somewhat acrimonious. The distinctions between "U" and "non-U" language and behavior became something of a national parlor game, a sort of linguistic "How to Tell Your Friends from the Apes." The demand for copies of Miss Mitford's article was so great that *Encounter*, which cannot be called a popular magazine (it is published in London by the Committee on Cultural Freedom, and its literary editor is Stephen Spender), sold out the edition "immediately after publication."

There is little to be gained by adumbrating in this introduction the distinctions between U and non-U, which you will find explored and exploded in the essays in this volume. But the extent and nature of the response they evoked are entertaining, and a hint of the meaning of the terms is necessary to introduce them. It is U, for example, to say "lavatory paper," but non-U to say "toilet paper" (which makes all Americans non-U), but "writing paper" is U and "note paper" is non-U; "wealthy" is non-U and "rich" is U. According to Miss Mitford, it is profoundly and inexcusably non-U to say "Cheers" before drinking, and it is sufficient cause to tear up a letter without reading it if the salutation reads "Dear Nancy Mitford"; Dear Miss Mitford, or Dear Nancy, but Dear Nancy Mitford, never!

Some of the most entertaining and infuriated responses to Miss Mitford's essay are contained in this book, though it is only fair to John Betjeman to note that his verses, "How to Get on in Society," appeared in *Time and Tide* many months before Miss Mitford's piece was published. But there was a great deal that appeared elsewhere afterward, and I would like to quote some of it to justify Mr. Philip Toynbee's use of the word *frenzy*.

Graham Greene in a letter to the *Observer* wrote:

4. "As the co-founder, with my sister Jessica, of the Hons Club, I would like to point out that . . . the word *Hon* meant "Hen" in Honnish. . . . We were very fond of chickens and on the whole preferred their company to that of human beings." Deborah Devonshire (Duchess of Devonshire) in a letter to *Encounter*.

Sir,—It is sad to find that by Miss Mitford's exacting standard Henry
James was often Non-U in his correspondence. Frequently he followed the "unspeakable usage" of writing to someone as "Dear X X."

Many examples will be found in the last edition of his letters: "Dear
Walter Besant," "Dear Auguste Monod," and surely most shocking of
all to Miss Mitford, "Dear Margot Asquith."

To this Miss Mitford replied in a letter that also appeared in the
Observer: "As for Henry James writing 'dear Margot Asquith,' he
was an American." Which seems to take care of that, and of us.

Another correspondent to the *Observer*, P. B. S. Andrews (how
many initials, I wonder, does it take to make one U?), wrote:

Sir—Mr. Philip Toynbee has been hunting through a dictionary of
quotations in order to rebut Miss Mitford's "extraordinary claim that
the U circumlocution, 'looking glass,' should be preferred to the apparently non-U 'Mirror.' " There is surely no need to look far for the
perfect comment on the difference between Miss Mitford's pretentiousness and what used to be called the King's English:—

King Richard:
An if my word be sterling yet in England
Let it command a mirror hither straight. . . .

Bolingbroke:
Go some of you and fetch a looking-glass.

Shakespeare, *Richard II*

To this Miss Mitford replied: "It is probable that Richard II, like
many monarchs, was Non-U."

Malcolm Muggeridge, the editor of *Punch*, who knows a band-
wagon when he sees one, devoted almost an entire issue of his
magazine to Miss Mitford's little tempest. Its cover bore a mock
coat of arms and the device "Snoblesse Oblige," and a coronet was
printed at the top of each page of the issue. The book review section (except for a piece on Saint-Simon, who "staggered even Louis
XIV by the emphasis he put on rank and pedigree," and one on
Lady Waldegrave) was devoted entirely to books by peers reviewed
by other peers. In a piece called "Aunt Nancy's Casebook *(Correspondents requiring a private reply should enclose a stamped, embossed
envelope)''* were such delightful questions and answers as:

My mother forbids me to use the word "Tuesday"; she says it is common. What can I say instead?

"Morbid," Wylye Valley

Your mother is quite right. Tuesday is a very Non-U word,[5] indicating the day people who stay on after a Friday to Monday fail to leave.

Edna St. Vincent Millay, once a U poet whose reputation has become rather non-U in recent years, wrote inaccurately that there are no islands any more. The charm of the essays in this book is at least partly their insularity. This is a family joke told in family language, but like most good jokes it is easily translated into one's own experience.

Direct translation is, of course, impossible. A boot does not fit a foot that is used to a shoe, or a bonnet a car that is used to a hood. A society that perpetuates an inherited aristocracy, even though it often makes fun of its behavior, does not joke about its ruling class in at all the same way that we joke about our tycoons and politicians and F.F.V's. The tone of voice is as different as the substance of the joke. But the nature of English snobbery on which this book is based is less different from our own than one might think. We live, as these essays demonstrate beyond the shadow of a doubt, in an age of Reverse Snobbism.

We are somewhat more direct in our antisnobbism, and lest we seem to be snobbish, we tend to affect the language and manners of the people we are with. The chairman of the board, for example, is almost, but distinctly not quite, as slangy and back-slapping as his salesman when he is at a sales conference, though his manner and his language with his board of directors is dignified, proper, and filled with the U phrases of top management. The reverse is likely to be true of his wife, whose language at a company outing is apt to be rather more U than when she is with her intimates; at such moments she is very conscious of being the wife of the chairman and feels the responsibilities of noblesse oblige.

Class mannerisms of speech in America are difficult to pin down; regional differences are so much more important. A Bostonian can get away with mannerisms of speech that would be intolerable in a New Yorker or a Charlestonian. If there are usages that betray class distinctions in America, they are likely to be of the very same

---

5. So, according to a letter to *Encounter,* is the word *weekend.*

kind that Miss Mitford has singled out—the use of a fancy phrase when a simple one does as well.

The analogy is far from exact, but in some respects our Nancy Mitford is Emily Post, who has for many years occupied a kind of quasi-official position as arbiter of U behavior in America. In the latest edition of *Etiquette: The Blue Book of Social Usage,* Miss Post in a tone of voice not much different from Miss Mitford's devotes a chapter to U and non-U (under another name) words and phrases. It is called "The Words We Use and How to Choose Them." Here is a sample.

WORDS AND PHRASES TO WATCH OUT FOR

Never say	*Say instead*
I desire to purchase	I would like to buy
I presume	I suppose
Tendered him a banquet	Gave a dinner for him
Mansion	Big house

UNINTENTIONAL VULGARITIES

Lovely food	Good food, or delicious food
Elegant home	Beautiful house or place

IN VERY BAD TASTE

Formals	Formal clothes
Boy *(when over twenty-one years of age)*[6]	Man
Drapes—*this word is an inexcusable vulgarism*	Curtains *are hung at a window;* hangings *as decoration for walls. It is true,* draperies *would be correct for many loopings or shirrings or pleatings, especially on a woman's dress.*

6. "Years of age" seems to me rather non-U. "Old" would be U, I should think.

Corsage	*A word cherished by many, but distasteful to the fastidious who prefer the phrase* flowers to wear.
Going steady with	*There is no proper equivalent for the phrase because according to etiquette the situation does not exist; no man is given the exclusive right to be devoted to any girl unless engaged to her.*

It is obvious that Mrs. Post plays by the same rules as Miss Mitford. But it is unlikely that anyone who is U in America would think of quoting Miss Post as an authority on manners of speech or, even worse, of deigning to argue with her. "In best—meaning most distinguished—society no one arises, or retires, or resides in a residence," according to Mrs. Post. "One gets up, takes a bath,[7] goes to bed, and lives in a house." It may be a rather circumscribed formula for daily existence, but, as Mrs. Post adds, "Everything that is simple and direct is better form than the cumbersome and pretentious."

As you will see, there is trenchant disagreement among the U's who have contributed to this book, as there will be equally sharp controversy about what is U and non-U in America. Recently a friend in London sent me the clippings from which I have quoted above, and he wrote: "Altogether I think it is fair to say the articles have caused a great deal of light-hearted controversy. I rather think that when they come out in a book the tone of the comment will change. . . . These shibboleths will come to the attention of thousands of people who have been happily talking about serviettes and toilets all their lives without realizing that they were writing themselves off, in certain eyes, as socially benighted, beyond the pale, outcasts. This may make them, justifiably, sore. For my own part," he added, "I think there could be nothing more hopelessly Non-U than to write a book about it."

He may be quite right, but there is something pleasantly U about importing such a book to America, where one man's U is another man's U-all.

New York, 1956

---

7. It is non-U to bathe, but presumably it is downright vulgar not to.

Kudos for Clutter

I was relieved to read in my morning paper recently that "clutter," indeed "English clutter," is back as an approved attribute of the decoration of houses. I was unaware that clutter had been away, much less gone to England. It has certainly not been away from my house, but as a conscientious observer of taste, I find it comforting to know that what I am innately unable to avoid is approved by at least some of today's tastemakers. It once seemed to me that one measure of a man's taste is what he'll put up with (and perhaps one measure of a woman's taste is what she'll expect a man to put up with), and clutter is one of those things I would far rather put up with than pretend I can control.

The return of clutter as a decorative virtue rather than as an outrage (as Edith Wharton, in her book *The Decoration of Houses*, insisted it was) seems to me to represent an unusual example of fashion yielding to common sense. It may, of course, merely be an example of "if you can't lick 'em, join 'em," since clutter is almost as much a part of the human condition as political confusion, but it seems to me that it is a reaction to a reaction.

Let me explain. The kind of clutter that Mrs. Wharton and her disciple, Elsie de Wolfe, wanted to sweep out of the American household was that comfortable, often sentimental accumulation of sometimes pretty, sometimes hideous objects that Victorians scattered about their parlors and dining rooms and boudoirs. A surface that was not a garden of bibelots, ornamental boxes, photographs in monogrammed frames, floral paperweights, and jars of potpourri was considered as uncivilized and barren as a curtain without fringe and tassels, a carpet without cabbage roses, or a porch without ferns in hanging brass pots. This kind of clutter, taken item by item, was as much a family record as the family Bible had once been. The objects were the souvenirs by which it was possible to keep track of the past, a catalogue of places and events and persons, albums without covers, private museums of travel and nostalgia.

About 1890, fashion said this was a lot of nonsense. It was not only unhygienic but, worse than that, it was unsuitable. Clutter must go!

Of course it didn't; it just went into hiding. "Good taste" in the first decades of this century cleared off the tabletops, except for a discreet placement of the "best" things, abolished fringe and tassels and tailored lambrequins, relegated the floral Brussels carpet to the attic (if it was in too good condition to throw away), and stowed away in cupboards the fancy china that had been displayed in the dining room on plate rails. Walls, once painted with heavy colors or covered with elaborately patterned papers or Lincrusta Walton (imitation Spanish leather), now turned pale, and woodwork, once oak or mahogany (real or fake), was painted white.

This wasn't enough for the purists—not by a long shot. Those who took the functional tenets of the Bauhaus to heart skinned their houses to the bone. They painted their walls flat white; ornament on silver and glass and china was looked upon as very nearly immoral; bibelots vanished. To break the monotony, rubber plants and other forms of tropical vegetation stood in corners or on tables as pure as milk. Mantels disappeared along with the clocks and the candlesticks and the porcelain animals that embellished them, and bookcases of the open-ended sort that continually threaten to spill their volumes replaced the conventional, reassuring, built-in kind. It was all very honest and sincere.

But where did the clutter go? What happened to the traces of human indecision and the detritus of pleasant experience? In old houses it went into the attic; in modern houses onto the top shelves of closets or into the cellar or the garage or sometimes to thrift shops and rummage sales in the name of charity. (Today, charity beginning at home, much of it is disposed of by garage sales or, in my part of the country, tag sales.)

Every household, no matter how orderly it appears on the surface, has its precious secrets. It is secrets, I believe, that make a house a home: cupboards where the broken or outgrown toys are put away; where one earring is kept with hope; where are sequestered ribbons too pretty to throw away, razors now outmoded, old sneakers that might do for a weekend guest who forgot to bring any, small baskets and tin boxes of inconsequential miscellany such as brooches with the pin missing, ornamental buttons, old and faded family photographs ("Can that be my father when he was a boy?") and useful objects, from whisk brooms to string to the leashes for long-departed dogs. The maxim of clutter is "You can never tell when it will come in handy," and just often enough it does. It is also a record of indecision. I came on a little basket recently that might once have been a party favor, and in it was a "Bundles for Britain" pin from World War II, a silver dollar my father carried as a "pocket piece," a string of glass worry beads given to me by my host at dinner in Athens, an Indian-head penny, two glass marbles, a yellow golf tee, and a penknife with one blade missing. I put the basket back where I found it.

But this kind of clutter is not coming back into fashion; it never went out and never will. It has only to do with frailty, not fashion. What is evidently meant by revived clutter is "organized clutter," clutter for clutter's sake, clutter that invites the eye and therefore invites rumination, clutter that enlivens and provokes and stimulates, and that keeps the past in the present. The nature of clutter in any house is the key to the personality and often to the history of its inhabitants. It is visual autobiography, though it is frequently edited for public consumption. Nonetheless it is a giveaway. Clutter happens; it cannot be faked, and when it is superimposed on a house by someone not living in it, it is a deception—a fashionable, not an open, face.

Architectural Digest, 1985

On Getting Rid of Things

*W*hy is it that in today's consumer society so many of us are so inept at *de*consuming? I do not mean just major disposal problems like toxic and radioactive waste, though I fail to understand why if chemists and physicists are clever enough to come up with such horrors they aren't also bright enough, these geniuses of "I can break it but I can't fix it," to reverse the process and neutralize them. I do not mean big waste problems. I mean those on the scale of the broken-but-possibly-fixable bicycle that has been cluttering up the garage, the wedding-present tea set that has lurked for years in excelsior on a closet floor, and the very slightly warped tennis racket that is almost too good to throw away. That sort of thing—our closet (literally) secrets that we will scarcely admit to ourselves.

It happens that I am on a museum's deaccessioning committee which is made up of a small group of compliant if marginal experts to whom the curators submit objects they do not think worthy of the museum's collection. We are asked if they can be disposed of. I cannot remember when we failed to agree, usually with enthusiasm. Sometimes they are in such poor condition (and presumably were when someone who didn't know what else to do with them donated them) that they are not worth the time and trouble to repair. Sometimes they are objects it would be nice to take home, and it is a relief to know that is a temptation to which we cannot yield. The law does not allow it.

Perhaps every family should have a deaccessioning committee with the head of the household (and there must still be households that have a head) as chairman, or I should say chairperson. It should be the least sentimental member of the family, the one who can cut through nostalgia and argue most convincingly for good sense without losing sight of the virtues of sensibility; someone who knows that objects are often important for maintaining the pleasures and strengths of continuity.

I imagine that a deaccession meeting in my house could last for days, what with children and grandchildren, the variety of our temperaments and ages, and the kinds of interests and personal blind spots we represent. (Blind spots are very important to deaccessioning.) I have a feeling that it might come down to a sort of auction in reverse, no bids meaning high priority for good riddance. The big problems will be those objects, whether they are broken or not, that have acquired a kind of patina of affection, but that to all intents and purposes have become invisible because no one looks at them anymore. When they are brought out and presented to the committee, someone is bound to exclaim, "Oh, that! I haven't thought of it in years. I wouldn't part with it for anything."

Let's say it is a small bowl with a slight chip in its rim that long ago came from Florence. It has been invisible because, while it has been regularly dusted where it has sat on the living room mantelpiece, it has not been looked at. Movable objects that do not get moved have a way of disappearing into what might be called the domestic landscape—pictures on walls, figurines in bookshelves, coffee-table books on coffee tables, which is probably not where their authors imagined they would be.

There are many other categories of potential disposables—children's toys, for example—that are outgrown but which, for deeply personal reasons, grown-up children regard as sewn into their personalities with threads of remembrance. Then there are grown-up toys. I have five golf clubs: a mashie, a niblick, a putter, a midiron and what would now be called a 3 wood but was once known as a spoon. All of them have wooden shafts. Does that mean they are deaccessionable because useless? Such things are not serious problems; they are just nostalgic detritus or, put less pretentiously, friendly junk.

Nonjunk is a real problem, the almost-still-useful objects that might be readily fixed. Take, for example, the hand-propelled lawn mower that if sharpened could take the place of the power mower if it breaks down and if, of course, anyone can be bribed to push it, if anyone can be found to sharpen it. There must be thousands of such fixable tools lounging side by side in sheds and garages. They constitute a category that might be called Nostalgic Backup. Some cherished clothes also belong in this category. They ought to go to Goodwill, but the love of fellow man gets sidetracked by love of the private past.

Family pieces are especially unnerving—the out-of-sight, out-of-use pieces of china, furniture, linen, bibelots, and pictures. Slyly, on their own, they have crept into attics and cellars and the backs of closets. No one in the family truly wants them or knows what to do with them, but nobody is willing to be responsible for letting them go. Family pieces may be brought out of hiding for the committee's inspection, but sentiment abetted by indecision puts them back. Time, we know (though we don't mention it), will someday settle their hash as it will settle ours.

I have a personal deaccessioning problem with which nobody can help me. I mention it because, while it is eccentric in nature, it has a parallel in most people's experience. Twenty-seven years ago I wrote a little book called *Cadwallader: A Diversion.* It was a good-humored satire, and its characters were a family of amiable rats who lived in a New York brownstone and minded their own business. One upshot of this was a shower of little toy rats and mice from friends and readers—wooden ones, felt ones, rats and mice made of china, glass, plastic, and clay, some dressed as people, one beautifully carved. (There was not a single Mickey Mouse among them.) I have a cardboard carton filled with them. Can I deaccession them?

I do not expect an answer. I cannot submit my problem to a committee. Suppose everyone said, "Get rid of them." I would be right back where I started. One thing I seem incapable of throwing out is the whole deaccessioning problem. I shouldn't have brought it up. Obviously it is one of my blind spots.

Architectural Digest, 1986

Life in a Brownstone

*T*his is partly a story about an elusive cat named Horace, a black-and-white tabby, but it is mostly a story about New York brownstone row houses. In my experience they happened briefly to be inseparable.

The New York brownstone means many quite different things to New Yorkers. Basically, a brownstone is a particular kind of row house that dates back to the middle of the last century, when individual houses were as alike as peas (or, more accurately, as alike as kidney beans) in a pod. They were not "designed"; they were built by carpenters and masons for speculators who either "borrowed" some existing plan and stylish facade or adopted one and repeated it five or six or more times, cheek by jowl. Architects in New York were not only few in the 1850s when brownstones first appeared, they were employed on more important matters than housing the middle and working classes. They designed mansions for the rich, and churches and public edifices.

Houses in rows in New York before the brownstone era were mostly of brick, front as well as back, but it became fashionable to apply a veneer of brownstone (a soft, Triassic sandstone), from the quarries in Connecticut and New Jersey, over the brick on the front. Also added were deep cornices (often of stamped metal), fancy front doors, and lintels over the tall, usually narrow windows. But why brownstone?

The proximity of the quarries had something to do with it; so did economy. But there are many less pragmatic explanations. It is said that it suited the dark mood that hung over the nation before and after the Civil War. It is said by others that the drab color was suitable to the soot-filled atmosphere created by the factories of the then new Industrial Revolution. In any event, the entire city must have looked as though some dour deity had poured chocolate syrup over it. The interiors matched the exteriors in their "somber hues," as they were called—rich reds and purples, black horsehair on sofas, heavy curtains with ornate lambrequins, and ponderous oak furniture. It was all extremely genteel in a day when gentility was a virtue comparable to godliness, and all quite fussy.

Brownstones came in various widths: Some were "three-window" houses, twenty or perhaps twenty-five feet wide; some were "two-window" houses, fifteen or sixteen feet in width. The terms refer to the number of windows, side by side, on each floor facing the street and the backyard. Generally the brownstone had a cellar, a basement just below street level, and a stoop rising to a wide, double front door that opened into the parlor-floor hall. Above this were two floors of bedrooms.

We have lived in our remodeled two-window brownstone (originally one of six identical ones built with high stoops in about 1875) for thirty-seven years. Its facade had been stripped, its stoop removed, and its entrance was a step below sidewalk level. In a burst of eccentricity some years ago, we had it painted white.

But about Horace, the cat. My wife and I were in the Berkshires when our son, who keeps an eye on the house while we're away, called and said, "I just stopped by, and I thought you'd be interested to know that you have a cat. It's black and sooty-white and I can't figure out how it got in the house. He was in the front living room when I first saw him, and when I tried to pick him up, he nipped down the stairs to the hall and then down the cellar stairs and vanished. I searched the cellar. I even got a flashlight to see what he might have got behind. Didn't even leave a smile—obviously not a Cheshire."

The cat appeared and disappeared just as mysteriously several times. Once I cornered him and put him out the back door into the garden; he sat for a moment staring daggers at me, then disappeared behind the magnolia, and in a flash was over the high fence into our neighbor's garden. That afternoon I found him asleep on the love seat in our back living room.

Life in a New York brownstone is a way of living, but so vastly different are the ways people live in them that it is not what some, who don't know any better, call a life-style. Others live more luxuriously, possibly more comfortably, and surely more elaborately, in their apartment house rabbit warrens than we do behind our quiet, impersonal facades, but no one lives more pleasantly or more privately. A brownstone is a strictly urban, strictly Eastern Seaboard declaration of independence.

A brownstone is a fastness from which to watch the city shrink here and grow there, to hear its frequent shrieks and its continuous hum. Its sounds, like its skyline, change. The roar of the Third Avenue El gave way some years ago to the roar of the jets from La-Guardia, stopping conversation in the garden in summer. There were street criers when we moved in, and on Saturday mornings we heard a singsong voice calling "woe-a-wope," which we finally learned was the cry of a man selling rope and pulleys for the laundry lines that stretched by the dozens from the windows of neighboring buildings to tall black poles in the areas behind them. Monday was a sort of domestic flag day, with all the colors of the spectrum flying from the ropes. In the backyard of the house next to us, a man raised rabbits for food; this was at the end of World War II, when there was meat rationing. What was once just an expanse of sky above low buildings is now punctuated with multi-balconied apartment houses with wooden water tanks as topknots. We are luckier than many brownstone dwellers; the high rises do not hem us in. Our block is now lined by plane trees with flowers at their bases, and a block association fights a successful holding action against the shrapnel of urban decline.

The rigidly foursquare box, which is the basic brownstone shape, is more flexible than you might think, and some of those that have been remodeled have had their insides ripped out entirely and asymmetrical tricks played with their spaces. Ours retains its restful formality of shapes without the fussy formalisms of Victorian style. Books and paintings and drawings, which, partly for professional reasons and partly for love, flock to us like steel filings to a magnet, have had more to do with determining the nature of our surroundings than any conscientious efforts at "creating an environment." Our house is an accretion—not, strictly speaking, a furnishing or a collection; it is as much a place of work as of relaxation, where it is hard to tell where the one stops and the other takes over. Our life is like that, and we wouldn't have it otherwise.

Only Horace has violated our privacy. The cat, we finally discovered, belonged next door. What Horace had discovered that we hadn't (nor had our neighbors) was a pipe that went from their cellar to ours, through which he could squeeze. Horace was mysteriously a two-brownstone cat. Indeed, it was the small daughter of our neighbors who said, "Horace isn't a he, he's a she."

Architectural Digest, 1981

On Being a Photographer

*F*ifty years ago, when I started taking photographs for my own amusement and, I hoped, for the amusement of my friends, the 35mm camera was not yet a universal tool of the trade. I had a bulky, boxlike contraption with a sort of reverse black funnel that I looked down into to see what its lens saw. It was a Graflex, and it was lent me by Julien Levy, the art dealer who brought Surrealism to America and had the first serious gallery (after Alfred Stieglitz's famous "291") in which to show and sell photographs to collectors. He sold very few, but many whose prints he hung on the gallery's curved walls (considered very avant-garde then) were young men and women who have become "old masters"—Walker Evans, Berenice Abbott, Henri Cartier-Bresson, George Platt Lynes (my older brother), Man Ray, Clarence White, and others whose works are now sanctified by museums. In those days museums spurned photographs, as fifty years earlier they had looked down their noses at etchings. A few showed them, sparingly, but almost none collected them.

The reason Levy lent me the Graflex had nothing to do with my being a photographer, in his meaning of the word. The artist Eugene Berman, whose paintings he exhibited, had recently arrived in New York, and Levy hoped he would do some pictures of New York for his next show. Levy asked me if I would introduce Berman to the New York waterfront and take some pictures that might be useful as documents and reminders. Berman, who later became famous as a designer of sets and costumes for ballet and opera (including the Met and La Scala), intended, I believe, to oblige Levy, and we prowled the docks below Brooklyn Bridge while I aimed the Graflex at what I hoped had the romantic and somewhat decadent atmosphere of Berman's paintings. He seemed pleased with them, but when he went to work to prepare for his show, what came from his easel were still more of his imaginary Baroque ruins.

To my astonishment Levy decided that I was, in his terms, a potential photographer, and he let me keep the camera for a couple of years until I bought a far more convenient 2¼ × 2¼ Rolleiflex. (I still have it.) I had no intention of being a photographer. I was working for a publisher, as a clerk, and I meant to be an editor and writer. I had, however, got the habit of picture taking and of happily obliging friends who needed pictures for books they were putting together or to put on book jackets. Since film and processing were expensive on my wages (which could scarcely be called a salary), I insisted on having my costs covered. The first picture I sold, a photograph of a tier of iron balconies on the old Murray Hill Hotel, was bought by the editors of a book called *Metropolis*. That was in 1933, and the print, which I retrieved, is now in the archives of the New-York Historical Society. It was the earliest print in a recent exhibition called "Russell Lynes Observes: Fifty Years of a Writer's Photographs," an occasion that would have surprised my late brother at least as much as it did me.

George Bernard Shaw, who enjoyed using a camera and did so with skill, wrote in *Camera Work*, Stieglitz's magazine, in 1906: "Technically good negatives are more often the result of survival than of special creation. The photographer is like the cod, which produces a million eggs in order that one may reach maturity." Most photographers know in their hearts that this is essentially true, though some are obviously more codlike than others.

My brother liked to work with a view camera, a bulky box with bellows, in which the image is seen upside down on the 5 × 7 or 8 × 10 ground glass and peered at under a black cloth. He regarded those who used 35mm cameras as "buckshot photographers," who believed that if you sprayed a subject with exposures, something good was likely to turn up on a negative. Cods' eggs were not for him.

Public attitudes toward photographs have changed radically in the last fifty years, and so, of course, have the means of taking photographs. At the time when Agnes Rogers, Frederick Lewis Allen, and Edward Moffat Weyer were compiling *Metropolis*, for example, shots taken in nightclubs with "available light" were as fuzzy and exciting as they were rare. Film was slow, so were lenses, and "candid" shots were a new craze. Photographers will understand—

but there is no reason anyone else should—what it means when I say that the film we used in the 1930s had an ASA speed of 25; now it is commonly ten or twenty times that and can be a hundred times more. The Rolleiflex I loved in the 1930s and still use with pleasure is an oxcart by comparison with today's battery-propelled sleek little robots that do most of the photographer's thinking for him. That is not to say the robots take more interesting or more beautiful pictures, though they do take new kinds.

In the 1930s the question of whether photography was an art or, even at its best, a craft was still hotly disputed, though I do not recall that the photographers I knew worried about being artists. Why should they? The word *artist* had been depreciated. Anybody who could lay out an advertisement or draw a cartoon was a commercial "artist," and anyone who painted on canvas, however routinely, was a "fine artist." It seems to me—and this is surely an oversimplification—that the distinction between the photographer who is an artist and the one who is not is the difference between the picture maker and the picture taker. Anyone who can point a camera and push a button can call himself a photographer, can be a picture taker.

The picture maker, however, adds to his skill his temperament and the vast vocabulary of visual images and judgments he has stored in his memory. This warehouse, plundered from wherever he has been, from paintings, and from photographs, is his visual past. To this he adds his sense of proportion—visual, moral, and historical—and his humor, wit, and intelligence. But above all, it is the photographer's unfailing ability to be surprised by the commonplace and his ability to reveal its singularity that separate the picture maker from the picture taker. I like to believe that for fifty years I have been more often a maker than a taker, but that is for time and others to decide.

Architectural Digest, 1985

Life among the Philistines

*T*here are those who think a work of art is sacrosanct and those who think it is a commodity like any other man-made product, sometimes good, sometimes not so good, sometimes frightful. Those who believe in art's inviolability are likely to think of those who disagree with them as Philistines—an epithet fortunately heard less often than it used to be.

A Philistine, according to my nearest dictionary, means "a smug, ignorant, especially middle-class person who is held to be indifferent or antagonistic to artistic and cultural values." Taken literally that would seem to include, in our middle-class nation, almost everyone at one time or another—anyone who happens to disagree with artistic and cultural values as perceived by a limited group of intellectuals posing as aesthetic policemen.

But artistic values change rapidly today. Look, for example, at what has happened to painterly values since Picasso, Matisse, and their precursors upset the nineteenth-century applecart of romantic realism. Look at what the Bauhaus did when it skinned ornament off architecture and preached "functionalism" at the expense of beaux-arts classicism. And consider how many of these "cultural revolutions" are now interesting primarily as history.

There was a time when the artistic elite, as they thought of themselves, tarred with the brush of Philistinism anyone who spoke out against abstract painting. The same brush smeared those who in the 1940s liked the Chrysler Building but thought the Museum of Modern Art was nothing but a "flat-chested" factory building, or who had the effrontery to scoff at Le Corbusier's concept of a house as "a machine for living." To qualify as a true Philistine it was necessary to speak out, and the most dangerous Philistine was the one who knew enough to talk back to the aesthetic policemen. I learned this more than forty years ago when I published an article called "Architects in Glass Houses." I thought it was good-hu-mored. The cultural cops did not.

A group of New Yorkers also learned this when they took artic-ulate issue with a sculpture called *Tilted Arc,* by Richard Serra, which bisects a downtown plaza. These particular Philistines were only secondarily concerned with art, if they were concerned with it at all. They were not taking offense at artistic values but defending an open space in a crowded urban setting, which, to be sure, is a cul-tural artifact not to be despised.

In a general sense the Philistine, like beauty, exists only in the eyes of beholders. An abstract artist's Philistine may well be a fig-urative painter's cherished aesthete, just as one collector's treasure may be another collector's trash. But *Philistine* is an epithet used just as loosely as the word *aesthete* is, and both are pejorative. To the aesthete the Philistine is a bully; to the Philistine the aesthete is a dilettante.

How Philistines became identified as enemies of art puzzles me. In the Bible the Philistines connived with Delilah to cut Samson's hair and reduce him from macho to mouse. They could not have had anything further from their minds than culture. It was appar-ently Matthew Arnold who first used the term in its modern, anti-cultural sense. This poet-essayist, who said that the bourgeoisie were Philistines and aristocrats barbarians, took the meaning of Philistine from a word used by German university students to describe "townies" in the days of town-and-gown riots. The word was *phil-ister,* and this is how the connection with the biblical Philistines came about. There was a town-and-gown riot in Jena in 1689 that resulted in several deaths, and the university preacher took for his text "The Philistines be upon thee," a quotation from Judges 16. The philisters, in other words, were the anti-intellectual boobs the students and the university preacher looked down upon.

The aesthete, as far as I know, has no biblical roots. The dictio-nary defines an aesthete as "one who cultivates a superior appre-ciation of the beautiful; an effete person, one whose pursuit and admiration of beauty is thought to be excessive or affected." (This seems to me unnecessarily harsh.) The aesthete's roots are basically in the French "art for art's sake" movement of the nineteenth cen-tury and in England's Aesthetic Movement—which prompted W. S. Gilbert in his libretto for *Patience* to write: "You can't get high aesthetic tastes, like trousers ready made." The art-for-art's-sake adherents were deadly serious. Art to them was not a means to an end but an end in itself. Theophile Gautier, a spokesman of the cult, wrote: "What is really beautiful can be no other than good for nothing; anything that is useful is ugly because it expresses some need." A work of art, in other words, was pure, sacrosanct, and, by implication, useless.

It is this nineteenth-century doctrine of the distinction of a work of art from any other reality that persists in the insistence of Serra and his defenders who say that *Tilted Arc* is sacrosanct and not to be moved. Those who think otherwise are Philistines. But the world is not divided into Philistines and aesthetes. There are probably more Philistines than aesthetes in our society (which is not much different from any other society in that respect), though I am not sure. Look at the crowds that for whatever reason jam museums, go regularly to concerts, and support art for the sake of supporting art. Or the millions of young people who give their hearts and treasure to rock concerts, and if there ever was any purer art for art's sake than rock, I don't know what it can be. It is certainly useless. Are those adorers of an art that leaves many of us old parties cold to be called Philistines or aesthetes? To them rock and its performers are sacrosanct.

Or take another kind of art for art's sake that enthralls millions of Americans: the ubiquitous piece of abstract public sculpture known as the automobile. It is the design and craftsmanship of the finest cars, not the hidden chassis, that bring the light of aesthetic joy (and envy, too, no doubt) to eyes that would shy away from an abstract sculpture by Calder. The Calder performs an aesthetic function just as the Corvette does—and for many of the same mysterious reasons.

It would seem that in some degree all of us are Philistines and all of us are aesthetes, and that one man's Philistine is another man's aesthete and vice versa. It is the contest between one man's good and another man's evil that keeps our cultural broth bubbling, tasty, and nourishing.

Architectural Digest, 1986

The Truth about Status

*O*ne of these days some conscientious historian of costume is
going to trace the rise and fall of bell-bottom trousers from
the navies of the world to Carnaby Street to points west, and back
to the navy. From it he will deduce some seemingly profound social
truths.

I was put in mind of this tidy cycle of taste (for that is what it
is) by a piece I clipped out of a newspaper last year and which since
then has been pinned on my bulletin board. It was a story that
began: "The Navy announced today that it was returning the traditional uniform of bell-bottom trousers and white caps to its lower
enlisted men." The reasons given for this suggest more than just
convenience, though it is true that the enlisted men found it difficult to keep their new uniforms neat. The more likely reasons have
to do with status, tradition, and manners, as all matters of dress
seem to. If this question of men's clothes seems somewhat far-
fetched in a magazine devoted largely to where and how some people live, I would suggest that a man's pants tell nearly as much
about him as his living room does.

During World War II, I worked for what was then called the
War Department, and I had occasion, in the course of my duties,
to talk with the major in command of an induction center in New
York. Qualified draftees at that moment were given a choice of being
assigned to the navy, which was short of its quota, or the army,
and many more chose the latter. I asked why, and the officer
shrugged his shoulders and said, "A lot of them don't want to get
into those sailor suits with the floppy pants and the middies. They
think they'd look silly, especially the slightly older ones."

What the navy set out to do in 1971 when it put its "lower
enlisted ranks" in coats and trousers, white shirts, black ties, and
peaked caps was to try to look more democratic without being more

democratic. It is considered democratic for a so-called classless society like ours to make egalitarian gestures of this sort, though nobody puts much stock in them—not, that is, until someone's status
is threatened. In this case it was the chief petty officers who, according to the story, were "bothered by the fact that the distinction
they once enjoyed when wearing coats and peaked caps disappeared when all enlisted men began to dress in the same way."

For a nonmilitary (even antimilitary) nation, we set enormous
store by uniforms, and we judge each other by degrees of uniformity. Not that we want everyone to conform to the same things; we
merely want to be able to tell our friends from our antipathies and
our social inferiors.

No one in America admits to social betters, only to social inferiors. One way we make this distinction is by how we dress—not
how casually or formally, but by the ways we try to look like the
people we want to be identified with. It has something to do with
that tacky expression "life-style," but there is more to it than that.

I happen to be one of those adults who think they should dress
their age, and I'd feel as silly in fringed blue jeans as I would in
rompers. I feel the same way about "bells." Not long ago I went
into a men's shop in the Berkshires to get a pair of slacks, and I
said I wanted them cut straight. I was offered instead "executive
bells," as being suitable to my age and what the salesman apparently considered my station. I have nothing against executives per
se, but I don't want anybody to take me for one. Somebody might
get a false impression of my capabilities and aspirations, and wonder why, if I'm an executive, I hang around a typewriter so much
of the time. Still, I don't want to look like a writer and have people
wonder why, on the one hand, I'm not in Hollywood or, on the
other, why I'm not being serious and living on pasta, grants, and
fellowships.

In other words, I want to wear the uniform of anonymity, or so
I tell myself. It is a forlorn hope. There seems to be no such thing.
Society demands that we show our rank as well as our class in our
clothes and in the surroundings we make for ourselves or make do
with. Society insists on knowing whether we are enlisted men or
petty officers or commissioned officers, but more than just that, it
wants to know from our uniforms our innermost thoughts, our
prejudices and our preferences, our standards of what constitutes
the good life, and our sexual mores. We comply. We flaunt what

we would like people to think is the truth about ourselves, and in doing so we rarely conceal the truth itself.

I suppose the truth of the matter, as the navy's return to bell-bottoms and blouses demonstrates, is that our manner of dressing ourselves, which we think of as a kind of camouflage, is, like our houses, an intentional giveaway. Camouflage is a game we all like to play, but our secrets are as surely revealed by what we want to seem to be as by what we want to conceal. Our uniforms kid nobody but ourselves. The navy found this out.

Architectural Digest, 1977

Packaged Fantasies

A few years ago I ordered a genuine Irish tweed hat—not from Ireland but from the auld sod of Oregon. In so doing I not only covered my gray hair with raffish waterproofing, I opened the door to a new land—a world, indeed, of fantasy. Perhaps it was not the hat but something else that did it—a flannel shirt from Maine, or a kit to make a revolving bookcase that is my pride and joy and, next to my typewriter, the most useful object in my study. But whatever it was, my life has not been the same since.

Every time I go to my house in the Berkshires, the mailbox is filled with catalogues: little compact ones on pulp paper and large glossy ones filled with color. Each is a window on a world I have very little to do with; each is a lesson on the limits—if there are any—of American fantasy and the "upper" and "lower" reaches of our national taste. I say this without disparagement, for I am, as any historian of taste can't help but be, wary of didactic judgments. This year's vulgarity has an uncomfortable way of becoming the kitsch or camp of a decade or two from now, and its products collected and cherished as artifacts of an era's social, and sometimes aesthetic, climate.

For example: After a brisk shower this morning in my personal massage parlor, I sit down to eat my Wheaties—since I am a sort of household champion—from a white porcelain fedora hat; I pour coffee into my "Gertrude Stein," turn on my plastic hamburger to get the news. If it is a dark morning, I read my paper by the light of a lifesize goose that "glows all over," and when I'm through with the paper, I turn it into a log for the fireplace.

I can do all these astonishing things by taking the advice of a single catalogue. The "massage parlor" is a shower curtain with those words on it in very large letters. The porcelain fedora, the glowing goose, the "Gertrude Stein"—the author's features are molded on its surface—and the "singing hamburger" are exactly what I say they are, no frills added by me. This is a world I wot not of. Do you?

Since I do not have to live in this world, I wouldn't miss it on paper for anything. It delineates an aspect of American taste that is inhabited by many of the very same people I watch soaking their dentures and having their digestions soothed, on television. It is also a world I do not laugh at without a certain self-consciousness, for one man's vulgarity is another man's pretension.

One of my favorite catalogues comes from a small town in New Hampshire, and it offers primarily "hard-to-find tools." While I am no more of a carpenter or mechanic than the next fellow, I pore over this catalogue with its hundreds of uncommon wrenches, screwdrivers, and delicate and sturdy files. I scarcely ever buy anything from its pages; my pleasure is atavistic, I guess. The man who invented the flail to beat his grain comes out in me, and my reaction to any elegant tool conceived for a specific purpose is automatic admiration.

In recent months I have had occasion to spend a good deal of time in the Cooper-Hewitt Museum of Design in New York, and I have had the chance to look at a great many aged objects of the sort that today might be sold by mail order. An important aspect of the museum's collections is what we call household goods—porcelains, textiles for furniture, boxes to hold everything from snuff to precious stones to needles, wallpapers, paperweights, chairs, and commodes. What these objects have in common is not always a high degree of opulence but a very high quality of craftsmanship and of design, characteristic of the ages in which they were made. They represent what generations of men and women could not bring themselves to throw away, even if the articles were put out of sight in closets and attics because they were out of fashion. They are not all artifacts of "high taste" or "chic taste"; some of them are what anyone could afford, like the cheapest Export china, kept because it was useful, with no notion that it would one day be cherished by collectors.

Among the primary documents of the late-twentieth-century's taste will be the catalogues that clutter my mailbox, just as the early Sears, Roebuck catalogues, now greatly valued by social historians, are primary documents of the taste of eighty years ago. Every generation gives part of its taste to illusions and fantasies—things designed to look like something they are not, the goose that glows, the hamburger that is a radio. At the Cooper-Hewitt, for example, there is an eighteenth-century chair that is a bidet, a Gothic castle that is a bird cage, a jewel casket that is a music box. It is an old, recurring story, a nursery story perhaps, but one adults never get over.

One of the illusions nourished by those of us who think of ourselves as sophisticated is that our time produces a greater variety of tasteless and vulgar objects than any before ours. I see no reason to fall for this propaganda of the tastemakers, any more than to fall for what we find distasteful in the catalogues. Where taste is concerned, I believe in love and let love.

Architectural Digest, 1978

Things

A French sociologist named Georges Perec has written a novel called *Les Choses* that has recently been published in this country under the title *Les Choses*, which goes to show how international things are becoming. The novel, essentially an elaborately embroidered household inventory, sold 100,000 copies in France and won one of their innumerable literary prizes, the Prix Renaudot. It is about a young couple named Jerome and Sylvie, who must be one of the most boring couples in French, or any other, literature. These young people are impressed by things, all sorts and manner of things, so long as they bespeak the good life, which to them is the life of the upper classes (though they also seem to settle for what we might call Upper Bohemians). And they are voyeurs, because they are too lazy to earn enough money to buy the things they letch after. I am devoted to things myself, up to a point, but I left Jerome and Sylvie staring into a shop window along about page fifty, and I hope never to meet them again.

One thing that 100,000 Frenchmen are not wrong about is that this is an age uncommonly concerned with things, with their manufacture, their distribution, their acquisition. Things are endowed with mystical powers beyond the dreams of those who make them, with social influence, political significance, international prestige. The world has become, if you will excuse the expression, a *thingdom*, and the importance of its several provinces is more and more determined by how many things they can make, consume, waste, and have left over to sell (or, even better, to give) to other provinces. In general, things (more viable today than ideas) are divided into two principal categories—consumer goods and military hardware—and it is a toss-up which has more international status. The great debate in most provinces of thingdom is which category shall be allocated the greater part of the wealth.

It is infra dig for a "great nation" today not to have the most destructive thing of all, and scientific progress (or who's ahead) is measured by how many things a nation can put into orbit and how big they are. Less great nations settle for dams to create power to make things, and emerging nations momentarily settle for a jet transport (which is called an airline) or a railroad: things that will transport other things when there are any to transport. Total progress is measured by improved standard of living, which, of course, is measured primarily by things—refrigerators, clothes, automobiles, houses, furniture—not by education, say, or health. We even take nonthings like food and by processing them, freezing them, packaging them, make them into things. A thing is easier to cope with than a fact of nature in the raw. You can store it, break it, put it on the mantelpiece, forget it. If you can't think of anything else to do with it, you can use it, or if you're a great nation you can negotiate about not using it.

There is a story of a little boy who was given a couple of chocolate rabbits at Easter that, I think, must have a profound meaning for our thing-ridden society. By the end of the day the rabbits had disappeared, and the boy's mother asked him what had become of them. "They got too dirty to play with," he said, "so I ate them."

If more of us could establish as logical and direct a relationship with things as this, think what a different world we would live in. There are some people who give the appearance of staying a pace or two ahead of things, men, for example, whose desks are always neat and uncluttered, tidy altars ornamented with the ritual accoutrements of business—the onyx-based pen stand with gold swivels, the monogrammed silver frame with pictures of wife and children, the tooled leather portfolio, the empty in and the full out baskets, symbols of decisiveness, of mastery over things. I am suspicious of such desks and darkly believe that beneath their pristine surfaces the drawers groan with indecisions—undigested memorandums, knots of rubber bands, dried-up erasers, pennies, unused date books with one's name stamped on them in gold letters by insurance brokers: things, in other words, that are in *my* desk and seem impossible to throw away and, no matter how dirty, are impossible to eat.

We are creatures of clutter in an age of clutter. Clutter is what happens to things when they become useless but friendly. The Victorians made it into an ideal of decoration, a nice try at turning man's natural instinct for indecision into a domestic virtue. Emerson, who lived through the height of that Age of Clutter said, "Things are in the saddle, and ride mankind." The history of civilization is the history of things—things made of stone, of bronze, of iron, of clay and glass and precious metals, things for survival and for vanity. The history of mankind is one big desk drawer.

I sometimes think that the world would be a better (certainly a more orderly) place if man could take it with him to the grave—especially his indecisions. Consider, for example, the problem of wire clothes hangers. Do you save them or throw them away? Or do you save the ones with the cardboard still on them and throw the others away? It is a little thing, but it is symptomatic. There is something of the pack rat in all of us.

We are forced, however, to make decisions about things lest we be defeated by them, lest, as consumers, we become consumed, buried, overwhelmed. Every so often one has to turn over a new leaf, start fresh, face the facts, and perform (or try to) other such clichés of salvation. This very day I am going to start ruthlessly throwing away things, and as a symbol of my emancipation, the first thing I am going to throw away is *Les Choses*.

Horizon, 1968

II

Leisure and Style

Some years before Edith Wharton undertook to explore the manners and foibles of her age as a novelist, she was already greatly concerned with matters of taste and style. A very well-bred and properly brought up young lady with a sharp eye and an equally sharp wit, she had a taste for elegance and a distaste for stuffiness. In the 1890s, when she was in her early thirties, she and her husband bought a house called Land's End at Newport, Rhode Island, in its day the most fashionable resort in the country. The house was, she recalled in her autobiography, "incurably ugly" on the outside, but it seemed possible that it might respond to surgery on the inside. She convinced a young Boston architect, Ogden Codman, to do the interior and so set a new precedent.

"The architects of that day," she wrote, "looked down on house decoration as a branch of dressmaking and left the field to upholsterers, who crammed every room with curtains, lambrequins, jardinieres of artificial plants, wobbly velvet-covered tables littered with silver gewgaws and festoons of lace on mantelpieces and dressing tables." Indeed, she not only played a role in changing the profession of interior design, but in the course of it she produced her first book. It was called *The Decoration of Houses,* and the young architect was her coauthor. That was in 1897.

Those were days when leisure and style belonged to what was called the leisure class, or so they thought, a relatively small coterie of fashionable people who took their leisure so seriously that they scarcely had a moment to enjoy it. Men, even the very rich, thought it improper to work fewer than six days a week, but their wives, when not changing their costumes—morning demanded one, lunch another, paying calls or motoring in the afternoon still others, tea another, and then dinner, of course, still another—spent their leisure on details of social and domestic organization that would chal-

lenge the ingenuity of a systems engineer. Leisure was circumscribed by well-defined rituals whose rules were invented and
understood, if sometimes ignored, by those who were socially secure or could be learned by rote from dozens of approved books of
etiquette.

The nature of leisure has changed in ways that would have astonished Mrs. Wharton, though she would not, I believe, have been
shocked by them. She was no prig. She would have been surprised
to find that in our day nearly everyone belongs to the leisure class.
Since this is true, there is no leisure class to which people look for
an example of what constitutes style, not even the so-called beautiful people. Because of the shorter work week—it used to be about
sixty hours in 1900 and is now between thirty and forty—a more
affluent society, and the lengthening of vacations, there are vast
numbers of people with time on their hands: time to play, to putter,
to sit for hours in endless lines of weekend traffic, to lie by the sides
of pools, to pursue culture or trout, to cultivate their gardens or
their minds, to struggle up mountains or social ladders.

The life-styles of a great many people are fashionable, but the
life-style that has style is rare indeed. A somewhat younger contemporary of Mrs. Wharton, Edna Woolman Chase, for many years
the editor of *Vogue,* was a wise woman and a clever one—wise in
the ways of human vanity and clever in exploiting it. "Fashion can
be bought," she said. "Style one must possess." It is an elegant
summary.

One is inclined to identify style with high style, something only
the rich can afford when, in indisputable fact, one of the great hazards to style is wealth. Those who try to achieve style by the lavish
use of money are, on the one hand, likely to achieve vulgarity or,
on the other, "good taste," both of which are the antithesis of style.
Vulgarity is mindless ostentation; good taste is educated timidity.
Style has conviction, arrogance, and egotism and a dash of chutzpah
and gall. It has self-confidence.

Trying to define style is as fruitless an exercise as any I know.
How do you explain why the old Metropolitan Opera House in
New York had it, and the new one does not? Fred Astaire has it;
so did New York's rascally Mayor Jimmy Walker. The present mayor
has none. Both Roosevelts, Teddy and F.D.R., had it in abundance;
Truman had it. The San Francisco Palace of the Legion of Honor
has it; Hearst's castle, San Simeon, defies it. Many sloops and yawls

and schooners have it; few of their owners do. One recognizes it on sight in a ball player, a cowpuncher, or a parson.

Our increased leisure, I'm afraid, has produced less style than one might have hoped. It has produced a great deal of vulgar ostentation in houses and hotels and in some gaudy cultural centers. It has also produced many efforts at good taste in our quaint and cozy houses and in our Early American and Spanish Mission motels which lurk on the aprons of interstate highways from Maine to the Mexican border, as out of place as a lady in a crinoline and bonnet operating a drill press. In some respects the very multiplicity of styles of life is the most encouraging aspect of our new leisure. The more the merrier; the better the odds. The followers of fashion will always be the multitude, the possessors of style the fortunate few. There are enough of them, however, to set the style of our age. We may be criticized for our vulgarity and the timid nostalgia of our taste. But we will be remembered, I dearly hope, not for that but, as ages in the past have been remembered, for our style.

Architectural Digest, 1974

The Cult of the Environment

*E*very now and then words explicit in their original meanings seep into general usage, turn into movements and fads, and excite people to passionate behavior. They become political or moral slogans, and any word that takes on political or moral overtones arouses opposition. Look out for catchwords. They grab and hold.

Environment, until quite recently, was a word that summoned up pleasant visions of gardens and glades, of nature working out its sometimes friendly, sometimes dog-eat-dog inevitabilities, its cycles and seasons, its natural wonders and equally natural horrors. Now *environment* is a word that raises hackles, a contentious pistol of a word. "The environment" is something of a cult, like Zen. A place used to be a place; a room a room; a house a house. No longer. A place, a room, a house, is now an environment, for better or for worse, for richer or for poorer. Personally, I find this tiresome.

Not long ago, in the introduction to a catalogue of a museum exhibition that had to do with design in many of its manifestations—design of useful and decorative objects, design of cities, of means of transportation, of clothing—its author, no mean designer himself, spoke of contemporary design as being concerned with "the totality of the environment." The architect (actually he is a landscape architect) of the proposed Franklin Delano Roosevelt memorial for the city of Washington described his plan as an attempt to "create a memorial environment as a total living experience." A *what?* Meaningless phrases like these make my heart sink. They are like whipping a trout stream with a sinker instead of a fly. The thud is enough to drive nature's creatures fleeing for cover.

As words go, *environment* is not an old one. Its usage, according to the *Oxford English Dictionary,* dates back only to Thomas Carlyle, writing in the 1830s. To be snobbish about it, it is a word of good breeding, with stalwart French antecedents in the word *environs*, which means "vicinity, neighborhood, surroundings, outskirts."

It is only recently that the environment has become quasi-sacred. To be for the environment is like being against sin, and to question the virtue of the environment is like questioning the virtue of motherhood.

To trace, not the word, but its intentions, to its literary origins suggests something different. The original "planned environment" was created in a frightful hurry and on a very large scale. Its parlor, so to speak, was the Garden of Eden, which was, as its original inhabitants soon found out, too good to be true. Or rather, they were not good enough to be true to it. So they moved out into what the rest of us have lived with ever since. You can be sure that Adam, when he "gave names to all cattle, and to the fowl of the air, and to every beast of the field," did not name the place they all had to make do with, "the environment."

Since man was not good enough even for what he was shooed into, it occurred to him, by way of making life on earth supportable, that there must be something worse, so he thought up Hell. As Dante in *The Divine Comedy* is at some trouble to explain in detail, Hell was a thoroughly planned environment with all the charm of a public housing development. To be sure, it had no energy problem, but then it had no air conditioning.

From the very beginnings of history, man has been trying to get the better of the world that was handed to him. He has done so in ways that have been dictated by expediency, as in the building of towns and cities; or by pride, in the building of palaces; or by fear of vengeful gods, in the building of temples. One of the worst planned and most beautiful cities is Rome; one of the worst planned and most fascinating palaces is at Windsor; one of the worst hodge-podges of temples is on the Acropolis. They are products of accretion that no modern environmentalist would tolerate, except for their historical record of man's ambition, and his submission, for heaven knows what reason, to the inspiration of artists. Age lends charm to error. It lends charm to art, too.

There is something smug about the environmentalists. They give the impression of knowing better than anyone else what is good for the rest of us. There is also something illogical about them. They are all for preserving the mistakes of the past, if that past was long enough ago. In this respect they are sentimentalists, whose judgments are emotional and who think they can protect us from the future by canonizing the past.

There need to be guardians, of course, against despoiling the world we live in—its history, its monuments, its streams and wood-lands and mountains, and the air we breathe. It is not the guardians I object to, it's the pretentious garments of language in which they adorn themselves, words that are meant to be armor against criti-cism. A year ago I hired three young artists who were paid cash to paint my house. "We're glad to work on a writer's environment," they said. See what I mean?

Architectural Digest, 1978

The Landmarks Dilemma

*L*andmarks are not what they once were—emphatic objects by which you could tell where you were, mountains and lighthouses and towers and other conspicuous, usually tall, natural or man-made exclamation points in the landscape. By being always where you expected them to be, they were comforting, partly because they were timeless and partly because in their impersonal way they were welcoming. The old landmarks have not lost their meaning, but they have been joined by hosts of what are called "designated landmarks." Time and custom did not decide they were landmarks; the landmarkers did.

I speak as a somewhat disenchanted landmarker. The designation of landmark buildings and so-called historic districts has, from the very first, which was not so long ago, been a can of worms. Not only do the people concerned often disagree basically about the quality—architectural or historic—of proposed landmarks, but their judgment is colored by many considerations that have nothing whatever to do with history or architecture or aesthetics, but can be casually included in that basket of a word *environment.*

I learned this at firsthand as a founding member of the Landmarks Preservation Commission of the City of New York, one of the first such commissions with a comprehensive law to support it. For seven years (1966–72) I listened to arguments, often impassioned, pro and con. I heard a parish priest testify that he approved of having his beautiful little church designated a landmark, and his bishop, who wondered what would happen to the value of that piece of real estate if the parish dwindled away to nothing, argue against it. I listened to owners of property on which distinguished buildings stood argue that those structures were of no historic or aesthetic interest and should be demolished so that they could be replaced by more profitable ones. I heard committees seeking the

designation of an entire area of New York as a "historic district"—
an act that would thereby prevent any owner of a house or business structure in the district from making any exterior alteration,
however small it might be, without the review and permission of
the Landmarks Commission.

An early such district was Greenwich Village, which, as I listened to the discussions, seemed to me as much a state of mind as
a place. It was, and is, full of commercial structures—warehouses,
service stations, cheaply built apartment houses—that surely do not
deserve to be saved along with the many charming, and some elegant, nineteenth-century dwellings and public buildings. (Just the
other day, a friend who has a house in the Village told me she was
outraged because several of her neighbors were painting their houses
in bright colors, thereby "spoiling" the neighborhood. I suggested
that this same sort of thing had happened in recent years in parts
of San Francisco and had, in fact, added greatly to its sprightliness
and charm.)

The arguments for landmarks preservation, reduced to their
simplest terms, have been the need to save our heritage of architectural styles, the homes of heroes (statesmen, authors, artists), the
sites of historic events, and historically interesting groups of buildings. Opposed to this is the right of citizens within the restraints of
zoning laws to do as they please with their property. That seems
simple enough: *Pro bono publico* versus individual rights, an ancient
and honorable confrontation resolved in different times and cul-
tures in a great variety of ways, not all of them, by our standards,
equitable.

But it is by no means as simple as that; nothing is that is com-
pounded of sentiment, taste, status, comfort, nostalgia, pride, money,
and politics—and the designation of landmarks involves all of these.
Is the greater benefit of the city accomplished by preserving as landmarks structures that stand in the way of creating amenities for a
large number of citizens? Are creating these landmarks justifica-
tions for letting taste and ambition and enterprise take off on their
own to pursue unpredictable fancies? In the narrow area of landmarks preservation, just what *is* the public interest?

The question was answered, in the bluntest of terms, at an early
meeting of the New York Landmarks Commission, by a member—
a historian of the city—who said, "If this commission had existed a
century and more ago, there wouldn't be any New York today."

He had a point, but not one he meant to press. By this same token, however, one wonders what nostalgic Parisians thought when the emperor Napoleon III let the baron Haussmann tear down much of Paris to make splendid boulevards and open spaces and vistas and parks. Some years before that happened, Philip Hone, the mayor of New York, wrote in his diary in 1831: "The city is now undergoing its usual annual metamorphosis; many stores and houses are being pulled down, and others altered, to make every inch of ground productive to its utmost extent." Much of what was built then is now Greenwich Village. The presumption is that this village would not have been built if there had been a Landmarks Commission in Mayor Hone's administration.

The function of the Landmarks Commission in any city is to adjudicate disputes over which landmark sites and buildings are worth protecting and preserving. Protecting them is the city's business; preserving them, unless the city owns them, is essentially private business. "Historic preservation speaks to properties of architectural, historical and cultural significance," Beverly Moss Spatt, a former chairman of the commission, wrote recently in the *New York Times*. "Yet people are requesting and gaining designation for a whole array of other reasons: to maintain the status quo, to prevent development, to revitalize an area . . . to gain tax benefits."

Landmarks laws are fragile things, subject to attack by any property owners who dispute the designations of their buildings. The fact that the United States Supreme Court upheld the constitutionality of the New York law in a dispute over the Grand Central Terminal, a major victory for landmarkers, does not mean that abuse of the law will not put it in jeopardy again.

Legislation that attempts to administer taste is always fair game for Philistines and aesthetes alike, and in some respects it becomes increasingly evident that some of the landmarks law's most enthusiastic and energetic friends are also its most dangerous enemies.

Architectural Digest, 1981

Landmarks—The Bright Side

*F*ifteen years or so ago I drove from New York with two friends to the city of Hudson, once a thriving river port about a hundred miles north of the metropolis. Our destination was a house called Olana, built in the 1860s by the then (now again) famous landscape painter Frederic E. Church. I had paid a casual visit to this "Persian villa" some years before, when the house was still occupied by Church's daughter-in-law, a lady then in her nineties, but at that time I thought it discreet not to ask to see the interior. The villa was designed by Church himself, with the aid of the architect Calvert Vaux. It is a romantic building in a romantic setting, high on a manicured hill looking down the river that gave its name to a school of painters that includes Church.

We had heard that the house, with its bright Victorian plumage, was an endangered species and that in every interior detail it was precisely as it had been when Church had died in 1900. We were not prepared to discover that every object in it was tagged with a lot number. The contents of the villa were about to be sold at auction; the house and land were up for sale. To the executors of the Church estate, Olana was a very large white elephant—in size and uselessness—and just as exotic.

How Olana was saved, eventually being taken under the wing of New York State to become a magnet for thousands upon thousands of visitors each year, is a complex story of political maneuvering, benefit exhibitions, magazine and newspaper articles, local pride, and abundant goodwill and financial backing. Our visit that day had something to do with getting the ball rolling or, to be more literal, stopping the wrecker's ball from flying. Let it merely be said that Olana is a remarkable nineteenth-century treasure, full of Church's work and the evidence of his exotic taste and restless spirit. Pure chance froze it as the artist conceived, made, and lived in it.

Deciding what to do with Olana, if indeed it could be saved, was not a problem that faced its rescuers. There are historic houses that are successfully used as museums, but there are very few that bear the distinctive stamp of those who built them. Olana is one; Vizcaya in Miami is another: a kind of Venetian palazzo facing Biscayne Bay, built around 1914 for James Deering by the architect F. Burall Hoffman, with magnificent formal gardens and rich holdings of European sculpture and decorative arts. Both Vizcaya and Olana, different as they were in every respect of style, taste, and site, needed only repair and refurbishing to convert them into public museums. The current revival of interest in nineteenth-century exuberance and Edwardian elegance makes these sorts of pleasure palaces somehow both remote and comforting today. "Escape" is written all over them; Church and Deering meant it to be. Both buildings were created with a sense of adventure and fun, and as indulgences in private fantasy, not as symbols of status.

The question that faces most efforts at preservation is one of use: "What do we do with it now that we have rescued it?" Is it enough that a landmark building be a whiff of the quality of life that once abounded in it? Is it enough that it is an example of style and taste of a past conviction? Usually its function is a passive one— to be treasured by the nostalgic, to be scrutinized by the curious, and to be analyzed by historians.

But landmark buildings are also images against which to judge the present (sometimes favorably, although it is my impression that most preservationists think otherwise) and—since styles have a way of recurring in defiance of technology—to suggest the possible future. As voices of "the good old days," landmarks are tellers of tall tales, for they recall only the surface of the life they witnessed, its ornaments and tools.

Landmarks have a way of tidying up the past, much as Currier & Ives tidied up the nineteenth century. George Eliot, in *Middlemarch* (1872), called it "that softening influence of the fine arts which makes other people's hardships picturesque."

On the other hand, pleasantly practical uses are increasingly found for buildings that have been given up by almost everyone but preservationists and an occasional imaginative pragmatist who sees economic ways of revitalizing what is generally considered obsolete. Preservationists are quite aware that there is a limit to how many endearing old buildings can be converted into museums for local historical societies or into cultural centers. The cry these days is "Adaptive Reuse!" (I don't suggest you try to cry it; it isn't a slogan to stir the blood.) "What we are trying to do," one preservationist declared at a conference, "is rehabilitate the environment so that older properties remain economically viable." Submerged in this jargon is good sense.

Increasingly there are examples of adaptive reuse almost everywhere you look. Some of them are official, in the sense that preservationists have promoted them; some are entirely unofficial, because some imaginative people have come to recognize their commercial or community or domestic possibilities.

Within a few miles of where I write in rural Massachusetts, there is a charming nineteenth-century "bracketed" railroad station, which, a few years ago—when the trains stopped running—became the home for the local Visiting Nurse Association. Edith Wharton's house, The Mount in Lenox, abandoned for a decade or so, has been taken over by Shakespeare & Company, a theatrical group, and—with some government and some private funds—is being rehabilitated in a way that Mrs. Wharton would approve. There is a nearby board-and-batten "Gothick" church of about 1850, which has recently been discreetly and handsomely remodeled to house a family. These are small adaptations.

Cities have vast ones, like the Jefferson Market Courthouse in New York's Greenwich Village, which was made over inside to become a very handsome modern library. Boston has its Quincy Market, which was to be abandoned and destroyed and is now a thriving enclave—of shops and markets and restaurants—bursting with life that has spread to neighboring old buildings and inspired *their* rehabilitation. San Francisco has recently commissioned I. M. Pei & Partners, architects of the new East Building of the National Gallery of Art in Washington, to give new life to its Ferry Building, built in 1896, a proud landmark with a splendid tower and arcaded facade. Miami, by contrast, is agonizing over what to do with its Freedom Tower, a 1925 building that initially comprised the offices of the *Miami News*, and after that the Cuban Refugee Center, and which now is threatened with demolition, though its structure is sound.

The landmarks climate has changed dramatically since we agonized over how to save Olana fifteen years ago, and almost always for the better. Landmarks, it has been demonstrated (with the vital help of the National Trust for Historic Preservation), are not just the scolding fingers of the past, telling us to mind our manners, but centers of profitable enterprise. Some of the profit goes to business, but the most important part of it goes to improve the quality of our villages, towns, and cities, and thus, the quality of our lives.

Architectural Digest, 1981

The Culturettes

*T*here is a segment of the art world, not generally recognized as belonging to it, which I like to call "the culturettes." Like the farmerettes of World War I who tilled the soil for food, they till the soil of the arts so that those who are fighting on the museum and concert fronts can eat. Like the Rockettes of Radio City Music Hall, they dance in unison (more or less) to the tunes played by museum directors, conductors, and boards of trustees. If they were to vanish into some other sort of good works, more artists would starve, lecture halls would be dark, concert series would go unsubscribed, and a great deal less tea would be drunk across the nation and far fewer thin sandwiches eaten in the name of culture.

The culturettes, who are usually well-coiffed upper middle-brows, speak in well-modulated voices that have a tone of executive assurance somewhat belying the scent of their perfume. They can be spotted in almost any cultural center by their air of belonging, the way they smile at the custodians and call them by name, and the unconscious assurance with which they walk through the galleries as though they were walking through their own living rooms. They are unawed by the presence of Art, though they are very likely to be uneasy in the presence of artists. Their station wagons, parked behind the museum, are likely to be full of envelopes for them to address and announce the next season's special privileges for members.

There is an inclination on the part of artists and performers of various serious sorts to consider the culturettes as "part of the price we pay" to be permitted by society to do "our thing." In the best of all possible worlds they would just pay us and leave us alone—which, of course, is nonsense. If they were to leave us alone what would happen to our Public and hence to our vanity? We know we need them, but they have to be taught that they need us. Very few of them come to the arts because of a thirst for their life-giving waters; they come because they are taught that it is their duty and that it is a taste that with effort can be acquired.

In this age of choosing up cultural sides (either you are for art or you are a Philistine), the culturettes have thrown in their lot with uplift, and for whatever satisfactions they derive from their choice they pay dearly. I was brought up in a rectory in New England (my father was an Episcopal minister), and it is not strange that I should equate the culturettes with the church's Ladies Aid Society and the Altar Guild. It would have been impossible to get the day-by-day chores of the parish done without them. They hovered about my father as the culturettes hover about the director of a museum. There was a missionary zeal about them which I think sprang more from personal social need than from deep faith, and they were bent on spreading the gospel. It is much this same kind of zeal that is now bent on bringing the culturally unwashed to the temples of art.

Recently I had a long conversation with the director of a small but distinguished museum in upstate New York. I will not name him, but I am sure that what he said would apply to small-city (and some metropolitan) museums anywhere in America.

"Tell me about your culturettes," I said.

"Ha," he replied, "ha! HA!"

The word was not familiar to him, but the concept obviously was; he knew at once what I meant.

"Well," he said, "we have a Members Council of about a hundred and fifty people, all women. They have to be at least ten-dollar members of the museum, and they are invited to join the council."

I asked him to what wheels this considerable force of womanpower put its shoulder.

"They do all the dinners, tea parties, coffee hours; they are responsible for hospitality and social functions for exhibitions and the lecture series, and they are hostesses on their own."

This sentence came out as though it has been as well rehearsed as a politicians' spontaneous reply to a planted question. His particular museum has a very small professional staff which performs the curatorial functions for the collections, arranges special exhibitions and lectures, and runs art classes.

"They are not," he said emphatically, "involved in programs. The professional staff does all that; they are purely auxiliary."

It must take a steady hand to keep so powerful a force from dabbling in the programs and policies of the museum, but there seemed no doubt in this director's mind where the line was drawn between the sacred and the profane.

"They're important for fund-raising," he said. "Last year they had an art auction—well, not strictly art, of course, everything from a chair made of elephant tusks to, well, you know, a fake Corot, and ten lessons in metal sculpture. They raised fifty-eight hundred dollars, and that, let me tell you, is not hay."

"Not hay," I echoed.

"And two years ago they organized an art trip to Italy preceded by five lectures. This was just for members, and they ran a James Beard cooking school to help raise funds to furnish our new kitchen and serving pantry to the tune of thirty thousand dollars."

Food for thought is obviously not all that issues from a museum's enclave. I was reminded of church suppers in my father's parish house.

"Who are these remarkable women?" I asked. "Where do they come from?"

"They're not the old Helen Hokinson types of the past," he said, using a cliché for busty clubwomen-in-hats familiar to all regular readers of the *New Yorker* over forty. "They're from all backgrounds—university people, college girls, girls who grow out of the Junior League, garden-club members. Did you ever read a story by Edith Wharton called 'Xingu'?"

I said I hadn't.

"You should," he said. "It's about a man, I think it was, who lectures about a river in Africa called Xingu and about his audiences. If I remember correctly, Wharton says something about women not daring to face culture alone; they can only bear to face it in groups."

"I'll look it up," I said, but the point was clear.

Culturettes have a strong herding instinct. It may be that they do not feel sufficiently sure of their taste to be left alone in the presence of art—or what somebody who is supposed to know tells them is art. You will never hear a culturette say, "I don't know anything about art, but I know what I like." That would be Philistine, and culturettes are dutiful handmaidens.

The rewards they garner for their devotion—for selling postcards in the museum shop, for guiding tours, for pouring tea and taking tickets—are few. As they climb the ladder of their Establishment they are on a first-name basis with museum directors and an occasional maestro. They meet artists and lecturers at airports and for a few frightening moments have them all to themselves. They are guests at dinners where a "nationally known figure" sometimes makes an effort and sometimes just sulks. Some culturettes are allowed to penetrate by just a little the tight circle of local creative artists and theater people, and the more daring among them occasionally sit on the floor of their studios and drink wine. Could the arts in our society get along without them? Heaven forbid!

Art in America, January 1970

Corn, Glorious Corn

*C*orn is an inescapable element in the texture of American Life—good corn and bad corn, entertaining, enlivening, mawkish, and vulgar corn. We are surrounded by every sort of it every day, and often we dismiss it as irrelevant or unimportant when it is in fact neither. Corn is big business and small-c culture. There are markets and warehouses bursting with it, but whatever else it may be (and it can be anything), it is not vicious. Its intent is to amuse, to titillate, to titivate, and to lead us into harmless (if sometimes expensive) temptation.

To some, corn confirms the "I-wouldn't-be-caught-dead" fastidiousness of their taste. To others, it defines class or caste—highbrow, middlebrow, lowbrow. To still others it reveals much of the nature of the twentieth century, as shards tell much of the Aztecs. And for those who like to stand back and observe, as I do, it is a constant source of entertainment and revelation of man's foibles, particularly my own.

For many years I exchanged items of corn with a friend who was a museum director. I never knew what might turn up in my mail any more than he knew what might appear in his. We did not exchange postcards or greeting cards, the very essence of which is too often corn and therefore too obvious. We exchanged objects come upon by chance almost anywhere we happened to travel. The last one I received from him was a small inflatable plastic palm tree from Florida (it soon wilted). I had sent him a yellow plastic tray with a flying Virgo (nude) on it, from a roadside cafe near Mantua. He had an amused eye for sincere bad taste, objects that were meant to be art but turned out to be corn, often expertly executed, and were without the intentionally cute, hoked-up, or ruthlessly quaint qualities inherent in most commercial corn.

There is, admittedly, something snobbish about judging corn that other people take to their hearts, but everyone is a snob of some sort—intellectual, social, physical, spiritual, you name it (as I tried to thirty-five years ago in a little book called *Snobs*).

Corn is an American term, but it is by no means limited to our continental borders. It is related, as you would expect, to *corny*, which one dictionary tells me comes from "corn-fed [music] played in country style, out of date, hillbilly." This definition dates the dictionary, as country style is obviously one of today's most up-to-date and prevalent kinds of musical corn. Another dictionary says that *corny* means "old-fashioned and sentimental" and that *corn* is anything considered "trite, dated, melodramatic, or unduly sentimental." Still others give *corn* such attributes as "lacking in subtlety and full of clichés" and "mawkish," a word that, according to this source, originally meant "nauseating."

There is, to be sure, corn that is nauseating. Think of the commercials that turn up on or about Mother's Day, when otherwise healthy sentiment gets downright gluey. But for the most part corn is silly, soupy, healthy, and cheerful. Along with the Kewpie doll, pink plastic flamingoes, and teddy bears, America invented and seeded the nation with that most outrageous and corniest of cultural symbols, the movie palace, the blithe and financially redoubtable conception of Marcus Loew. He understood the American appetite for glitter and pastry-cone architecture, for three-dimensional corn on a scale of magnificence. For some it was the essence of bad taste; for many of us it was the epitome of delightful nonsense, the best kind of corn; for others it was a temporary dreamworld accessible to anyone for seventy-five cents or less. The theater, presumably from the days of Euripides, has been a purveyor of both rude and sophisticated corn, and opera plots often seem the apotheosis of the mawkish, overblown, trite, and sentimental.

The point at which high art and corn meet is often where art celebrates abstract virtues, like Justice, or where the artist sets himself the task (or is commissioned to perform it) of personifying a victory or the glories of a hero. One of the great artists of the nineteenth century was in my estimation also, when he set his mind to it, one of the corniest. I give you J.A.D. Ingres, whose magnificent portraits are anything but corny. But consider a painting called *Apotheosis of Napoleon I*—a nude emperor in a chariot drawn through the heavens by four steeds, accompanied by a female with a trumpet who holds a garland over his head, which is already adorned with a laurel wreath.

I have another favorite, also a celebration of royalty in a most unlikely circumstance. It is a 1940s painting by English artist Rex Whistler called *Allegory: H.R.H., The Prince Regent Awakening the Spirit of Brighton.* (Brighton, you will remember, is where the prince regent built his elaborate, onion-domed, quasi-Oriental Royal Pavilion.) The prince, a plump fellow with wings and a double chin, is clothed only in a very slight veil, strategically placed by the winds of decency, and a blue satin ribbon to which is attached the Star of the Order of the Garter resting on his nether end. The garter clasps his right leg above the calf, and he wears pumps. He is half kneeling and plucking at the edge of a sheet that evidently, until he got hold of it, covered the Spirit of Brighton, a slender young maiden reclining on what may be pillows on the ground. She is clad only with a narrow pink ribbon around her waist. Behind them is an evening seascape capped with rosy, whipped-cream clouds.

I am not sure of the size of the painting (I describe it from a color postcard sent me by a corn fancier), but the carved label on the frame suggests that it must be quite large—five by eight feet perhaps. Whatever its size, it is corn in full flower, quintessential corn.

Of the myriad manifestations of corn with which our society is plagued or enlivened, depending on your aesthetic reflexes, there is one that though not overlooked needs to be named. It is the cornification of villages and sections of cities. Everyone is aware of what has recently come to be called *gentrification* (a word so new that it does not appear in the 1975 edition of the *American Heritage Dictionary*), which means the upgrading of real-estate values by sprucing up neighborhoods to look genteel—that is, like the homes of gentry. Cornification often goes hand in hand with gentrification. It means (I should know, I just made it up: *vt* cornify; *n* cornification) the cornying-up of a neighborhood or perhaps a shopping street to make it look old-fashioned and cute. (The British have been doing this for years.)

Colonial Williamsburg is an example of Early American cornification. The corn is not in the conscientious and valuable archaeology practiced there; it is in such cosmetic devices as dressing up the servitors, docents, and craftsmen like period dolls, superimposing the fake on the real to achieve the quaint and corny. Something of the sort happened in St. Louis a couple of decades ago when it cornified a run-down part of the city and called it, as I recall, the Gas Light Square District. (It came to wish it hadn't.)

There is a bit of cornification in New York City's South Street Seaport, a rehabilitation of the old Fulton Fish Market district. There is some of it in the Quincy Market in Boston, a delightful recapture of a part of town that had badly deteriorated. It is even happening on the block where I live in New York. My esteemed neighbors on the block association have voted to replace perfectly efficient modern streetlights with imitation Victorian ones. That, patient reader, is what I mean by *cornification*.

Architectural Digest, 1987

The Tyranny of Cyclops

*S*everal years ago in Venice I shared a motorboat taxi with a couple I did not know, going from a hotel on the Grand Canal across the lagoon to the airport. Venice is a city that seems always to be moving, its facades reflected in the ripples of its canals, its approach sometimes shimmering in the morning mist, sometimes brittle against bright skies filled with clouds that seem to have been painted and left there by Tiepolo. It is a city of skyscrapers rising out of a bed of jewels, campaniles above Gothic and Renaissance and Baroque gems shaped by love and faith and greed. To approach it from the airport is to see it emerge from the quiet water as though it had not been there until you saw it. To leave it is to look back on its slow absorption into the sky. It never stands still to have its picture taken.

As my fellow passengers stepped into the motorboat, the lady said to her husband, "Have you got all your toys, darling?" His "toys," it was immediately apparent, were his cameras and tripod and gadget bag. He laughed and assured her that he had them all, and we departed.

This pleasant couple with whom I chatted (he said that he had been photographing "buildings, mostly") were a modern Cyclops and his patient wife. The Cyclopes, you'll remember, were a mythological race of one-eyed giants, whose three progenitors were said to have forged thunderbolts for Zeus—a sort of cottage industry armaments supplier that stockpiled weapons for an easily infuriated god. By contrast, the modern Cyclopes are Pygmies, one-eyed travelers who look at the world through the lens of a camera and attempt to capture it bit by bit (usually in color, these days) to take home to plague their friends and neighbors. I admit that I am a part-time Cyclops myself, but I do not ask my friends, or even my relations, to waste time looking at my slides. There is not a projector or a screen or even a bare white wall in my house.

Travelers' photographs, to be sure, constitute a sort of diary of a trip, and as private reminders of occasions enjoyed and sights seen, they have an amiable validity. They are useful tools of private nostalgia; they are, however, commonly used as public tools of one-upmanship. It is well to remember that our forebears who kept diaries of their travels did not, I believe, sit their friends down in the living room or parlor after dinner and read aloud to them their impressions of architecture, picnics, landscapes, restaurants, and traveling companions. Perhaps some ladies shared their sketches of the Alps and bits of pressed edelweiss with intimate friends, but those who took photographs—as travelers have been doing since George Eastman, in the 1880s, began to market the Kodak with the slogan "You Press the Button, We Do the Rest"—pasted their prints into black-paper albums held together with black string.

Far be it from me to tell others how not to torture their friends. I confess to a certain bias in this matter, and so does a friend of mine, who said (to my amusement and apparently to her host's), when asked if she would like to see his slides of Portugal, "I'd love to look at your ten best."

"I suppose that was a rude thing to say," she said to me later, "but why can't people edit their pictures to do themselves justice? Why do they think that just because a picture isn't underexposed or overexposed it is interesting to look at? By the law of averages, his ten best are very probably interesting. The trouble is that most people are in love with their slides, and their love spilleth over— without restraint or self-criticism—into three or four carousels."

I do not know how my boat companion made out with his "buildings, mostly," but I have found from my own travels that a camera can be a hindrance to understanding and enjoyment, rather than a help. I am not alone in believing this, not by a long shot. The great architect Le Corbusier, who filled dozens of notebooks with pencil sketches and watercolors, used to say to his pupils, "Don't take photographs, draw; photography interferes with seeing, drawing etches into the mind."

Not everyone can draw, of course, and not everyone knows intuitively how to look at architecture. One takes skill, the other, accumulated acquaintance. But I have found it is true that when I look at a building through the lens of a camera, it is not the building I see; it is a framed image, a flat image, and a potential photo-graph. Architecture is three-dimensional, and a building cannot be experienced in two dimensions. All good architectural photogra-phers know this. To understand a building or a living room or a garden, or any defined and enclosed space, it must be walked through, and the quality of its space must be felt as well as seen. The exterior of a building, by the same token, must be walked around, so that its volume, structure, and detail can be seen as parts of a whole. A building is far more than the sum of its parts, and the expert photographer looks at it first without his camera, not for its pictorial quality, but for its architectural quality, its physical con-text (how it relates to its site), and its social context (what it means to those who use it or pass by it daily). He may then be ready to look at it through a lens, as a two-dimensional image or series of images, but not before.

I learned this the hard way years ago, and since I like taking photographs (by which I mean making pictures, not just records) as much as the next Cyclops, I arrived at a simple solution, which I recommend to those who enjoy the subtleties as well as the pa-nache of buildings. I make a distinction between sight-seeing and picture taking, and treat them as two distinct pleasures, not to be confused one with the other. When I go sight-seeing, I leave my camera behind; when I go picture taking, I leave my guidebooks. It is an easy formula. It improves both sorts of pleasure, and in the long run it is kinder to one's friends.

Architectural Digest, 1981

Putting Artists in Their Places

*A*rt historians—and this includes museum curators and a majority of conscientious dealers—find it useful to put artists in pigeonholes. They like to categorize them, give them descriptive tags, and assign them to movements, and it takes an artist of unique character to escape them. Some years ago, for example, scholars of nineteenth-century American landscape painting hit on "Luminism" as a name for a style, and the National Gallery in Washington hung a vast exhibition called "American Light: The Luminist Movement, 1850–1875." That put the cork in the bottle once and for all. It firmly trapped and pigeonholed a great many painters and photographers who henceforth will be known, no matter what they may have had in mind when they stood at their easels or snapped their shutters, as Luminists.

There are obvious reasons for this kind of pigeonholing. From the dealer's point of view, the buyer wants to be told where the picture or sculpture he adds to his collection fits into the artistic scheme of things. If he buys an Impressionist painting, then he knows—or ought to—that it belongs to what was considered an outrage by the Academic artists of the nineteenth century and is now as safe as a church. If he owns a Church (Frederic E.), he has a picture of the Hudson River School, though it may well be of a South American volcano. Church is tagged, for better or worse, as a Hudson River School painter. To be sure, his magnificent Persian villa, Olana, looks down the Hudson from a high eminence, and at some times of day in some seasons the river looks so like paintings of it that nature seems to be imitating art.

Anyone who is anybody knows that the Hudson River School is "in" and that such pictures bring whopping prices. To minor members of the school, it most certainly never seemed that they were members of any school whatsoever. They were just painters of what they saw, or rearranged on their canvases, and hoped to sell. Now that it is too late for them to enjoy it, they are basking in the glory of their more lustrous contemporaries, and their works bring prices they never dreamed of. If a contemporary of John Frederick Kensett or Martin Johnson Heade or Albert Bierstadt had said to any one of them, "You're a Luminist," the painter unquestionably would have replied, "I'm a *what?*"

Collectors, except those with the most eclectic and adventurous taste, like pigeonholes. I know a woman who has a remarkable collection of Futurist paintings. The Futurists, of course, were a group of Italian artists active early in the twentieth century, and, in this case, they invented their own pigeonhole and issued manifestos to define it. I also know a couple who collect the Ashcan School, a group of painters active in New York around 1910. The name was given by critics who thought the paintings of alleys and laundry lines were a parody, or worse, of art and what was suitable to the concern of artists.

These collectors, and there are many like them, are very knowledgeable. Their judgment is discerning, and their collections can unhesitatingly be pigeonholed as "important." As they stick closely to their choice pigeonholes, their collections increase and acquire for professional pigeonholers the value of historical "documents" essential to the study of the particular school they encompass. When someone mentions the X collection or the Y collection, the knowing will nod their heads, for they understand precisely the nature of the art each contains. This not only impresses other collectors, it also impresses curators, who will then lay polite traps to capture the works for their museums.

Sometimes pigeonholes are precise and neat; sometimes they are loose, more like market baskets that will take a miscellaneous assortment of casually related artists than like small tidy boxes. The New York School of the 1950s and the School of Paris of the 1920s (roughly) are of the grab-bag sort. The New York School was a group of painters who took off in new directions after World War II—each in his or her own direction, which was inward—and astonished the art world here and abroad. In a very real sense, men like Jackson Pollock, Arshile Gorky, Mark Rothko, Robert Motherwell, and Barnett Newman stole the leadership in painting from a tired, disillusioned Paris. They also stole the market, but it was not they who thought of themselves as a school. That was the pigeonhole into which critics and dealers put them. The School of Paris in turn was merely a convenient package in which to wrap a batch of smaller schools: the Fauves (Matisse, Derain) and the Cubists (Picasso, Braque, Gris), who preceded the Neo-Romantics (Berman, Bérard, Tchelitchew).

It was not until art history stopped being an exercise in art appreciation, as it used to be called in schools, and became a social science of a sort in the hands of German academics that categorizing became one of the tools of the game. This was in the late years of the nineteenth century, long after Linnaeus, the Swedish botanist (1707–1778), had created a revolution in the study of plants by his system of categorizing them. It was also long after Ruskin's beautiful effusions about the arts and Walter Pater's precious illuminations of masterpieces. Indeed, there were no such creatures as art historians—as distinct from social and political, religious and economic historians—until such serious scholars as Heinrich Wölfflin, Erwin Panofsky, and Walter Friedlaender made the history of art a respectable academic discipline. They did this to a considerable extent by categorizing art and pigeonholing the artists by schools. A subject that once had been considered a mere stepchild of history took on the aura of an exact science—or if not exact, at least exacting. Art history became distinct from art criticism in the same way that literary history is distinct from book reviewing.

One of the great categorizers of our time has been the Museum of Modern Art. It almost seems as though if you can't label it you can't see it, a thesis Tom Wolfe explored differently in *The Painted Word*. Not long ago I received a mailing tube from the museum, and when I pried the cap off one end I could see nothing rolled inside. I took off the cap on the other end and looked again. It contained nothing but a column of air.

Is MoMA tring to tell me something?, I wondered. Is this what Minimalism has finally come to? The empty pigeonhole?

Architectural Digest, 1982

Let's Face It!

"*T*o sit for one's portrait," said the Scottish poet Alexander Smith about a century ago, "is to be present at one's own creation." He would not be likely to say such a thing if he were to pose for those painters today who are dedicated makers of art and to whom portrait painting is merely one way to exercise their larger subjective gifts. In the context of the present he would be more likely to say: "To sit for one's portrait is to be present at one's own autopsy."

There is, to be sure, a revival of interest among avant-garde artists in America in painting the human face and figure, something that their counterparts of a decade or so ago, the Abstract Expressionists and Action painters, would not have considered for a moment as anything but debasing. But within the revival there lurks an ancient antipathy of artist for patron and portraitist for sitter, with the canvas on which a portrait is painted as the battlefield where they meet and where the painter has all the weapons . . . except the ultimate one—cash.

In a recent issue of *Art in America* devoted largely to portraiture ancient and modern, the artist Elaine de Kooning said with some (but not total) accuracy, "I adore Goya. Every portrait he ever did is a kind of attack, but in the attack he is also understanding the person." By no means were all Goya's portraits attacks, any more than Velázquez's were, though he was more than a little rough on the Spanish royal family whose court painter he became. Attack was a gesture of independence and defiance (if it was attack, not just search) that he did not feel the need to exert when he painted the *Maja* on whom his eyes feasted with obvious relish, an act of submission rather than aggression. The idea of attack (except in the ancient art of caricature) is a modern one. Search has always been the key to great portrait painting. "It is for the artist . . . in portrait painting," Whistler said, "to put on canvas something more than the face the model wears that one day, to paint the man, in short, as well as his features."

The modern English novelist, critic, and editor Cyril Connolly declared that in every fat man a thin man is screaming to get out. By the same token, in every portrait painter a disappointed or disillusioned artist seems to be screaming to get out. Most artists, from the beginning of the Rennaissance at least, have regarded portraits as second strings to their bows, hackwork, repellents against the familiar wolves at their doors—but they took pride, if not always pleasure, in their ability both to probe and to please. When the advent of the camera in the 1840s deprived a great many artists of their financial mainstay, only the rich or the self-important or public figures commissioned painted and sculpted portraits. To them the artist's primary social function had always been portraiture, whatever his aesthetic function might have been. They were, however, aware that the more important an artist was as a creator of other kinds of paintings and sculptures, the more prestige reflected on the sitter.

Some characteristic in man makes him want to have his mask pierced, his public face seen through, the self disclosed that no one else sees—but only a little, only to that shallow point just beneath the surface where he believes (or hopes) that something noble lingers. He wants to meet posterity with his best face forward, and it still seems to be true that not even the most penetrating or complimentary photograph has the same value in his eyes as a painting or a sculpture. The very time and effort that an artist must devote to a portrait is one contribution to its value to the sitter, and this contribution is vastly increased if the artist is held in high esteem. Max Beerbohm, the novelist who was also a caricaturist, wrote some years ago: "It seems to be a law of nature that no man is ever loath to sit for his portrait. A man may be old, he may be ugly, he may be burdened with grave responsibilities to the nation, and that nation in a crisis of its history; but none of these considerations, nor all of them together, will deter him from sitting for his portrait."

The last thing that a sitter wants is a true likeness. He wants a suggestion of a resemblance. A portrait is not a fact; it is a symbol. Portraits are illusions. If they are paintings, they are two dimensions pretending to be three. If they are sculpture, they are bronze or marble or plastic pretending to be flesh. In a nice parody of this

Claes Oldenburg made a plaster mold of his face ten years ago and cast it in Jello. But whatever they are, they are not, and no one wants them to be, the truth. A suggestion of the truth, to be sure, is what is asked for—a reminder of it, not a revelation.

Only truly vain men and women want to be portrayed as they are. When Oliver Cromwell asked Sir Peter Lely to paint his portrait a little more than three hundred years ago, he said, "I desire you to use all your skill to paint my picture truly like me, and not flatter me at all; but remark all those roughnesses, pimples, warts and everything as you see me; otherwise I will never pay one farthing for it." Ah, but what about character? Do you think the artist would have been paid had he not made Cromwell appear noble and intelligent?

It seems to me that the best portraits today are not attacks played out on a battlefield of canvas: they are neither contests between personalities, on the one hand, nor sycophantic panderings to vanity, on the other. The attack portrait is essentially a propaganda picture ("I'll expose the rascal!") just as the official, boardroom portrait is a public relations picture ("The surface is what counts!"). These are the easiest kinds of portraits to come by today—the autopsy or the apotheosis. The rarest portrait, and in the long run the most durable, is the one in which the subject and the artist agree that the ultimate aim is not merely a superficial likeness but a work of art based on the artist's penetrating search of himself as well as his subject. Thus both sitter and artist are present at their own creation.

Architectural Digest, 1975

Dilettantes

Waste no pity on the dilettante; he's better off than many of us, unless we are willing to classify ourselves as dilettantes and have the right to do so. Dilettantism is not a state that is easily or casually achieved. It is a state of grace, and more. It is a cultural necessity, which can be, and often is, a very pleasant state as well.

If this seems to you outrageous, bear with me for a moment; let me try to dispel your concern and perhaps entice you to join in the fun and satisfaction. If it weren't for dilettantes, the world would be a less interesting and entertaining place, the arts would be in the doldrums, music would be monotonous, even sports would suffer from indifference.

Dilettante is a word that has lost its once erect posture, its dignity, and its guts—and nothing has come to replace it. It once meant "connoisseur," but it has come to mean "dabbler" and, as an adjective, "superficial or amateurish." I would settle for something between expert and tyro because it occupies that center ground of knowledge and enthusiasm on which the arts depend for encouragement, appreciation, pleasure, controversy, and, especially, intelligent support.

The word comes from the Society of the Dilettanti, a group of Englishmen in the eighteenth century who met to discuss the arts and sciences seriously but informally, and it was out of the Dilettanti that the royal academies of the arts and sciences seem to have been born. These dilettantes were concerned with the preservation, examination, and encouragement of knowledge.

A few months ago I had the pleasure of meeting with a group of dilettantes (though it hadn't occurred to them to call themselves that) in New Haven, Connecticut; they call themselves Friends of American Arts at Yale. In the past several years they have met periodically as a group for three days of serious study and the inter-

change of ideas and experience. Some of them are justifiably classified as experts, but most of them are dilettantes. The experts are
professional scholars and curators; the dilettantes are concerned
collectors and amateurs—in the true sense of that word—of the arts
of our country. They are part of an important American tradition,
a tradition that has made the arts viable and available.

The Yale University Art Gallery, where these dilettantes meet,
wouldn't be what it is—a collection of great range and exceedingly
high quality—if it were not for dilettantes. One of them, for example, was James Jackson Jarves, the eccentric, prickly, sharp-eyed
son of the founder of the Sandwich Glass Company. After dabbling
in a variety of careers (businessman, newspaper editor, diplomat),
Jarves went to Paris in the 1850s and discovered the Louvre, which
stunned him into becoming a dedicated and effective dilettante. He
was hooked. Then he moved to Florence and started to immerse
himself in Renaissance painting. It was a time when scholarship in
art history was as primitive as the paintings that attracted him, and
he began to buy and to write about what he saw in the hope of
opening the eyes of his contemporary Americans to what his vision
had captured. Jarves's eloquent and discerning articles were published in *Harper's New Monthly Magazine* and collected in books, *The
Art Idea* and *Art Hints;* his collection became a nucleus of the Yale
Art Gallery. The Jarves Collection is one of the finest groups of
Italian primitives anywhere outside Italy.

Another dilettante of a very different stripe was a contemporary
of Jarves, Luman Reed, a New York wholesale grocer. Reed was an
upstate boy who came to New York in his teens and by the time
he was forty had made a considerable fortune. He built himself a
splendid mansion and had a brief go at buying old masters, but,
realizing that fakes were being palmed off on him by an unscrupulous dealer, he turned his attention to his contemporary American artists. His special pleasure was in Asher B. Durand, who has
been called the father of the Hudson River School, and in Thomas
Cole, one of America's most accomplished nineteenth-century artists. Reed not only bought the work of these and other artists but
helped support them and in some cases paid for their travel to Europe to study. He did this because, he said, "The artists are my
friends, and it is a means of encouragement of better men than
myself." On the top floor of his house on Greenwich Street Reed
had an art gallery, which he opened to the public. He commis-

sioned Cole to paint a series of five very large pictures called *The Course of Empire,* and he paid the magnificent sum of five thousand dollars for them. Since it was a long and painstaking job for Cole, who lived in the Catskills, Reed wrote him, "Draw on me for whatever funds you may need during the winter. . . . You must not hesitate to call on me and you will not be disappointed." Like Jarves's enthusiasm, Reed's created a treasure that is still intact. The Luman Reed Collection is one of the great assemblages of nineteenth-century American paintings, and it is displayed at the New-York Historical Society, one of the most delightful of New York's museums.

America has produced, and still produces, hundreds—indeed hundreds of thousands—of dilettantes of the arts, without whom its museums and concert halls, opera houses and ballet theaters would be drab or nonexistent. Relatively few of them have been important patrons and collectors like Jarves and Reed; by all odds the largest number have constituted the equally important audience for the arts. It is because of the eyes and ears of conscientious dilettantes—their concerns, discretion, knowledge, and finely honed sensibilities that demand the highest performance—that the arts flourish in our society today. They give encouragement and understanding, and are repaid by the satisfaction of their educated and adventurous appetites, and by abundant delight.

Dilettante comes from the Latin *dilectare,* meaning "to delight," and who would quarrel with delight? Not you or I or any other dilettante.

Architectural Digest, 1980

Mirror Images

*T*he architect Leone Battista Alberti, who built churches in such noble cities as Florence and Mantua about five hundred years ago, and who wrote the first printed book on architecture, declared that "Narcissus, who saw his reflection in the water and trembled at the beauty of his own face, was the real inventor of painting."

It is an unkind conceit by an artist—himself not remembered for his modesty—based on the myth of the young man who spurned the adoration of the nymph Echo, leaving her, you might say, almost speechless. She could only repeat the last words spoken to her—a sad fate for a chatterbox, which she was said to be. The goddess Diana, protectress of the nymphs, saw to it that Narcissus fell in love with his evasive reflection in a woodland pool, and as Thomas Bulfinch wrote in the *The Age of Fable*, he "pined away and died."

I came on Alberti's snide observation about painters in a book of *Five Hundred Self-Portraits*, published nearly fifty years ago in Vienna. I was searching for a self-portrait of Jacques-Louis David that I remembered only vaguely, and I ended by looking at all five hundred pictures of how artists have appeared to themselves, or how they wanted to appear to their contemporaries and to posterity. Narcissus, to be sure, had something to do with the paintings and drawings and sculptures that looked back at me from the printed page, but so did honesty and economy. By no means all the portraits were acts of self-adulation or the camouflage of flattery. A few were cold-blooded statements on the ravages of age, many seemed honest searchings for whatever truth can be deduced from surface appearances, and still others were conscientious exercises in the crafts of painting and sculpture.

The earliest known self-portrait, I was interested to learn from this book, is an Egyptian tomb relief that scholars have dated 2650

B.C. In it the sculptor is a spectator of a busy scene of farming and fighting. He sits on his haunches, drinking from a vessel offered him by a servant, and he has gone to the trouble of signing his name, Ni-ankh-Ptah, in the stone above him. That he was allowed to get away with putting his signature into a place inhabited by deities must say something about the respect with which artists were regarded by the rich and powerful in that distant day. He may, I suppose, have been the equivalent of the pampered court painters of some four thousand years later—masters like Rigaud at Versailles and Velázquez in Madrid.

Inserting oneself as a relatively inconspicuous figure in a religious or secular scene is an older trick than I had known. It was not uncommon in the Renaissance for an artist to make himself one of a crowd of spectators (he can often be spotted, because he is the figure looking directly at you, full face, as he saw himself in a mirror), or to use himself as the model for one of the principal characters. One legend, that Saint Luke painted a portrait of the Virgin, gave a number of artists the opportunity to show *themselves* painting the Virgin—every bit as large as she. It was an exercise in what might ungenerously be called spiritual vanity, an exercise in which the Flemish masters of the fifteenth century particularly indulged. Saint Luke was looked upon as the patron saint of artists, who felt themselves fortunate to be watched over by one so important, and made the most of it.

One Italian master even found a way to upstage Christ Himself. Veronese, in the magnificent and vast *Feast in the House of Levi*, which hangs in the Accademia in Venice, is the most prominent figure in his own painting. He stands in the foreground in half-profile with arms outspread. This boldness may have contributed to the trouble he got into with the Inquisition over the painting.

There is a famous instance of self-portraiture for a legal purpose. On the wall of Jan van Eyck's remarkable double portrait of Mr. and Mrs. Arnolfini, painted in 1434 and now in the National Gallery in London, there is a convex mirror in which the backs of the couple and two tiny figures facing them are reflected. One of those figures is van Eyck. Above the mirror are the words, in Latin, "Jan van Eyck was here," along with the date. The couple are holding hands in the presence of witnesses to solemnize their marriage. The painting, a sort of wedding certificate, was commissioned by Arnolfini, a banker on business in Flanders, who most likely planned to send it to his family in Italy to assure them that he was legally married.

The handiest and cheapest model in any artist's studio is, of course, the artist himself or herself, and artists not only record their own features but often pose for figures they want to incorporate into their paintings. Albrecht Durer often did this, prettying up and solemnizing his own features to represent holy faces. Velázquez, in one of the best known self-portraits, stands with brush and palette in hand before a large canvas. He is painting the infanta with her entourage, thereby establishing himself as an honored member of the royal household. Occasionally an artist is inspired, by a dark wit, to use his head in strange ways. In Caravaggio's *David with the Head of Goliath*, the severed head—held by the hair, at arm's length—is Caravaggio himself. I recently saw a drawing by an old friend, Paul Cadmus, in which he has used his own features, distorted, in the same context.

Sometimes artists painted themselves amid a collection of friends, as Courbet did in his *L'Atelier du peintre*, and sometimes, as Charles Willson Peale did, with their families. Self-portraits turn up in surprising places. The bald head of Ghiberti protrudes from a sort of porthole in the bronze "Gates of Paradise" he designed for the Baptistery in Florence, and portraits of some wood-carvers look out from choir stalls and organ cases. Until the invention of the camera early in the last century, the self-portrait was the only way an artist could be sure his features would be preserved for posterity, unless he could persuade a fellow artist to record them. Some, like Rubens—an uncommonly handsome man, if we are to believe his pictures—depicted themselves with dash; some, like Rembrandt, whose self-portraits are many, have recorded with unexampled honesty the increasing puffiness and blurring of their features as they grew old.

The camera seems not to have halted the art of self-portraiture—far from it—though it may have made that art more honest and more subjective. Artists know truths about themselves that others only suspect. Frivolous artists depict themselves frivolously; abstract artists schematically; solemn painters harshly; vain painters prettily; dishonest artists glossily. Like Echo, unlike Narcissus, when artists paint or sculpt or draw themselves, they have the last word—false or true.

Architectural Digest, 1984

The "Culture Industry"

*I*t is very probably old-fashioned of me to think of culture and industry as separate and distinct from one another, though I am aware that culture is a salable commodity and that its commercialization is not unique to our century. I was, however, surprised when someone recently handed me a copy of a report of a survey called "The Non-Profit Arts and Cultural Industry." *Industry?*

On the face of it, it seemed to me absurd to call the service of the muses an industry, but as I read the survey, what emerged from the statistics and the language was indeed the picture of a multibillion-dollar industry with all the accoutrements associated with, let us say, the pharmaceutical industry. It has research departments, management consultants, distribution systems, government lobbies, public relations departments, interlocking boards of directors, and outlets large and small. It is a vast hungry conglomerate of orchestras, museums, ballet and opera companies, civic theaters, academies, and cultural centers. It differs in one vital respect from other industries: It is in the business of losing money, not of making it. It fears the vitiating influence of the mass market, at the same time that it woos it with missionary zeal.

Since "the industry" is in the business of losing money (when it doesn't, it is suspected of having gone over to the enemy), it must constantly expand its overhead. It builds vast centers and their smaller satellites, and makes converts to the high aesthetic purposes for which it stands. The culture business today is, in fact, a great deal more like a new "established church" than like an industry. Its municipal centers, built to the glory of art—and civic pride—are its new cathedrals; our great museums are its basilicas; the thousands of converted barns and movie houses for the performing arts and the many hundreds of small museums are its parish churches.

A large part of the troubles this industry/church faces comes from

105

the fact that those who administer it cannot decide whether they are running a church or an industry, a religion or a business. The high priests and priestesses of the arts—the museum directors, symphony conductors, opera impresarios, ballet masters and their acolytes, the performing and creative artists—know very well that it is a church they serve and that serves them. Those laymen who raise the funds, negotiate the contracts, sit on the boards, and needle the public know very well that they are engaged in an industry, even if it is a perverse one with its head buried in the clouds.

And so there exists between these two factions certain tensions. One of the tensions is that nobody knows who is boss—or, rather, everyone thinks he or she is boss.

On the one hand, the director of an artistic organization usually believes that art must be served first and the public second, that art is more important than the people who look at or listen to it. It is his primary function to preserve and perform the miracles created by artists, to study them and to make them available to the truly interested few. The other faction, the operative laymen, are most often concerned first with the public—the more the merrier—and second with the quality of the bait that attracts them. I wonder if any work of art is as interesting to them as a long line of people waiting to see it.

When these opposing points of view become irreconcilable, it is the director who is fired. The board may be his temporal boss, but his conscience and convictions are his spiritual bosses. Such head-on collisions have occurred with increasing frequency in recent years.

One of the most powerful centers of this nonprofit cultural industry has decided to play it both ways by admitting that it is a business first and a temple of art second. The board of the Metropolitan Museum in New York, "the greatest treasure house in the Western Hemisphere," as it likes to call itself, has decided that in the future it will be managed by a paid president, a retired diplomat who has boasted that one of his qualifications is that he does not pretend to know anything about art, and therefore will not interfere with artistic policy. Under him will be a director, who will be in charge of aesthetics and doctrine, of acquisitions and exhibitions.

This is looked on with the darkest suspicion and foreboding by a large segment of the art world who regard this move as demeaning, a put-down. The arguments on both sides are too elaborate and too subtle to explore here, but my own opinion is that the odds are strongly against putting the ultimate power in the hands of the laymen, rather than the clergy, of our new cultural church. I am reminded of a statement made some years ago by Lincoln Kirstein, very possibly the most brilliant and effective patron of the arts in our time and the man who nurtured the New York City Ballet to its preeminence. He has asked why he wasn't more businesslike in the operation of the company. He replied, "If we were businesslike, we wouldn't be in business."

Architectural Digest, 1978

The Art Epidemic

*S*carcely a week goes by that the press fails to announce an auction that has established new record prices for works of art. There is a stack of clippings about such matters on my desk, and the one on the top of the pile reports that a Japanese collector just paid $2.156 million for a painting by the Dutch artist Piet Mondrian executed in 1930. It was, according to the *New York Times*, "the highest price ever paid at auction for a work of abstract art." There seemed an aesthetic logic in its being bought by a Japanese collector; no abstract artist was more meticulous, more formally polite, or more chastely controlled in the exactitude of his abstractions than Mondrian. He built his paintings the way the Japanese build their houses—spare and geometric.

Just below that clipping on my pile is one that tells of a sale two weeks earlier, in which a painting by Mary Cassatt of a woman reading a newspaper brought a record price—for her—of $1.1 million, and a pastel by Degas fetched $3.74 million. The latter was bought jointly by the Getty Museum in Malibu and the Norton Simon Museum in Pasadena. It was the highest price ever paid for a pastel at any auction. And this was not the first time the Norton Simon and the Getty had shared the purchase of a masterpiece; a magnificent Poussin is also sometimes at home at one and sometimes at the other.

The apparently exorbitant prices paid for some works of art are, of course, merely symptoms of the art boom: solid, highly visible symptoms that everyone—except artists, who can't quite believe it—can understand. The art boom is commonly measured in numbers, since figuring out what art truly means to the public is next to impossible. We know we are enjoying an art boom, because we can put the evidence in a computer: How many people go to museums, compared with the number who go to the ballpark? How many millions do corporations donate to art institutions? How many cities today are building museums or adding wings to meet the demands of civic pride? I can think of four in New York alone. In this sense the art boom lends itself more readily to interpretation by statisticians than by social historians, art historians, and other humanists who are more interested in why than in how much or how many.

High art, like high tech, is obviously "in," and reasons having nothing to do with inflation make it so. Only a tiny percentage of those who collect art do so as a hedge against the fluctuations of the stock market or the value of the dollar. To be sure, the startling sums collectors and museums are willing to pay make news, and where museums are concerned, it is the kind of news that brings the public flocking. Some years ago, when the Metropolitan Museum of Art bought Rembrandt's *Aristotle Contemplating the Bust of Homer* for the then astonishing price of $2.3 million, staff members at the museum were delighted by an enthusiastic young boy who turned up at the information desk and asked, "Where's the hundred dollar picture?" The art boom is only superficially a financial and aesthetic phenomenon. It is essentially a social phenomenon that involves far more than just art lovers.

When some thirty years ago, Francis Henry Taylor, then the director of the Metropolitan, wrote "Art museums are the cathedrals of the twentieth century," he was thinking of museums as places where the faithful congregated to pay homage and to refresh their spirits. To be sure, not all who came could be counted among the faithful. Many came, as they still do, because they thought it was a social obligation, an obeisance to art they could tell their friends they had duly paid. Some came out of curiosity to see what all the expensive fuss was about. Many others came because museum-going was an inexpensive way to kill a weekend morning or afternoon.

Art is catching, the way many enthusiasms are. No one is totally immune to it, as there are arts for all tastes and all degrees of sophistication. If, however, the statistics about attendance at museums, their proliferation, their budgets (and deficits), the increase in cultural centers sponsoring opera, theater, and dance, in cities small and large, are true—and I'm sure they are—something has happened to the American character that cannot be measured by computers. The fact is that America is in the clutches of what can only be called an art epidemic.

This agreeable epidemic started some years ago at a time when the art market, far from its present effulgence, was in the doldrums, when art was looked on as the province of the elite, and artists were viewed by most Americans with suspicion, as bohemians in ivory towers and not quite to be trusted. A depression seems an unlikely incubator of an art boom, but it was in the 1930s that it germinated, and it has been nourished by the social, political, and technical changes that in half a century have so remarkably transformed our views of the pursuit of happiness and the ways in which we pursue it.

Architectural Digest, 1984

The Birth of the Boom

*T*he art epidemic that happily engulfs us today germinated in the dark days of the 1930s. Many artists, even the most gifted ones, were out of money, if not out of work—which is to say that there was no market for what came willy-nilly from their brushes and burins and chisels.

"Hell!" declared Harry Hopkins, FDR's administrator for federal relief projects, in 1935. "They've got to eat, just like other people!"

This observation was made in response to those who looked with misgivings on the government's several public art projects, the first of which the Treasury Department initiated in 1933. It came about at the instigation of George Biddle, a respected artist and a friend and classmate of President Roosevelt at Groton; it was put into action by Henry Morgenthau, secretary of the Treasury, whose wife was "an art enthusiast."

In the next few years, all across the country, in small cities and towns and in big ones, local citizens by the thousands watched artists at work decorating post offices and other public buildings and discovered that just like other people, artists on scaffolds did not live in the clouds but were hardworking, meticulous craftsmen. The murals often provoked intense arguments, usually about subject matter—folks took exception to how their local mores and histories were interpreted—but their existence opened many eyes to art as a living process, not just a historical fact.

The Treasury projects and the WPA, which came along in 1935, may have been responsible for a great deal of second-rate art, but they produced some paintings and prints that are now, with the revival of interest in the thirties, looked on with fresh, approving eyes. There was scarcely an artist among the group known as the New York School, which emerged with fanfare after World War II, who had not been carried by "the project." It was WPA artists who

111

transformed the silk screen—used only commercially to print on such things as milk bottles—into an art medium (serigraphy) and turned out "multiple originals," as they called them, by the thousands. The WPA also set up Community Art Centers, where anyone could come to paint and sculpt and work at crafts.

The approach of World War II and rearmament gradually brought an end to these projects, and war itself created new ones. The army and navy commissioned "combat artists"; the Treasury Department and the Office of War Information now commissioned hundreds of posters, and magazines like *Life* and *Collier's* employed artists as war correspondents, just as *Harper's Weekly* had dispatched young Winslow Homer to report the Civil War. Activities like these, along with the appalling reports of art looted by the Nazis and the spiriting of masterpieces out of museums to sequester them from bombings, sharply focused popular attention on the importance of art.

After seeing a slump in attendance during the thirties, museum directors were delighted to watch the crowds swell during the war. Many who came were men and women in uniform exploring the sights of great cities they had never visited before. Many others, because of gas rationing and other restrictions on travel, took advantage of local enticements. It was not long after hostilities ceased that thousands of students on the G.I. Bill swelled the enrollment in art schools and graduate schools of art history, a newly popular subject.

Galleries selling modern art of every sort and quality sprang up where few had existed before, and a new enthusiasm for collecting seized many young people who, if they could not afford paintings, bought prints and drawings. The art market came to life, and because of the vitality of its young artists and the eagerness of its collectors, New York City discovered it had replaced Paris as the center of the art world. As artists had for years gravitated to Europe, they now came to America to be at the vortex of the excitement.

But the art epidemic, whose seeds were sown in the Depression and curiously nourished by the war, would not have proliferated to its present extent had it not been for the remarkable changes in the ways our society uses its time. The decade following the war brought with it a usually happy dilemma called the "new leisure." We had time on our hands, a situation freighted with unaccustomed problems. Leisure, like work, we discovered, had its pressures as well as its pleasures.

The work week dropped from forty-eight hours to forty for some, and for others from forty to thirty-five. Men and women who had worked on Saturdays won the dreamed-of two-day weekend, and they looked around for all sorts of ways to occupy their leisure. Resorts flourished, and so did old and new industries that manufactured means for passing the time: television sets (a novelty then); boats of all sizes; sports equipment; do-it-yourself kits. Adult education courses in every conceivable subject abounded, and thousands took to the potter's wheel, the loom, the workbench, and the easel. Sunday was no longer just a day to rest up for Monday. Everybody belonged to the new leisure class now.

It was this new freedom of time that accelerated the spread of the art epidemic. The art boom, as it is dramatized by the very large sums of money that change hands today for works of art, has some of the transitory character of a real estate boom. The art epidemic, on the other hand, while some of it is more show than substance, is the happy consequence of half a century of living with the arts in harmony and respect, and of being instructed, enlivened, and generously enriched by them.

Architectural Digest, 1984

Baiting the Museum Trap

*L*ast autumn I was in Paris when the vast exhibition of works by Picasso opened in the Grand Palais. It opened on a Saturday evening to the official world of diplomats and politicians and dignitaries of the arts, and I went early the next day, along with what seemed to be half the Parisians who get up on Sunday mornings. The exhibition consisted of some six hundred works by the "master," given to the Republic by his heirs in lieu of death duties. My recollection of this occasion, several months later, is of the backs of heads, of profiles and coifs and murmured comments in almost every language.

Exhibitions like this one and the horses of San Marco and the treasures from Dresden—to which crowds come by the mob—are known as blockbusters in the museum world. Since almost all museums these days live at least partially on grants from the National Endowment for the Arts and from state arts councils, and put on the blockbusters with grants from large corporations—often with the help of private foundations—the door count (how big the mob is) is of basic importance to curators and trustees when it comes to justifying the need for support.

A result of this is a bind in which museums are sometimes caught: between their educational function and showmanship; between art and artifice; between introspection, which art is uniquely qualified to inspire, and exploitation, which is, or should be, none of its business.

Pity the poor curator. Consider his problem as it affects you and me. He (and, increasingly, she) is a personality split a great many ways—part scholar, part educator, part money raiser, part sleuth, part seducer of collectors whose possessions he covets for his collection, part author, and part display artist—a glorified window dresser, a showman. His merchandise, not for sale, but for con-

114

sumption all the same, is something he wants to make as attractive, nay, seductive, as possible. He wants what he shows not only to catch the eye but to hold it long enough to evoke more than snap judgments. In recent years he has developed remarkable techniques in order to do just this.

The curator starts with a space that is essentially an empty box, its nature determined by an architect who, one can suppose without being unjust, is more interested in the shape of the space he encloses than in the objects he predicts will be displayed there. It may be used for large paintings or small drawings, sculpture the size of horses or as small as Byzantine ivories. Recently, the curator has partially solved this dilemma by designing flexible spaces within which it is possible to build false walls and ceilings, as I. M. Pei did in the so-called house museums in the new East Building of the National Gallery in Washington, and as Gordon Bunshaft arranged for his circular Hirshhorn Museum on the Mall. It is the curator's first problem to lick the box, to get the better of its shape and character in order to make it work for small objects or big ones, delicate or bold ones, brilliant or all-but-colorless ones, and sometimes all of these together. He hopes to lead the visitor from one object to the next by some sort of visual or chronological or stylistic logic, so that one object or group of objects contributes to the understanding of those that come next. He must do this without allowing the display to overwhelm what it is meant to complement.

When the elements of architecture, art, and display come together in harmony they combine to create a unique delight. During the past winter such an alliance was enacted between some very ancient bronze horses and the very modern Lehman Pavilion of New York's Metropolitan Museum of Art, with what seemed to me faultless results. It happened that I had seen this exhibition, called "The Horses of San Marco," in Burlington House, the home of the Royal Academy in London, where it had looked handsome. In the Lehman wing it was magnificent.

A single golden horse from the four that for centuries have graced the facade of the basilica of San Marco in Venice was the centerpiece of the show, and it was accompanied by other ancient bronze horses, horses' heads, flanks, and tails (fragments, that is) and with drawings (including several by Leonardo from the Queen's collection), small equestrian bronzes, and appropriate ancient ceramics. The golden horse stood alone, and he could be seen from afar—as

one sees him in the Piazza San Marco—or at arm's length, his remarkable splendor and dignity hovered over by an air of mystery.
No one knows where or when the magnificent horses of San Marco
were made. They may have been cast in Greece as early as the
fourth century B.C. or in Rome as late as the fourth century A.D. It
is known that Venetian soldiers in the Fourth Crusade "liberated"
them from the Turks and brought them back to Venice from Con-
stantinople in 1204, and that fifty years later they were set above
the main portal of San Marco. Nearly six centuries later the French
army made off with them and took them to Paris. Venice reclaimed
them in 1815 after Napoleon's final defeat.

Just one of the horses was in New York; all four of them were
suffering from the ravages of pollution and have been removed for
restoration and study. They will be replaced on the facade of the
basilica by copies, and the ancient steeds themselves will be stabled
safely within Venetian walls.

Blockbusters like this one are, in a sense, temporary museums
within permanent museums. They are surrogates for travel and
challenges to the ingenuity of curators and installers. And if one is
not in a hurry, there are ways of enjoying them without being
trampled underfoot. The trouble with the Picasso show in Paris was
me; it would be around for a long while, but I couldn't be. I waited
until the horses had been at home to the public for some weeks, I
went at the moment the museum doors opened for the day, and I
left when the mob arrived. Of course I didn't have to worry about
one-upping my friends. After all, I had seen it in London.

Architectural Digest, 1980

Does MoMA Know Best?

A few months ago, a New York savings bank sponsored a full-page ad in the *New York Times* with the headline "When it comes to identifying the masters of modern art, MoMA knows best. How about you?"

The occasion for this ad was the celebration of the fiftieth anniversary of the founding of the Museum of Modern Art, called MoMA by an in-group of millions. It opened in 1929 with an exhibition of those then little-known masters Cézanne, Gauguin, Seurat, and van Gogh. From the very first, MoMA knew best, and she has never been reluctant to say so.

For me to take MoMA apart would be an unfriendly act. She is an old friend—and, in some respects, an old enemy—of mine, and now that she is middle-aged, it is sad to see her running to fat, both physically and intellectually, and one shouldn't, perhaps, tease her. But middle age overtakes institutions, too.

When the museum opened, only a handful of dealers anywhere in America were exhibiting what was Modern, and scarcely any museum was willing to stick its neck out. Artists like the ones that MoMA chose to show first, though it is hard to believe now, were still considered outrageous by all but a few Americans. Impressionism had been difficult for the nineteenth century to accept. It was just as hard for the early twentieth century to accept Postimpressionism.

The founders of MoMA decided it was best to ease the public into what it was really up to by showing works of "the founders of modern painting," and then progressing to more recent and "advanced" art. (In case you are in any doubt about when Modern Art started, it began with Cézanne. How do I know? MoMA told me so.)

Once MoMA cut loose, she was a very spry girl indeed—adventurous, headstrong, ambitious, and delightfully outrageous. She was doctrinaire, didactic, and determined, a zealous proselytizer who would have been as lost without her Philistines as a missionary without his cannibals. The Word had been given to her.

The Word came down from Alfred H. Barr, Jr., the museum's first director. As patriarchs go, he was an extraordinary one; among his entourage he enjoyed a papal infallibility. What he said was art was art, and the museum, for as many years as he was either its director or curator of the museum's collections (which is what he was called after the president of the museum's board fired him and he wouldn't go away), was a mirror image of his taste. Early in his career he decided that a number of things that other people thought of as entertainment, like movies, were art. He also thought that ball bearings, propellers, insulators, and coil springs were art, and exhibited them as such. And we cried "Amen!"

I stopped in at the museum the other day to refresh my memory. I had spent a great deal of time there a few years ago when I was writing a history of the place and as much of the soap opera that is its true story as I thought proper (*Good Old Modern*, Atheneum, 1973). I wanted to get the feel of it again. As I walked through the galleries, I thought, "This isn't a museum of modern art. This is the Alfred H. Barr, Jr., Museum of Art, and they ought to call it that and stop kidding themselves." It was modern once. It is now a historic shrine.

No such thing will happen, alas. The fiftieth anniversary is being celebrated by a drive for fifty-five million dollars in order to expand the museum's facilities. A new forty-four-story tower for "luxury apartments" is to be built above part of it (they sold the air rights for seventeen million dollars), and the rents (tax-free to the museum) will be used to help support it for a few years, until it decides again that it isn't big enough. The anniversary is also being celebrated by a series of exhibitions that might be gathered under the title "Contemplating Our Navel."

Two of these are "major exhibitions," to use MoMA's term. Next year, starting in May, there will be a mammoth Picasso "retrospective, unprecedented in scale . . . with works from public and private collections all over the world." Currently, there is an exhibition of "Art of the Twenties," which has been assembled by William S. Lieberman, who has contributed his discernment and scholarship as a curator to many aspects of the museum's collections for many years. This is his swan song. He has been appointed chairman of the Department of Twentieth-Century Art at the Metropolitan Museum—a good thing for it and, I trust, for him. No one, I guess, can say he is leaving a sinking ship, though the ship seems to me intellectually becalmed. Of his final fling at MoMA, Lieberman says: "The exhibition is a tribute to the vision, conviction, and achievement of Alfred H. Barr, Jr., the first director of the museum and the man who founded its collections and by definition established their scope."

As Mayor Hylan's wife is reputed to have said to Queen Marie of Rumania when Her Majesty visited New York in the twenties, "Queen, you said a mouthful."

Architectural Digest, 1979

The Caretakers

*C*urators, especially curators in art museums, lead lives on the edge of a precipice, aware that almost no one will notice them unless they slip and take a header. As a rule, the press pays them no attention unless they have made, or seem to have made, a blunder that involves quite a lot of money and a loss of face. It does not matter whether the accusations brought against them are true or false. A curator who buys a painting or a sculpture or an antique tapestry or chair that either is, or is suspected of being, a forgery can be sure of getting into the papers, something that rarely happens to the curator who discovers a masterpiece with whose authenticity no one can find fault.

Two years ago, you will remember, CBS News attacked the validity of a painting bought in 1960 for $675,000 by the Metropolitan Museum of Art. Attributed to Georges de La Tour, it was called *The Fortune Teller*. The story surfaced on "Sixty Minutes" on the say-so (or say-no) of "experts" who contended that the picture was an obvious fake. The press took up the dispute and had a field day with the ensuing arguments pro and con. (It seemed to me that the Met won this argument hands down on the evidence its curators presented.) The incident is worth mentioning here merely because of what it says about the public's pleasure when an art expert is accused of the kind of fallibility taken for granted in economists, politicians, and demographers. On such occasions curators become more interesting than the artworks that are their daily (and midnight) concern.

It would be easy to say, "Pity the poor curator," but in my estimation it is more appropriate to say "Envy him," or, increasingly, "her." (Many of today's curators are women; some, like Agnes Mongan, the great expert on old-master drawings, have been eminent for two generations.)

120

A curator is part handmaiden, part nanny, part teacher, part hoarder, part writer, part showman, part crystal gazer, part historian, part snoop, part missionary, and part toady. The curator worth his or her salt is engaged in a perpetual love affair with things. It is not often that those of us who are outsiders see a curator busy curating. It is characteristic of curators to be publicly invisible, unobservable but felt presences. Some of them, like swimmers exploring under the surface of the water, can be known only by their bubbles. They are looking for things that are out of sight to most of us. If the thing the curator surfaces with is beautiful, we don't bother to ask her name or his.

The curator occupies an essential if ambiguous position in the hierarchy of a museum. If he has the first word when it comes to adding an item to the collection, he never has the last word. There are two layers of decision above him. His boss is the director. The director's boss is the board of trustees, and as someone has observed, every museum trustee is a curator manqué, and most of them enjoy exercising their own taste when it comes to approving or disapproving an addition to the collection.

Furthermore, as a vice-director of the Metropolitan once said to me, "A museum is like a collection of duchies." He meant by this that each department is in competition with every other department for funds. So the curator must have acute peripheral vision to keep an eye on his colleagues as well as sharp eyes for searching out quality.

The attitude of curators to most trustees is one of resigned suspicion. Theirs is the mistrust of the professional for the judgment of the amateur. Curators know they cannot bully trustees, so they must seduce them, often with flattery, to accept their recommendations. When they are not seducing trustees, they are making eyes at collectors whom they hope to convert into donors, or flirting with foundations and corporations in the hope of getting the funds for special exhibitions.

The curator's view of the museum is bifocal. The distant view is of people crowding the galleries over which his department holds title—the estates of his duchy. The close-up view, which he prefers, is of the objects it is his responsibility to know more closely than he knows his friends and family—objects he must study and care for, and, when necessary, commit to the museum's hospital, its department of conservation. He is a scholar with a taste for the intrigue and the rough-and-tumble of the art market, with the instincts of a ferret and the doggedness of a sleuth. He must be sensitive to the vagaries of fashion and able to anticipate where it will alight next. To a very considerable extent, curators and dealers not only create the audience for the arts, they lead it by the nose.

You and I are either won or lost by the curator. His skill as a showman must be subtle, as he is dealing with subtle things; it must be unobtrusive, to give the things a convincing voice; and it must be instructive without being intrusive. The late A. Hyatt Mayor, curator of prints at the Metropolitan, the most accomplished curator I have known and an essayist of great skill, wrote that a "show can be explained in the foreword to a catalogue, but most visitors will get more out of very brief notes, in the style of telegrams, scattered here and there like a paper chase. In such diminutive essays every word must act like a fishhook to catch the visitor as he drifts along. One hook ill baited, a paragraph that looks long, and the visitor is on his way elsewhere." Proper baiting of the hooks can be achieved, like the hanging of a show, only with love, knowledge, and reticence. A showy curator is a contradiction in both terms and style.

There are two kinds of us fish who swim through museums: those who look first at an object and then at the label, and those who read the label first to decide whether to look at the object. Those who look first have come for pleasure; those who read first probably shouldn't have come at all. Curators know that, but the good ones don't let on.

Architectural Digest, 1984

Assessing the Museum Boom

Some years ago a friend of mine, who was a dealer in old masters and a few contemporary artists he thought distinguished, said to me of what was then the beginning of the art boom, "All it means is less art for more people." This was in the 1950s. It was a clever, aphoristic remark that struck me because it sounded as though it ought to mean something profound, but I wasn't quite sure exactly what.

It is plain, though, that if he were still alive he would not have changed his mind. There is certainly no less art (he might think it of less distinguished quality), but what there is appears to attract a great many more people than were interested, or professed to be, thirty-odd years ago. You obviously cannot measure the cultural importance of art by a nose count, and you cannot measure it by what has happened and is happening in the competitive growth of museums. What seemed to many of us like a refreshing breeze in the 1950s is now, by contrast, a driving gale.

One of the most commonly cited indicators of the health of the national economy, if we can believe the pundits (and of course I do), is "housing starts." Whether they are up or down a few percentage points compared with last year tells me whether my optimism quotient should be up or down. If we were to use "museum starts" as a comparable measure of the health of the visual arts, we would have to be bullish about their future. Museum starts are booming, not just in our most populous cities but in our smaller ones. The investment in recent years in art palaces and mansions (we settle for nothing less) is either appalling or inspiring, depending on whether you agree with my art-dealer friend that this means "less art for more people."

The art world, indeed the museum world, is not of a single mind about the building boom. In New York, for example, there are at the moment two unresolved, provocative museum-enlargement (call them "aggrandizement") projects that have deeply concerned parties at loggerheads. One of these is the scheme designed by Michael Graves, the guru of Postmodernism, for the expansion of the Whitney Museum of American Art. It is now housed (its third home) in a dour building designed by the late Marcel Breuer, a guru of Modernism, and Graves's proposal threatens to engulf it. The other is a seven-story addition designed by Gwathmey Siegel to rise in back of—and partly be cantilevered over—the Guggenheim, which was the creation of Frank Lloyd Wright. It is the only Wright building in New York, and by any sculptural standard it is one of the most beautiful he designed in his very long career. Whether it is a good museum building is another matter. It isn't.

These two projected structures (and I would be reluctant to bet on their ever being built as planned) are a drop in the bucket of New York money currently being poured into museum construction. A few blocks down Fifth Avenue from the Guggenheim, the Metropolitan Museum just opened the 110,000 square-foot Lila Acheson Wallace Wing, to be devoted to the museum's collection of twentieth-century art. This new wing is bigger than the Guggenheim as it now stands. Just a couple of years ago MoMA doubled its exhibition space and added a building next door on Fifty-third Street with an apartment tower above it, the income from which the museum hopes will help solve its financial problems. Across the East River, the Brooklyn Museum—designed in 1893 by McKim, Mead & White with a five-hundred-foot facade—has announced that it plans to double its size at a cost of "between $50 million and $100 million" over a period of twenty years.

I have used New York examples because they are right under my nose. But look at Los Angeles, which has expanded its County Museum of Art, built a brand-new Museum of Contemporary Art, and will be adding another museum and research center to the Getty. Look at the new Museum of Art in Dallas; the new building for the High Museum in Atlanta; the Museum of Fine Arts in Houston; the addition to the Boston Museum of Fine Arts; the new Portland (Maine) Museum of Art. Look at Fort Lauderdale, Minneapolis, Baltimore, and colleges and universities almost everywhere, and you will see new art museums or newly expanded ones. Museum starts are startling.

Add to this the little and not-so-little museums that now occupy space in corporate headquarters, some, as in New York, branches of public museums, many others corporate collections to which the public as well as employees have access. The Business Committee for the Arts is a nonprofit organization based in New York that advises businesses on where and how to spend money supporting the arts. Its president, Judith A. Jedlicka, has said, "Art has become a business tool," by which she meant, I believe, an employee morale-booster and a corporate image-inflator. She estimated that in 1985 about a thousand corporations had permanent art collections. Some corporations, like PepsiCo, Chase Manhattan Bank, IBM, and Reader's Digest, have collections of very considerable size purchased at very considerable expense over quite a long period of time.

No one, as far as I know, objects to corporations purchasing works of art, though unquestionably some stockholders look upon it as an unnecessary business expense. There are, however, in the art community many articulate objectors to the way museums are putting their money into what used to be called bricks and mortar and today would better be called marble and glass.

Every museum I know of skates on a very thin financial edge and is constantly scrambling for money (civic, federal, foundation, and private) to keep its doors open. Every time it adds a wing or a new building, it increases its overhead and the squeeze becomes tighter. Its excuse for expanding is invariably to have more space to show its collection, a very large percentage of which is in storage (and much of this very large percentage is where it belongs). But essentially behind the scheme is the attractive but mistaken notion that bigger is better, and this is abetted by civic and intramuseum competition. If city A has a new museum that is bigger or gaudier than city B's, then B must build to keep its cultural socks up. This is nothing more than cultural one-upmanship.

The function of an art museum is often defined as to collect, display, conserve, and study works of art. Its mission is part educational, part scholarly, and part the stimulation and satisfaction of a very special kind of hunger. A museum is not a building; a building is merely a place. A museum is a collection, and its quality is what matters. It seems to me that the museum building boom has got its priorities backward. Art attracts art; fancy buildings attract curiosity seekers, politicians, boosters, and climbers. If museums were to mind their primary business of refining and improving their collections rather than building palaces, we would have not less art for more people but more and better art for more people to whom art, not gaudy display cases, is what matters.

Architectural Digest, 1987

Populism Versus Elitism in the Arts

*A*n old friend of mine, a retired museum director and accomplished fly fisherman, an authority on modern sculpture, who would rather watch a Red Sox game than the local repertory theater company, said to me at lunch recently, "Dammit. They've got quality and elitism mixed up. They say if you're for quality, you're an elitist. It's a lot of blasted nonsense." He was talking about the arts.

The "they" he was referring to are numerous these days. Some of them are politicians fighting to get government funds for their constituents who have pet projects that might conceivably come within the scope of arts councils. "They" are also some taxpayers who don't see why their tax dollars should be used to support certain cultural enterprises—grand opera, for example—which they do not happen to enjoy and believe to be vestigial remnants of embalmed arts. "They" are sociologists, who are more interested in "mass culture" than in what they refer to as "high culture." Some are critics in the Marxist tradition, who contend that only the privileged classes are well enough educated to enjoy anything that passes for fine—as opposed to popular—art, and that supporting the fine is robbing the poor to amuse the rich.

After lunch my friend and I watched a ball game. A second baseman, taking a toss from the shortstop, touched his base, leapt high to avoid a slide from first, and threw as he turned in the air to double the batter.

"That fellow," my friend said, "moves as beautifully as any ballet dancer and with as great control."

My friend by some definitions is an elitist. He admires quality and has spent his life searching for and isolating it, and making it available to the public. So are most baseball fans elitists. They go to

127

ball games as much to see perfection of performance as any bal-
letomane.

Not many years ago those who believed that high culture was
threatened by mass and middlebrow culture were at loggerheads
with those who saw in popular culture the promising wave of the
future. They argued in the little magazines, in academic conclaves,
indeed wherever the custodians of our sensibilities chose to dispute.
There were those who were convinced that catering to "the masses"
by "the media" was going to water down "all that is best" in our
culture. The serious arts were about to be swamped, they insisted,
by a wave of mediocrity. These critics were answered by those who
contended that popular culture is democratic culture, that American culture could not and should not be measured or constricted
by formulas imported from Europe, with its traditions of aristocratic
and autocratic and academic control of taste. The very flexibility
and social and intellectual mobility of our society fertilized the growth
of a great variety of audiences for the arts over which no one could
take control. It was a jolly confrontation of points of view which
served to change nothing.

The word *elite* occurred sparingly in these arguments. It has an
unpleasant ring in American ears. Now it has turned up, because
politics has gotten into the act.

What in the 1950s was a dispute, about high culture versus what
Dwight MacDonald nicknamed "midcult" and "masscult," has become a name-calling. "Elitist" and "Populist" have become epi-
thets. Money has changed the tune. When the high arts (that is,
the museums, symphonies, opera companies, and so on) were poorer,
their champions and detractors argued about philosophical matters;
now they argue about who ought to have first crack at the till.
Since the National Foundation for the Arts and the Humanities became a reality in 1965, the federal, state, and local subsidies to art
institutions have grown from almost nothing to about three hundred
million a year. On the one hand, the so-called elitists argue for the
maintenance of quality in both the established and experimental
arts, and on the other, the so-called populists argue that "the People" are not served by these arts, which are too recondite to contribute to their everyday fulfillment and their need for constructive
leisure. Moreover, they should get their share of tax dollars to promote popular arts and crafts. Obviously I oversimplify their posi-
tions, but so, it seems to me, do they.

The result is something that those of us who urged caution about the intrusion of government into the arts some years ago warned against. Tax dollars are political chips, whether they are for the arts or housing or highways. Politicians are going to get what they can for their constituents, and their taste is going to reflect their constituents' taste. The worst that can happen is that this might lead, as it did in the 1950s, to politically motivated decisions about which arts are good and which are bad. And this, in the democracy of the ball park or of the museum, is none of government's business.

Quality of life *is* its business, however, and quality should be the only measure by which funding for the arts, high and popular, should be divided.

Architectural Digest, 1978

Art and the Pleasure Principle

*I*f you want to raise the hackles of a collector, an art expert (including a historian, a curator, or a critic), an *antiquaire*, an art dealer, or a dedicated dilettante, all you need say is, "I don't see why an exact copy isn't as good as an original." You don't need to add, "I'd just as soon have the copy." The chances are you certainly wouldn't.

These are words that have provoked heated argument for almost as long as art has been purchased or stolen or, as happens in wars, plundered. In a recent book, *The Democratic Muse*, Edward C. Banfield, a professor of government at Harvard, raises this question in a discourse on whether government should support what he regards as the elitist arts. By elitist he means those that have aesthetic significance for a small percentage of the populace. "From a purely aesthetic standpoint," he argues, "it can make no difference when, where, or how a work was produced: all that matters is its quality as art. . . . There is no reason to believe that a copy—even a poor copy—cannot be an even *better* work of art than a very good original." He cites Michelangelo (Vasari is his source) as having made copies of old masters, "making them look old with smoke and other things so that they could not be distinguished from the original." (He didn't mention that these works were pen-and-ink copies of engravings at a time when, as one biographer of Michelangelo noted, "property of drawings had not become a topic of moral casuistry.")

There isn't room here to take issue with Professor Banfield's thesis about the role of government as an art patron, some of which I agree with. But it could be noted that only elitists of a sort are going to appreciate his government courses at Harvard, an institution which, like many museums, receives federal support. It also seems to me doubtful whether the good professor believes that an

130

approximate clone of himself would be as satisfactory as the original.

Be that as it may. There are many good human reasons why many people (and not just elitists) think that copies, however cleverly wrought, are no substitute for originals, however imperfectly made. The desire to own an original—that is to say, a unique product from an artist's or craftsman's hand—is to the serious collector almost as important as his or her own identity.

Each collector is one of a kind, and just as he cherishes his individuality, so he cherishes the singularity of the object to which he devotes his pursuit, his purse, his pride and, at best, his love. It speaks to him of another individual who applied his or her intellect, imagination, sensibility, and skill to the creation of a personal accomplishment no one else could make. Moreover, it ties the collector to a place and a time, sometimes distant and long gone, where a hand like his own performed a kind of magic that he is unable to achieve. Through the object—whether painting or sculpture, fragment of ancient textile or delicately carved bit of ornament—he shakes hands with the hand that made it and converses with the mind that conceived it.

A copy, however close it may be—it cannot be exact—may be pleasing and nice to have around, but it bears the same removal from the original work that a movie or a television show bears to a live performance. It is filtered through other minds, controlled by other hands, edited by other temperaments. It is seen with the eyes of the copyist. Copying is a performing art, an interpretive process, and each age interprets an earlier age differently, conditioned by its own prejudices, cultural atmosphere, and visual values. A copy of a Renaissance painting made by a twentieth-century copyist has a different look from a copy made by a Renaissance copyist, not just because of the difference in the materials used but in the way the world looked then and now to artists.

The collector's world is beset with booby traps. Until this century, copying old masters was part of every conscientious art student's training, and commissioning copies to ornament drawing rooms was a common practice in the days before the mechanical reproduction of paintings and sculptures. But the fakers of works of art are another matter, and so are the dealers who try to pass off copies as originals. Undoubtedly, Michelangelo's copies of engravings, which were intentional fakes, fooled his contemporaries, who looked with eyes that were conditioned like his own; it is most unlikely they would fool us.

It is a truism in the art world that forgeries come to light, very often, long after they were made. The remarkable fake Renaissance and ancient pieces made by the greatest forger of our century, Alceo Dossena, who learned his trade as the restorer of stone ornament on Venetian palaces, fooled his most sophisticated contemporaries for years. But after a while the pieces didn't seem quite right to discerning eyes. They reflected the sophisticated taste of the time in which they were made, and as ways of looking changed, their deception became apparent. Museums that had bought them whisked them out of sight; so did private collectors. They had become (and here is the nitty-gritty) not only less desirable but less beautiful to modern eyes. The sculptures had not changed; the eye of the beholder had, and beauty, as they say, is in the eye of the beholder. A thing of beauty is not necessarily a joy forever.

Collectors are determined beholders and believers. They believe in fine distinctions, and they also believe in the fallibility of their taste. (I exclude collectors who buy for speculation and those whose basic motive is the snobbism of one-upmanship.) What matters finally is the pleasure anyone takes in an object, whether he owns it or sees it in a friend's house, a museum, or a dealer's gallery. I doubt if there is any such thing as Professor Banfield's "purely aesthetic standpoint." The pleasure derived from a work of art is a complex of previous experiences, the mood of the moment, the game of making comparisons, and the pleasure of discovery, often sugared with sentiment and sometimes with sexual excitement.

One afternoon I was looking with great pleasure at a landscape by Camille Pissarro, the Impressionist painter, at the Metropolitan. A lady standing next to me said to a friend, "You know, I like the reproduction downstairs in the bookshop better than this one." My inclination was to laugh at her for being naive. On second thought it seemed to me none of my business. If she bought the copy and it gave her pleasure, it in no way reduced my pleasure in what came straight from the artist's hand. There are a lot of people who see things the way she does, but then there are a lot of people who see them somewhat, but not exactly, the way I do.

Architectural Digest, 1985

III

Art for Our Sake

We, meaning you and I, bought a painting several months ago for $4,070,000, a portrait of a young man with a large geranium plant. It was painted by the young man's older brother, Rembrandt Peale, 185 years ago, and it has aged gracefully. The geranium is there because the younger Peale, whose first name was Rubens, is said by legend to have planted the seeds for it, and it was the first geranium grown in America. The National Gallery of Art in Washington, D.C., bought the picture for us and is going to see that it is taken care of and that it will be there for us to look at whenever we please.

I am delighted that it now belongs to us rather than hanging over someone's mantel. It had been in private hands for years, and only rarely could we see it when it was generously lent to a museum, as its most recent owner, Mrs. Norman Woolworth, did in 1970 at the time of the Metropolitan Museum of Art's one hundredth birthday. I saw and enjoyed it then, but now I have a proprietary feeling about it. The National Gallery acquired it for us with funds from a fifty-five-million-dollar kitty it calls the Patrons' Permanent Fund. When J. Carter Brown, the gallery's director, bought the painting at auction in New York and the auctioneer announced the new owner to hearty applause, Mr. Brown stood up and said, "Any donations?" This was, I assume, greeted with friendly laughter.

In one remote way or another we all chipped in for this picture, partly through the taxes we pay (a tiny proportion of which goes to the support of the arts) and a great deal more through the taxes we do not pay—because donations to educational institutions, including museums, to an important extent are tax-deductible.* The

---

* Recent changes in the tax laws have sharply reduced the "important extent."

American system of patronizing the arts is, I guess, the most complex, subtle and, I contest, the most successful of any nation's in the world. It is certainly the most democratic. It is therefore worth taking a brief look at this system by way of explaining how we bought the painting of the young man and his geranium, and at some reasons the arts always seem to be on the brink of bankruptcy but never seem to go broke. (Do I hear catcalls from the balcony?)

We are all art patrons whether we like it or not. I like it, and what is more I take it for granted, as I believe most of us do, though some people do so grudgingly, some indifferently, and some with great enthusiasm. Our particular form of indirect art patronage goes back to 1917 and the First World War, when a provision for deducting a share of charitable donations in computing income taxes was written into law. Personal income tax was a new thing then; compared with today's taxes it was peanuts and, furthermore, almost anyone who could read could understand the tax forms. Some wise senators foresaw that this new, unpopular tax, prompted by the costs of war, would encourage those who were accustomed to contributing to hospitals, colleges, and other such institutions to reduce their donations on the principle that charity begins at home. So, to oversimplify a complex story, the invitation to be a patron of culture was offered to every taxpayer, and it has remained so. If it was not so, the National Gallery almost surely would not have its kitty to buy the portrait of Rembrandt Peale's brother, and most orchestras and opera, dance, and theater companies would be silent.

Government funds to support the arts come today from the public sector; what we give as individuals, businesses, or foundations comes from the private sector. Where the arts are concerned neither sector, as far as I know, had a name until the federal government got involved with the establishment of the National Foundation for the Arts and Humanities in 1965. (Before this a few states and cities had already set up their own arts councils.) We think of the public sector as *them* and of the private sector as *us,* and we are right. We contribute vastly more in direct support than they do, and we do so as our interests and impulses guide us and, in some cases, as the Internal Revenue Service inspires us.

It would do us an injustice to imply that tax deductions are the motivating force in our support of the arts. We support them because we believe in them and need them. In Europe there are no such deductions. In England, for example, if you give your Rembrandt to the National Gallery, you are profusely thanked—period. This is also true in Italy, Belgium, and Germany. If, as the famous art dealer Lord Duveen of Millbank did, you pay to have the Elgin Marbles in the British Museum cleaned and give richly to museum collections, you might get a peerage and a gallery named for you, but not a tax deduction. In France a gift of a work of art to a national museum (in a sense all French art museums, unlike ours, are national and are administered as extensions of the Louvre) can have a pleasant effect on the donor's inheritance taxes but not on his income tax.

The richness of the collections in many of our museums long predates the seduction of tax deductibility. It has its roots in the judgment and acquisitiveness of such passionate collectors as J. P. Morgan, Mr. and Mrs. H. O. Havemeyer, and the merchant Benjamin Altman, who enriched the Metropolitan in New York; Mrs. Potter Palmer and Martin Ryerson in Chicago; Charles Lang Freer of the Freer Gallery in Washington; and the Misses Hewitt, whose decorative arts collection is the basis of the Cooper-Hewitt Museum in New York. There were hundreds of others.

Vanity, to be sure, made its contribution to the formation of many of these collections and to their having been given to you and me. These were collectors who were not gambling on the art market, though they were extremely canny in its ways. They were gambling instead on the quality of their perceptions and the sureness of their taste, testing their judgment against time, not against fashion. They were art lovers, not art flirts, as so many people who call themselves collectors are today.

Joseph H. Hirshhorn, whose collection has a museum to itself on the Mall in Washington, as does Mr. Freer's, was a small dynamo of a man who liked to explain himself. "I have bought art for the past forty-four years without any formal education," he wrote me in January 1975, three months after the museum opened. "I bought with a 'gut and heart' feeling. I felt I had some understanding—not buying what was 'fashionable.' I bought for a variety of reasons—mostly love." He scratched a postscript: "We have had 600,000 visitors up to yesterday."

Someday when you have a chance to enjoy our new Rembrandt

Peale at the National Gallery, walk a few hundred yards to the Freer Gallery and the Hirshhorn. They could scarcely be more different, but they have this in common: Each is the harvest of "mostly love," and the works they contain belong to you and me and the millions of us who merely by looking take possession of them.

Architectural Digest, 1986

Two Provincial Museums

*T*he word *provincial* too often has an unnecessarily pejorative meaning. In this day when regional differences are diminishing, it should be a compliment, not a put-down, and I use it as such. We can do with all the variety we can save, and we can also do with the excellence of smallness as a reminder of human scale.

I say this by way of introducing "two provincial" museums and the extraordinary delights that they, and others equally remote from our so-called cultural capitals, have to offer. Both of them happen to be in the northeast corner of the country, and they are mentioned less because they are likely to fall into your path than because there are almost surely museums near you, wherever you are, that can afford you similar pleasures. One is the Sterling and Francine Clark Art Institute in Williamstown, Massachusetts, a neighbor, but not a part, of Williams College. The other is very nearly at the top of Vermont in the town of St. Johnsbury.

The Clark Museum, as it is generally called, is essentially a one-man show, as the St. Johnsbury Athenaeum is also—one man's taste, that is, not one man's work. Mr. Clark, an army engineer by training and a horse fancier, had a very personal eye and unfashionable taste for his time. His collecting years were from 1912 to his death in 1956, and he thought his art collection was nobody's business but his own and his wife's. When he opened his museum to assure the collection a permanent home, he provided no budget for publicity, and the building itself seemed almost to defy entrance. It was a marble structure that might have been a mausoleum, the home of a secret society or a bastion of private banking.

The structure matters secondarily; its contents, which can only be hinted at, matter remarkably—thirty Renoirs, for example, some of the first quality. Have you ever had your eyes knocked out by a painting of six onions and a garlic bud? There are eleven Corots, small eighteenth-century drawing-room pictures, including a Fragonard, and little figure paintings by Millet of astonishing magnitude. There are Degas bronzes of horses, a great but tiny Degas self-portrait, and a small, magical Daumier. Most of these paintings are not as big as a sheet of typing paper. There are also Renaissance paintings—a Piero della Francesca, one of the three or four on this continent, a very bloody panel by Signorelli, a Mantegna, a Crivelli, two Goya portraits, one of them first quality, excellent Winslow Homers, Sargents, and so on by the dozens.

Clark's taste was nothing if not catholic, though he obviously had no use for his contemporaries. In one small gallery are three sturdy Gérômes, a much-sneered-at salon painter when Clark bought them, and two Bouguereaus that would gladden the heart of any barfly—big, lusty nudes with glowing flesh and generous attributes. I have not even mentioned the collection of English silver or the prints and drawings.

The St. Johnsbury Athenaeum gallery is an entirely different matter in scale and quality and interest. The Athenaeum is primarily a library, but on the back of it there is a gallery—one large, skylighted room. It is the only authentic 1870s American art gallery I know of anywhere in the country, and its charms are undeniable.

The room is dominated by a vast landscape, *Domes of the Yosemite,* by Albert Bierstadt, the so-called Hudson River School painter who rarely painted the Hudson but who loved vast expanses. The Brooklyn Museum acquired one last summer about the same size and is said to have paid $200,000 plus for it. With it are works by Cropsey, Asher Brown Durand, Worthington Whittredge, and other splendid practitioners, including a few sculptures of undeniable nineteenth-century sentimental nobility. Nothing has changed since Governor Horace Fairbanks of Vermont presented it to his hometown.

These two very different museums have an enchantment in common with each other and with many small provincial museums. The small museum invites, nay seduces, the eye to concentrate on the intimate object. The sculpture or painting or drawing that is so often overwhelmed not only by size but by numbers in major museums, though it may not be an important masterpiece, can speak quietly but authoritatively for itself.

Peripheral vision plays tricks in museums. A picture or sculpture half seen out of the corner of the eye often refuses to be spurned.

In the small museum it is never more than a few strides away, not galleries and marble halls and staircases and mobs of schoolchildren away. The pressure is off the visitor. The banquet may be rich, as it is at the Clark, but it is not endless. Though there may never be enough time to digest all the charms of more than a few especially delectable morsels, there is sufficient time to fall in love with them.

And certainly who would deny the pleasant delights of love in the provinces?

Architectural Digest, 1976

E. B. White, My Meat

*N*ear the beginning of his nice biography of E. B. (Andy) White, a very nice and very gifted man, Scott Elledge says, "White's long and interesting literary association with mice started early." I was inclined to say, "Oh, rats!" But my literary association as a reader with Mr. White's mice started early too.

It was nearly forty years ago that I first read *Stuart Little,* the story about the dignified and adventurous mouse born to the Frederick C. Little family of New York that so discombobulated children's librarians and delighted almost everyone else. I borrowed a copy from my three-year-old grandson. He hadn't got around to it yet, for it was still boxed with Mr. White's spider book, *Charlotte's Web,* and *The Trumpet of the Swan,* the one about the mute cygnet whose father swiped a trumpet for him from a music store. The three of them were still sealed like sliced bacon in plastic.

Mr. White's affinity with mice (he had a pet mouse when he was a small boy) was more than a child's fleeting interest in animals because they are little, timid with people, and resourceful when they are on their own. A mouse was a mirror to little Elwyn Brooks White, the youngest by a long shot (five years seemed a long shot) of six children, a shy, affectionate, and private child with a nose forever poking into things and an eye for capturing and keeping what he saw. A squirrel, a seedling, or a spider web delighted him equally. He was born in 1899 in Mount Vernon, a New York suburb, when that town was still about half country and half living quarters for commuters. His family was prosperous, if not rich, and he spent his childhood in a spacious Queen Anne house with wide porches and a corner tower. He explored on his bicycle, and he started early to write about what he saw and heard for *St. Nicholas* magazine. A gold medal from that children's publication sealed his occupational fate.

Mr. Elledge, who professes English at Cornell, has traced Mr. White's career at the typewriter from suburban childhood to a farm in Maine he bought years ago, where the ratio of puttering to writing has quite naturally increased with advancing age. As any biographer of a living myth must, he has talked with many of Mr. White's intimates and acquaintances. He quotes Mr. White's letters to his friends, wife, and son. He includes poems, many of which have the specific gravity (and often the delicacy and ensnaring quality) of a spider web, and pieces from *The New Yorker* that reveal their author as something of a spaniel that can't decide which side of the screen door it wants to be on. When he is in the city, Mr. White whimpers to be in Maine, and when he is in Maine, he looks sad-eyed to New York. Like Stuart Little, who pursues his love, a bird that has flown away to freedom, he expects to "be traveling north until the end of my days."

Mr. Elledge is fair, respectful, thorough, entertaining, skillful, and unpedantic. He has performed a splendid exercise in scholarship and literary analysis, and the result is fun. He does not pull his punches, because, it seems, there are no hard ones he wants to throw. He likes, admires, and is amused (but not bemused) by his subject, who is a sort of Eagle Scout of American letters. Mr. White has won all the merit badges, his heart is pure, he can tie and untie complicated knots, and he knows the names and habits of beast and fowl and sprout and loves them all. He is consistently on the side of the angels but flies a little below them, kept airborne by a precious and incorruptible sense of the ridiculous.

To be a writer was Mr. White's early ambition, and he drew a distinction between writer and author. Author seemed to him a noun with overtones of pretentiousness, and Mr. White was not (and is not) pretentious. He regards himself as a skilled craftsman, a user of tools for converting the visual world into verbal constructions that are both simple and workable. He has the greatest respect for his tools, and he keeps them clean and orderly and sharp. He is economical, and he eschews any ornament that detracts from clarity. He distrusts "fine writing" as a Bauhaus architect scorns curlicues. He can't help being funny even when he is being serious, and his humor invariably strengthens rather than dilutes his intention. "The whole duty of a writer is to please himself," Mr. White wrote, pleasing himself, "and the true writer always plays to an audience of one. Let him start sniffing the air, or glancing at the trend machine, and he is as good as dead, although he may make a nice living."

Mr. White started early to please more than just himself, even if the audience was just one other, a member of his family, a girl, a schoolmate, the editors of *St. Nicholas*. He was an editor of his high school paper; he was editor-in-chief of his college newspaper and "a big man on the hill" at Cornell. In his early twenties he sent poems to F.P.A.'s column, "The Conning Tower," thereby multiplying the audience of one by thousands.* To use a phrase he would never use, Mr. White "stayed loose," footloose, and he traveled across the country with a college friend in a Model T called Hotspur, picking up money wherever he could from odd jobs (some very odd—he sold roach powder for a few days) and selling pieces to local newspapers. It was an "exalted footlessness" made possible by the knowledge that he could appeal to his parents for help, though he managed not to.

Two things Mr. White faced squarely were his typewriter and his hypochondria, which, Mr. Elledge says, "appeared during his adolescence" and did not desert him. All through life, Mr. White seems to have thought of himself as ill, which was as bad, or as good, as being ill. Illness was a cocoon to which he retreated, carrying his typewriter with him. It was an excuse, a protection against the pressures of family and friends and work, but it was also a place for the germination of private seeds that produced public blossoms.

Mr. White was twenty-seven when Harold Ross, thirty-four, the founder and editor of *The New Yorker*, gave him a job he was not sure he wanted. Ross put him to work doing rewrites and editing "newsbreaks," which he continued to do until 1982. (When nothing else in the magazine was funny, they were.) He edited "Talk pieces" and "casuals" and soon was writing the "Notes and Comments" at the head of "Talk of the Town" in a manner no one has equaled. He was a sort of editorial handyman, hiding part of the time behind the editorial "we," which he did not like. His sidekick was James Thurber, and to most readers *The New Yorker* was for years their magazine. It was Mr. White who discovered Thurber's drawings, with which he strewed the floor of the little office they shared, and he persuaded a reluctant Ross to publish them. To-

*Franklin P. Adams, 1888–1960, whose column appeared in several New York newspapers from 1913 to 1941.

gether Mr. White and Thurber concocted a satire, *Is Sex Necessary?*, which sold well.

In 1928 he married Katharine Sergeant Angell, a colleague at *The New Yorker.* She was the fiction editor and a formidable influence on what came to be known, not always as a compliment, as "a *New Yorker* story." They bought a farm in Maine on Allen Cove, where he indulged his fondness for animals and the smell of salt water and sailed his boat alone while she cultivated her garden, read manuscripts for the magazine, and nursed her nostalgia for New York.

At heart Mr. White is an essayist (even his immensely successful children's books are essentially narrative essays), and he restored that literary form to a good name, something it had not enjoyed in journalistic circles since the Edwardians. Journalists wrote pieces or columns or articles; academics wrote papers. Essays were looked on as gentle exercises suitable for reading at literary teas. There was, however, no other name that accurately fitted Mr. White's pieces. They were sometimes gentle, sometimes vigorous, agreeably opinionated behind a mask of modesty, sly, and masterfully made. They were often very funny and sometimes very sentimental. (Mr. Elledge quotes snippets of them that do not appear in Mr. White's books.) It was in Maine that Mr. White wrote a series of essays for *Harper's Magazine* called "One Man's Meat" (later collected as a book), though he found a monthly deadline burdensome and the lead time between sending in his copy and its publication an unwelcome hindrance to timeliness.

The first of Mr. White's books for children, *Stuart Little,* was long in gestation, quick in birth. He had been making notes and writing episodes and had gone so far as to submit them to several publishers as suggestions of what might become a book. They were politely returned. In one of his *Harper's* essays, he had written "It must be a lot of fun to write for children—reasonably easy work, perhaps even important work." The children's book editor of Harper & Brothers, who had heard about the stories from Mrs. White, urged him to let her see them. "By March 1939," Mr. Elledge writes, "Stuart was reported to have 'taken everybody into camp' at Harper." It took Mr. White just eight weeks to pull the stories together and deliver a manuscript.

Children's librarians were dismayed at the wounds that might be inflicted on little minds by an ordinary mother's producing a mouse. One librarian who saw the galleys pleaded with Mr. White to withdraw the book. Stuart and his successors, Charlotte the spider and the mute swan Louis, became intimate friends of millions of children and their parents and, as far as I know, bugged none of them. *The Trumpet of the Swan* is Mr. White's longest sustained piece of prose. His other books (there are eleven in all) are collections of essays, memoirs, parodies, poems, letters. He was, as he insisted, a writer and, under pressure, an editor; not an author but an essayist and a poet; not a novelist, historian, or reporter.

"I feel that a writer has an obligation to transmit, as best he can, his love of life, his appreciation for the world," he said in 1970 when he was given an award. The next year, when he received the National Medal for Literature, he said, "Writing is an act of faith, nothing else. And it must be the writer, above all others, who keeps it alive—choked with laughter or with pain."

New York Times Book Review, 1984

Thurber's Bread and Butter

*H*arold Wallace Ross who conceived, founded, and for twenty-six years edited *The New Yorker*, a "comic weekly," as he called it, once put his head into the office of the checking department of his magazine and asked in all seriousness, "Is Moby-Dick the whale or the man?"

Ross was not in the least bothered by his ignorance. He made no pretense at being an educated man. He read almost nothing except what went into his magazine, and yet he was unquestionably one of the great editors of his day. He was, as James Thurber says of him in *The Years with Ross*—an extremely entertaining memoir—"a restless force" with a "magic gift for surrounding himself with some of the best talent in America, despite his own literary and artistic limitations."

Everything and everybody, Ross believed, conspired to make his life difficult, and his life was inseparable from the life of his magazine. World War II, he felt, was perpetrated just to make trouble for him, as were the occasional illnesses of the members of his staff and the disrupting affairs and marriages of his writers. He dreamed of an editorial office that ran like a perfect machine, and yet, Thurber says, "Ross was not Ross until he had churned the hour, any hour, into a froth of complaint and challenge." He "worried deeply about the state of the world, or a comma"; they were equally important to him.

He questioned everything, queried every detail on galley proofs, sometimes infuriating his writers, but always putting his finger on their weaknesses, and he worked himself into illness and exhaustion. (Once, Thurber says, when Ross took to a sanitarium for two weeks of rest, "a woman in the ninth month of hysterical pregnancy had been the doctors' and nurses' pet until, the legend has it, 'A man showed up who thought he was the editor of *The New Yorker.*' ")

If Ross didn't know whether Moby-Dick was a whale or a man, many readers, when they have finished Thurber's lively and extremely anecdotal memoir of himself and Ross, will not be quite sure whether Ross, a commanding behemoth in the deep waters of journalism, was a myth or a man.

No one can surround himself with as many gifted mythmakers as Ross did—with Thurber and E. B. White, with Aleck Woollcott (with whom he had an irreparable falling-out), with Marc Connelly, Peter Arno, Dorothy Parker, Helen Hokinson, Robert Benchley, John O'Hara, and a younger and equally brilliant generation of writers and artists—without becoming more myth than man. Ross was in every sense "good copy," but as editor he was also in a sense forbidden copy, and so the stories about him have proliferated by word of mouth into a garland of anecdotes through which it is difficult to see him clearly.

There is almost always something slightly condescending in the affection with which writers tell stories about editors. To a writer the measure of an editor is primarily whether the editor has the wit to recognize his (the writer's) genius and the talent to foster it. If he hasn't, then he is a clod, or precious, or only interested in money. If he has, then he is a precocious child to be humored. Thurber puts it this way, "I think the moths deserve most of the credit for discovering the flame."

Thurber joined the staff of *The New Yorker* two years after it first appeared in 1925. He applied for a job as a writer, and Ross said to him, "Writers are a dime a dozen, Thurber. What I want is an editor. I can't find editors. Nobody grows up. Do you know English?" Writers of Thurber's caliber are certainly not a dime a dozen, and he does know English. He knows it well enough, indeed, to tease it into performing all sorts of agreeable tricks for him, and this memoir fairly leaps with amusements, jumps through hoops of indiscretion with the greatest of ease and always lands lightly on its feet. There is not a dull page (though there are infuriating ones) in the book.

The Years with Ross is not, strictly speaking, a biography, and it is as much about Thurber as it is about his editor. It might almost be called "Ross's Years with Me," for Thurber, indeed, emerges more clearly than Ross, possibly because Thurber knows himself better and finds himself more interesting. In his [foreword] he makes his intention clear: "I determined that it [the book] should not become a formal schematic biography of the kind that begins: 'There was joy in the home of George and Ida Ross that November day in 1892 when their son Harold was born, and emitted his first cries of discontent and helplessness.' " But he does, in a series of chapters devoted to the secret life of *The New Yorker* and through "flashbacks and flashforwards," recount enough of Ross's life to satisfy anyone short of a biographer.

Ross was born in Aspen, Colorado. He got his first job on a newspaper (the *Salt Lake City Tribune*) when he was fourteen. He edited the *Stars and Stripes* in Paris for two years during World War I and, when he was discharged, worked on *Judge,* an earlier comic weekly, and on the *American Legion Weekly.* For two years he carried around the dummy of *The New Yorker* trying to find someone to put up the money to publish it, which Raoul Fleischmann did. During the first two years the magazine teetered on the edge of oblivion, but prosperity caught up with it (or it with prosperity), and the magazine has grown in wealth, size, and influence ever since.

It has weathered depressions and wars and recessions with urbanity, humor, diversity, meticulous attention to detail and, above all, quality of performance. It has made capital out of its parochialism at the same time that it has made the whole world its meat. It has changed the nature of American short fiction and the character of visual humor; its "profiles" (a word that originated with Ross) have set a standard for succinct biography, in the tradition of Lytton Strachey, that is the envy of editors of other magazines. Ross's comic weekly has frequently been called in the trade the best-edited magazine in America.

It has also been the most edited magazine. The success of *The New Yorker,* Thurber says, "was created out of the friction produced by Ross Positive and Ross Negative." It was "Ross' eternal questioning, his incurable discontent, and his psychological, if not indeed almost pathological, cycle of admiration and disillusionment," that made him such an extraordinary editor. But Ross could be swayed by other such remarkable editors as Katharine White (Mrs. E. B.), who was responsible for the introduction of fiction of quality into the magazine; by Gus Lobrano; by William Shawn, Ross's colleague for many years and his successor. "Ross," Thurber writes, "true to his stature as an editor, learned to change his mind and his magazine with the changing world and the temper of the times."

Ross surrounded himself with many of the wittiest men and women of his day, which was just yesterday (he died in 1951). It is these wits who people *The Years with Ross* in such a manner that life at *The New Yorker* emerges as a lovely sort of pageant of lunacy, of practical jokes, of feuds and foibles. It is an affectionate picture of scamps playing their games around a man who, for all his brusqueness, loved them, took care of them, pampered and scolded them like an irascible mother hen. It makes reading that will delight even those (if there are any) who have never heard of Ross's comic weekly.

After all, what difference does it make whether this is the way a magazine gets edited?

New York Times Book Review, 1959

Calder's Universe

A few weeks after the Calder exhibition opened at the Whitney Museum in New York, I found myself there in a vast elevator with about two dozen seven-year-olds. Being shut in an elevator with that many laughing, poking, shouting, giggling children off on a cultural spree the likes of which they had never dreamed of was probably the ideal introduction to the exhibition—one Sandy would have enjoyed enormously.

Here was joy, enthusiasm, innocence, surprise—everything (or almost everything except order) that greeted us as the doors of the elevator opened. Facing us was an object (perhaps it is better to say a complex) 33 × 55 feet, of aluminum plate, stainless steel, and a twist of pipe like an extended segment of a giant's telephone cord, which turned slowly. Indeed everything but the stainless-steel background moved, and the aluminum plates, in bright, almost primary, colors turned at varying speeds. Concealed in all this were seven motors, and it was called *Universe.*

It was not just Calder's universe but Everyman's. It was in constant motion, but it was not going anywhere. Indeed it seemed to consume itself without in any way decreasing itself. It might have been Einstein's universe.

Forty-three years ago Calder made another *Universe,* which Einstein saw at the Museum of Modern Art in New York. It was much smaller and quite different from this new one, and after the great physicist watched it for forty minutes as it was propelled through its ninety cycles by a tiny motor, he said, "I wish I had thought of that myself." In her catalogue of the exhibition (it is far more than that; it is a major work on Calder, with lots of plates, many in color, and as much fun, almost, as Calder himself) Jean Lipman, who directed the show, says that *Universe* "performs like a monumental abstract ballet."

In a sense, the entire exhibition was a ballet, a purposeful and lively and, above all, elegant dance of forms and shapes and colors with not a note of solemnity anywhere. It was a gala performance of the culmination of a serious artist's lifework, an occasion he enjoyed tremendously and at the opening of which, dressed in his inevitable red flannel shirt, he danced himself, a thing he loved to do. If he had a partner, so much the better; if not, he danced alone, though there is a precision and subtlety in the ways his mobiles dance that got obscured by his bearlike shuffling, no matter how precise the intentions in his head. His ebullience was equaled only by the dexterity of his powerful hands and the incisiveness of his intelligence.

I have never been to an exhibition where so many people were smiling. The children's smiles sometimes changed to looks of awe at the seemingly aimless but completely orderly movement of the hanging mobiles. On the other hand, they shrieked with pleasure at the toys made of tin cans and wire, and they watched with open mouths the film of Calder operating his famous circus. Elderly ladies, who walked with small, cautious steps, smiled shyly as though they didn't quite know whether to approve of this sort of thing in a museum and whether they should take it seriously as "art." Those between the children and the elderly grinned at the wire sculptures and wirelike drawings, simplifications at once humorous and elegant, distillations of the essence of character, anatomy, and movement. They looked at the mobiles as though hypnotized, and they gazed up at the stabiles, which were like gigantic friendly monsters.

Everywhere there were the primary colors children love. (Calder said that he never liked any school better than kindergarten, where he was encouraged to cut shapes out of colored paper.) His are the clear colors that adults have been taught to regard as unsubtle (which they are) and tasteless (which they are not). Calder exploits them with brazen subtlety and defiance and tosses them about as though he were Thor playing games with lightning. To one mobile he added a bit of thunder as well. Colored balls, hung from the ceiling on very fine wire, moved at random among a scattering of shallow metal bowls on the floor, and when the balls struck, which they did not do frequently, the bowls rang like gongs.

A couple of years ago I tried to define "style," how it has nothing to do with fashion or chic but stems from personal conviction, self-assurance, and independence that asserts itself sometimes for good, sometimes for evil, sometimes for fun. Style is amoral: Jesus and Allah had it, and so did Lucifer. So did Calder, who preached nothing but his joy in life, in a way that was uniquely his own. He is the closest thing to Picasso that America has produced in this century, and like Picasso, no one has successfully imitated him or been able to capture his spirit.

Architectural Digest, 1977

Steinberg's "Stuff"

A recent exhibition of Saul Steinberg painting-drawings, along with his carved and painted "drawing tables," at the Pace Gallery in New York was as full of surprises as each new show of Steinberg's inevitably is. It is not that he leaps from style to style; there is a logical progression from one sharp detonation of his talent to the next, as though his lifeline were a constantly burning fuse.

Some years ago Steinberg said to me, "Why do people call a cartoonist's work 'stuff'? They always say to me, 'I like your stuff.' "

I doubt if anyone today calls the remarkable products of Steinberg's eye and hand and obliquely incisive mind "stuff." I doubt if there are many people, even cursorily familiar with what comes from his pen, who think of him now as a cartoonist, though the shorthand he uses to describe his internal and external worlds has cartoon elements in it. His work is not like anyone else's. No other satirical intelligence is like his, and no other pen is propelled by such a combination of calligraphic mastery and a sure sense of what is socially and morally absurd. Critic Harold Rosenberg aptly spoke of Steinberg's work as "a kind of organized talk."

Steinberg's fascination with the manners and customs of America and Americans is inexhaustible. He looks at our lives as folklore with the detachment of an anthropologist and records and interprets what he sees like a social historian. He has an advantage that many of the most astute literary observers of America have had: He comes from a very different society, with a different class structure, social standards, and mores. He was born in Romania in 1914 and was trained as an architect in Italy, which he left in 1940. He made it circuitously to America and enlisted in the navy. His duties included teaching the Chinese about the construction of bridges, and since he did not speak their language, he made himself understood with drawings. In 1945 he settled with his wife, the artist Hedda Sterne, in New York. Here he was consumed with exploring the tribal rites of our American jungle.

Take, for example, his view of the American "national pasttime."

I stopped by his apartment one afternoon in the fifties when television was still quite young and baseball was not as expertly televised as it is now, and I found Steinberg watching a game for the first time.

"Tell me," he inquired, "is that man with the stick against those other three men?" I explained that it wasn't quite like that, drew a diagram of a diamond, and tried fruitlessly to explain what went on in the game.

"Is there a book I can read that will tell me all about it?" he asked. I said there was a rule book which would confuse him, as it would confuse anybody, and mentioned several how-to-play books my son had at home.

"I'll buy them," he said.

In 1954 *Life* magazine arranged for him to travel with the Milwaukee Braves, and he produced a remarkable set of what might reasonably be called baseball genre pictures—drawings with color. They ache with the often tiresome, occasionally explosive tensions of the game, its cumbersome ceremonial traditions, its poses, gestures, costumes—the helmeted armor of the catcher and plate umpire in contrast to the limp union suits of the infield and outfield and the plain blue uniforms of the base umpires.

"Baseball is an allegorical play about America," Steinberg has said, "a poetic, complex, and subtle play of courage, fear, good luck, mistakes, patience about fate, and sober self-esteem (batting average). It is impossible to understand America without a thorough knowledge of baseball."

This comment was quoted in the splendid catalogue of the large retrospective exhibition of Steinberg's work held at the Whitney Museum of American Art in New York in 1978. The show covered his work from the time he came to America to the present; it was the kind of tribute reserved for our most illustrious artists, one that is usually, in fact, posthumous. No one around the Whitney Museum at the time was talking about Steinberg's "stuff," you may be sure of that.

His recent show was a concentrated dose of the same kind of

visual elixir. There were American townscapes drawn largely with a ruler, the essence of dreary monotony. There were cityscapes exploding with the sound of planes above, and trucks and taxis and police cars in streets partly inhabited by reptiles and men with rabbits' ears. There were still lifes of flowers and pots and toys and the tools of Steinberg's craft. There were pictures about making pictures and parodies of documents, rubber-stamped; landscapes with lonely figures looking at horizons that could be the edge of the world. There were the painted drawing tables, some standing, some placed on the wall.

"Art can't be described by writing," Steinberg said to me when I went to see him after I'd seen the show at the Pace. "Art is one kind of metaphor; writing is a different kind. One metaphor can't explain another metaphor. One kind of symbol can't explain another kind of symbol. Writing can be a metaphor for history, not for art. The worst thing a writer can do to art is to describe it, to explain it, to serenade it."

He is quite right, of course, but that surely doesn't keep me from giving a long, low whistle of astonishment and delight.

Architectural Digest, 1982

Requiem for the Parlor

*T*he parlor as an amenity of the American house has vanished almost without a trace, but nostalgia for it seems to remain. I was in the American Wing of the Metropolitan Museum in New York one day a few months ago and the director of the department asked, "Would you like a peek at the new Gothic Revival room?" To get to it we walked between two parlors, one in the Greek Revival fashion of the early 1880s and the other Rococo Revival—one rather chaste, the other rather plush. Suitably, they were to be looked into, not walked around or sat down in. (I say "suitably" because parlors existed in the nineteenth century more for looks than for occupancy.) The new Gothic Revival room, from a house in upstate New York, is not, strictly speaking, a parlor but a library. Nonetheless, it has the formality of a parlor, the quiet dignity and feel of an imposing code of manners.

In its heyday, which lasted until the end of the nineteenth century, the parlor was a symbol of civilized living—if tight and formal living can, in our time of rampant informality, be looked upon as civilized. When we threw out the parlor (and that is just what we did) we threw out what we had come to regard as an outdated code of behavior. As codes of social behavior are dictated by convenience and fashion rather than by any standards of morality, the parlor became an inconvenience or an unnecessary luxury—even an embarrassment. It was made so by changes in architectural taste, the explosion of the suburbs, and the implosion of city living quarters. As apartments replaced houses in cities and suburbs increasingly became "developments" rather than sites for country houses (as they primarily were until about 1900), parlors came to be regarded as a waste of space. The gradual disappearance of live-in servants and their replacement by part-time help, mechanical gad-

157

gets, husbands (or their approximate equivalents), and children made the parlor obsolete.

In ample houses at the turn of the century, the drawing room took the place of the parlor as the site of formal gatherings; in smaller houses it was the living room that became both the place to entertain friends and what is now the "family room." The next step was to include the kitchen as an adjunct to the family room, so that whoever was working there need not be excluded from family intercourse. The parlor, in other words, lost out to progress—if loss of space, privacy, conversation, and quiet can reasonably be called progress.

It is the regression of those qualities, I believe, that prompts what nostalgia there is for the parlor, and they seem to be qualities not greatly cherished in our time. There is obviously not the slightest likelihood of the parlor being revived, but look with me for the moment at what the parlor meant to our great grandparents (add "greats" according to your age), whether they were farmers or city dwellers, professionals or tradesmen, new immigrants or old ones.

The parlor was a symbol within a symbol, the treasury in the family castle, a museum, the private room of the muses of painting and poetry and the decorative arts, a cabinet of archaeology and random geology. It was where the accumulation of the artifacts of family history were gathered and displayed, even if not frequently looked at. It was there that family portraits, if there were any (some of them might be tinted photographs), looked down out of black backgrounds from papered walls. There the family Bible, in which the births and marriages and deaths of the family were recorded, and perhaps a book or two of poetry sat on a center table covered, in Victorian times, with dark red serge trimmed with fringe that nearly touched the floor. There were the family's spinet, the "best" chairs, and possibly a love seat covered with damask or velvet. It was customary in the early years of the century to range the chairs along the walls—not, as today, placed for conversational convenience but intended to be moved.

Essentially, though, the parlor was static, the way galleries in museums used to be static. (You could go back year after year to look at your favorite paintings and find them always hung where you expected them to be. No longer, alas!) There the family bibelots gathered on little tables and on the mantelpiece, the rarest and most precious pieces behind glass in what was called the curio cabinet.

In such a cabinet in my family's house when I was a child there were pieces of Chinese money, several tortoiseshell fans, a blue-and-white porcelain jar filled with spicy potpourri. There was a piece of petrified wood, sliced and polished to show its rings (geology) and a Chinese Buddha, pocket sized, with traces of gilt (archaeology). There were mementos of travel, tintypes, a stereoscope that made photographs look three-dimensional. There was a drawer of parlor games—puzzles, cards, dominoes, checkers. There were no clothes or toys carelessly thrown down, no helter-skelter of magazines and comic books, no family detritus. The parlor was not a stop on the way to someplace. It was *the* place—domestically useless, perhaps, but essential nonetheless.

The parlor personified continuity, even in a society as footloose as ours. When pioneer families went west from New England to what we now call the Midwest and hacked out of forests pieces of land to till and built log cabins to live in, many took their parlors with them, or at least their precious possessions with which to make parlors. The fact that these possessions may have had little or no monetary value was beside the point. It was not unusual for a family, once settled, to build a second log cabin attached to the first by a breezeway. The original one remained the business part of the dwelling—the kitchen, bedroom, living room all in one; the second became the parlor, set apart for special occasions, such as visits from friends or the itinerant parson, for wooing, for family prayers, for solemn and frivolous gatherings. There treasures brought from home or acquired on the way or after arrival were displayed. There were the artifacts of continuity, however modest. The parlor was more than a place to show off: It was where the past met the present and promised the future.

As the origin of its name suggests, the parlor was a place to talk, a place for quiet conversation, an art nearly as out of fashion as the parlor itself.

Architectural Digest, 1987

The Austin Phenomenon

I am not sure how one accounts for a flurry of cultural activity in a certain unlikely place at a certain unlikely time. It is pleasant to think of it as the sparks that fly off a single individual that not only brighten the atmosphere but ignite others around him or her into a bonfire of activity that lights up the sky. When it happens, an individual is usually at the heart of the matter. I went back recently to the site of one of these happy conflagrations—in (you might say, "of all places") Hartford, Connecticut, "the insurance city." The embers are still comfortingly warm.

The fire happened during the Great Depression (which was not a time of depression in the arts—quite the contrary) a little more than fifty years ago. I was not one of those who threw ignitables on the fire, but its flames were certainly reflected in my nearby spectacles. The man with the match, to stretch the metaphor, was A. Everett Austin, Jr., "Chick" to his friends and everyone who knew him or knew of him in Hartford. He was the new, young (about thirty) director of the Wadsworth Atheneum, which is said to be "the oldest structure in America that has been used continuously as an art museum." It opened its massive Gothic portals in 1844, and in 1934 it opened the fourth of its five wings, the Bauhaus-Modern Avery Memorial. It was there that Chick set his fire.

Chick was one of a group of young men and women who had studied the arts at Harvard under the intense tutelage of Paul Sachs at the university's Fogg Museum—a clutch of aesthetes who shaped and led American art museums for about four decades. Their names are legendary in the then tight but now vastly expanded circle of arts purveyors. They might reasonably be called the old masters of the art boom. There were, for example, Alfred H. Barr, Jr., the first director and intellectual conscience of the Museum of Modern Art; Henry-Russell Hitchcock, the great architectural historian and mentor to Philip Johnson, who had been director of the architecture department of MoMA before he became an architect; James Rorimer, director of the Metropolitan Museum; Agnes Mongan, the foremost woman art historian and occasional museum director; and Agnes Rindge Claflin, the late duenna of Vassar's art gallery, a seedbed of critics and scholars.

To Chick Austin, Alfred Barr wrote: "You did everything sooner and more brilliantly than any of us." Composer and critic Virgil Thomson called him "a whole cultural movement in one man."

The most famous—or as it was then thought to be, most notorious—event that happened at Austin's instigation in the new Avery wing was the first performance in 1934 of *Four Saints in Three Acts,* the opera Virgil Thomson composed to a libretto by his friend Gertrude Stein. It was John Houseman's debut as a director. It was the first opera, a year before *Porgy and Bess,* with an all-black cast of singers and dancers. It was the first time the English choreographer Frederick Ashton did a production in the United States. As Eugene Gaddis, the museum's archivist, wrote of the occasion, "The arbiters of taste in art, music and literature—those whom the popular press commonly called 'the stream-lined intelligentsia'—arrived in Hartford for the premiere by Rolls Royce, airplane and specially-reserved parlor cars."

The performances of *Four Saints* may have made more people aware of Austin and his modern museum than other events planned and executed by him, but to the art community it was the delicious frosting on a very sound and nourishing cake. In 1934 Austin had hung in his galleries the first Picasso retrospective anywhere. His was the first exhibition in the United States of the Surrealists. He cooperated with Lincoln Kirstein in bringing Balanchine to New York to start a ballet school. He bought the Lifar collection of 182 oils, watercolors, and drawings by such artists as Bakst, Benois, Derain, Modigliani, Matisse, Picasso, Braque, Gris, Ernst, Rouault, and Tchelitchew for ten thousand dollars. Lifar was Diaghilev's last leading male dancer and had inherited the collection from him. (Evidently Chick's trustees had to swallow hard before approving the purchase price, which now seems ludicrously low for such a treasure.)

Lest he seem to be a modernist in his tastes—to the exclusion of the earlier arts—Chick organized the first exhibition of seventeenth-century painting in an American museum. It was a show of

Baroque pictures, a kind of art that had long resided in museum doghouses—unloved and unfashionable. Chick was an innovator and rediscoverer, ahead of his time; Janus fashion, he looked with equal intensity both forward and back and saw what others had not seen.

To achieve what Chick did in Hartford took considerable personal charm. He was an intense, entertaining impresario by profession, an actor by temperament, and a magician for the fun of it. He practiced the first with great seriousness and an eye for quality unparalleled, I believe, by any of his museum contemporaries. The second he indulged on the stage only occasionally, but it surfaced as naturally as breathing whenever and wherever he happened to be with people. The third, his magicianship, he performed primarily for the pleasure and benefit of children. He gave magic shows to raise money for art classes for children, an activity that some of the museum trustees thought disturbingly undignified.

About fifty years ago I was driving from New York to Boston, and I stopped in Hartford to see Chick and his museum. In his office was hanging a large seventeenth-century painting of St. Catherine of Alexandria by Bernardo Strozzi. It was a picture much publicized when Chick bought it, and I asked what it was doing in his office. "It's a copy," he said. He had seen the painting at an exhibition in Florence in 1922 and was greatly impressed. Eight years later it came on the market, and he got a dealer in Venice to buy it for the Atheneum. When it arrived he took one quick look and knew it was not the painting he had seen in 1922. It was a precise contemporary copy, possibly by Strozzi himself.

Chick eventually got the original he wanted, and I asked what he was going to do with the copy. "Destroy it, probably," he said. (In the end it was returned to the dealer.) Other friends of Chick's have slightly different versions of this story. None of them ceases to be astonished by the subtlety of his eye. St. Catherine is a star among many stars in the Atheneum's collection.

Austin left Hartford at the end of 1944 and became the first director of the Ringling Museum in Florida in 1946. There he imported from Italy the tiny, delicious Asolo Theater and rebuilt it adjacent to the museum.

One of the treasures he left behind in Hartford was the house he designed in 1930 for himself and his wife and two children. It was externally a steal, a Palladian villa based closely on one by

Scamozzi, Palladio's younger contemporary and rival. It sits luxuriously back from the road with the air of a stage set, a two-dimensional facade with shallow pilasters painted white on gray. It is a forerunner by half a century of today's postmodernism, with the added virtue of humor. The house is only one room deep, and behind it is a quiet stream and a sixteen-acre stand of woods—a tamed, suburban forest.

I had spent a night there many years ago, and to be in it again recently was as surprising and refreshing as to see it for the first time. Eugene Gaddis, who in addition to his duties as archivist is the curator of the Austin house (which Chick's heirs have given to the Atheneum), took my wife and me there. It is now a picture of shabby, eccentric elegance waiting to be revitalized—and it is about to be. Its dining room and living room are essentially Venetian eighteenth century, not just in style and feel but in authentic detail of boiserie and furniture, textiles and wall coverings. Upstairs the dressing rooms and baths are pure Bauhaus functional.

Austin would have laughed at being called "a Renaissance man," but my guess is that he would have enjoyed having it said of him that he was "a Baroque-Rococo man." The epithet would have suited his style, his sympathies, his inventiveness, the multiplicity of his interests, his remarkably contagious enthusiasm, and above all his exuberant panache.

Architectural Digest, 1987

Dossena's Hand Quicker Than an Eye

*A*lceo Dossena is not often on my mind, but two quite disparate occurrences have caused his cunning specter to surface once again. One was a letter from a clergyman in London who is writing about Dossena and asked me for clues to his career. The other was the recent unveiling by the J. Paul Getty Museum in Malibu, California, of an archaic Greek sculpture, a standing male nude, or kouros, presumed to be twenty-five hundred years old.

Dossena, who died just fifty years ago, was quite probably the greatest carver of fake antique and Renaissance sculpture who ever practiced that dark but illuminating art. Several years after his death I had what some regarded as the effrontery to write about him. When I had first looked into the matter, the people who knew most about Dossena were reluctant to talk. Some of them had been had, as they say, and were, I believe, unnecessarily embarrassed. Others had served in institutions, museums mostly, that had been taken in by the fakes and thought that the whole nasty business was better forgotten.

I hasten to disassociate Dossena from the Getty's acquisition. I have no earthly reason to suggest that the Getty has been duped, and my competence in such arcane matters is nil. What interested me was the simple fact of its emergence (its discovery and provenance are obscure) and the fact that the art world seemed ready to "round up the usual suspects" (as Claude Rains says in *Casablanca*). "If it looks good enough to be real," they seem to say, "it must be a fake."

This is not an unusual attitude in the art world. For all its facade of perfect confidence, it is skittish behind closed doors about its humanly fallible eye and its good but never total scholarship. The self-doubt comes from long experience in the shadowy business of dealing with aesthetic puzzles, of making didactic statements based

164

on a combination of connoisseurship and whether the hair stands up on the back of the neck when faced with a work of art. This self-doubt is based on the desire and the need to believe as well as on solid conviction, on trying to second-guess the future as well as the past, on wanting to recognize genius fore or aft. It is a question of knowing good from bad in a field where the lines are almost never absolutely clear, or of knowing whether time and taste change good to bad and bad to good, and when the tingling of the spine plays as large a role in making judgments as any amount of professional know-how.

But what about Dossena? Knowingly or unknowingly (he insisted it was unknowingly), he had a great many connoisseurs, curators, scholars, collectors, and dealers on the hip in the 1920s. As a young man he had worked as a restorer of marble balustrades and stone ornaments on churches and palaces and had acquired a sound knowledge of making new stone appear old, even ancient. He was remarkably skillful with his chisel and had an exceptionally discerning eye for style. After a tour in the Italian army in World War I, he was broke and unemployed, and he occupied himself with making and selling for a pittance sculptures in the Renaissance and antique manner. The first piece he sold, to an art dealer in a Rome cafe, was a low relief in marble of the head of the Virgin. This piece turned up by a devious route at a dealer's in New York, attributed to no less a giant than the fifteenth-century Florentine Donatello. It was subsequently bought as such by the St. Louis Art Museum, later repudiated and restitution made to the museum.

It was the first of twenty-odd pieces that turned up in American museums and private collections, an estimated $1.5 million worth (or not worth) of them. Some were spotted as forgeries shortly after they were purchased: a small, graceful archaic Greek maiden, for example, that the Metropolitan Museum bought; and two pieces, a Virgin and announcing angel, that Helen Frick (of the Frick Collection in New York) was convinced were by the Sienese painter Simone Martini, though he was not known to have made any sculpture. The pieces were attributed to him on "stylistic ground." The Cleveland Museum got caught; so, it appeared, did the Boston Museum of Fine Arts. Their mortuary monument, ascribed to Mino da Fiesole, was claimed to have been found near Siena in an abbey that was destroyed by an earthquake. None of these, you may be sure, were casual purchases. The pieces were reviewed, argued over, and tested at length by the authorities in such matters. Some were considered iffy but probable: others were flatly declared to be what they seemed—masterpieces.

A number of experts claimed to be the one who unmasked the forgeries and traced them to Dossena, a nice detective story with very abstruse clues too complex for the size of this column. Suffice it to say that Dossena, who claimed he did not know that his pieces were being palmed off as ancient masterpieces by unscrupulous dealers, became something of a national hero in Italy. The fact that his artistry had caused American collectors and museums to make monkeys of themselves delighted his compatriots, and he was not only showered with acclaim but with commissions for portraits and monuments. In 1933 an auction of known pieces by Dossena was held in the grand ballroom of the Plaza Hotel in New York. Works that had once brought many thousands went for a few hundred dollars, and it seems logical that some of them are still around and in circulation.

Dossena's genius was to assimilate and reproduce the style of a period and sometimes of a specific master without making copies of existing pieces. What exposed him was his inability to see with ancient eyes in the temper of ancient times and to feel with ancient prejudices and enthusiasm. "Forgeries must be served hot, as they come out of the oven," wrote art historian Max J. Friedlander in *On Art and Connoisseurship*. The forger fails, he says, because he tries to imitate a mood that he cannot feel and therefore "succumbs to the prejudices of taste that belong to his own period. . . . His pathos sounds hollow, theatrical and forced since it does not spring from emotion." As a result, one generation is likely to be appalled that the forgeries of an earlier generation took anyone in. How, we wonder, could they have been so gullible?

The Getty kouros, a target of suspicion as a matter of course (no such antique treasure could emerge today from a misty background without causing sophisticated eyebrows to twitch), has been subjected to tests and examinations that make Boston's analysis of its mortuary monument seem primitive by comparison. (The monument is now believed to be basically authentic but extensively "restored" by Dossena.) The Getty, which I am more than willing to believe knows what it is doing, also knows that the Metropolitan in New York has a magnificent kouros in pinkish marble that it bought many years ago. There are those who doubt its authenticity, and I dare say there always will be. I find myself on the side of the Boston Museum of Fine Arts, who said of their monument, "If that sarcophagus was ever a forgery, it is worth preserving. It is beautiful no matter who did it."

So be it. So be the Getty kouros. If Dossena is lurking in the shadows, so be the ghost of that remarkable master of dissemblance.

Architectural Digest, 1987

Ghosts of Sculpture Past

*T*he glossy white ghosts of ancient sculpture, which used to be the mainstay of American museums, are coming back to haunt these marble Edens of culture. They are old friends of mine. When I was a young man, every art museum that could afford them devoted a spacious gallery or lined a staircase or corridor with plaster casts of the works of ancient Greece and Rome and sometimes of the Renaissance—Venuses without arms, emperors and senators without noses, Victories with accidentally clipped wings, and a fragment or two from the so-called Elgin Marbles, the pediment sculptures that Lord Elgin "liberated" from the Parthenon. They stood about on pedestals with the blind-eyed casts of Michelangelo's colossal *David* scaled down to indoor size and his ponderous *Moses* and the figures of *Night* and *Day* from the Medici tomb in Florence.

It seems probable that my generation was the last to take casts seriously and also the one that got rid of them. They went out of fashion in the 1930s and 1940s, and museums gave them away (it cannot have been easy to find anyone who wanted them) or stored them in warehouses and other such depositories for objects of aesthetic indecision. Such is the superciliousness of taste that it was inevitable they should be so disposed of. They were not destroyed, which would have been an act of vandalism, whereas putting them where they might accidentally be damaged or permitted to disintegrate would not.

Many of them had been around for well over a century and had served their initial function: exposing Americans to the noblest of cultural artifacts. Original works of art, except those that were homemade and therefore considered inferior (usually for good reason), were unknown in American cultural centers—Boston, New York, and Philadelphia—at the beginning of the last century. There were copies of old masters—some by American artists who had gone to Europe to study, some daubs passed off by unscrupulous dealers as original masterpieces. Most famous works were known only from engravings, the quality of which ranged from dreadful to adequate.

Sculpture, however, could be more accurately known and understood from plaster casts made in Europe and shipped to the United States at considerable expense. It was thought to be not merely a civilizing influence in a nation that was modest indeed about its cultural sophistication but also a means of training native artists and encouraging merchants, politicians, and professionals to become patrons of the fine arts.

Casts were the basis of the first art institution established in America. The New York Academy of the Fine Arts opened its galleries in 1802, and with characteristic New York chutzpah changed its name shortly thereafter to the American Academy of the Fine Arts. It was the brainchild of a group of businessmen who, according to the artist-historian William Dunlap, organized the academy "with a view of raising the character of their countrymen by increasing their knowledge and taste." This was to be accomplished by "introducing casts from the antique into the country." Local artists, however, had a more practical purpose in mind. They encouraged aspiring young men and a very few women to learn to draw by copying these casts, a practice that persisted well into this century, as I know from experience. (I spent one afternoon a week for many months making inept charcoal drawings from casts at Yale when I was an undergraduate.) In New York the public soon grew weary of looking at the frosty emperors, goddesses, and gladiators, and the students, who were let in to draw only in the very early morning, grew restless. The academy closed its doors and the casts went into hiding. It seems likely that some of them were among the company of ancients that turned up in the Metropolitan Museum of Art when it opened its doors in 1870.

In Philadelphia, the Pennsylvania Academy of the Fine Arts, founded a few years later than the American Academy, had different problems with its collection of casts. When Mrs. Frances Trollope—the much-read and heartily despised Englishwoman who visited America in the 1820s and subsequently wrote *The Domestic Manners of the Americans*—was in Philadelphia, she was shocked by what she witnessed at the Pennsylvania Academy. Philadelphians were so prudish that they found the nudity of the casts of gods and goddesses offensive and would not allow men and women to see them at the same time. A day a week was set aside for female visitors, and on that day, it's been said, the nude figures were swathed from head to foot in muslin sheets. Mrs. Trollope was appalled, she wrote, at "the disgusting depravity which had led some of the visitors to mar and deface the casts in a most indecent and shameless manner." It was the result, she declared, of the "coarse-minded custom which sends alternate groups of males and females into the room."

Such prudery gradually abated (it is not likely ever to disappear), and by the middle of the century American sculptors like Hiram Powers and Erastus Dow Palmer produced marble statues of nude females that were made socially and morally acceptable to the public by being called *The Greek Slave* and *The White Captive*. Fig leaves, however, did not go out of fashion until some years later. As late as the 1880s Thomas Eakins was forced to resign from his job as head of the art school of the Pennsylvania Academy for insisting that students in his life classes draw from models who were totally nude.

There was a report several months ago in the *New York Times* that the despised and disparaged casts, which for several decades have languished in museum storage, are being cleaned up, repaired, and made presentable. Museums want them. Students and artists, presumably, want them.

About fifty years ago I spent an afternoon at the Metropolitan Museum with Arthur Lee—a very accomplished "academic" sculptor who is represented in the museum's collection—learning some rudimentary things about the art of sculpture in the presence of the Met's casts. Lee looked and pointed and ran his hands over the casts and talked; as he did so, the plaster took on life, and the subtlety, skill, and wisdom of the carvers of the marbles from which the casts were made took on reality, vitality, and wonder. It was a lesson in how to look that I have not forgotten and one that I could never have learned from two-dimensional slides or photographs. Masterpieces of sculpture at second hand became friends then and are still friends today. Some I have since met in person (in stone, that is); some I will never see. Some of those I met in plaster are closer to the sculptors' intentions than attempts at restoring the originals.

It seems to me that the casts of ancient sculptures are the only kinds of ghosts we can unashamedly believe in—dignified spooks that speak without utterance of vanished masters of the mallet and chisel.

Architectural Digest, 1987

Spreading the Wealth

*N*ow and then a "dirty word" turns up in museum parlance, or, to put it another way, a perfectly nice word takes on a publicly soiled meaning. *Deaccessioning* is such a word. Deaccessioning has been a common practice in museums and libraries and other public institutions of collecting, not just recently, but for many decades. It means, quite simply, to part with an item (or items) in the collection that curators and directors or librarians have decided no longer serves the institution's purposes or its plans for the future. Usually deaccessioning takes place in order to provide for the accessioning of something more pertinent. Sometimes the deaccessioned object is sold; sometimes it is traded (swapped) for an object in another institution or in the possession of a dealer.

The word came into disgrace in 1972 when the Metropolitan Museum in New York decided to sell a portion of a collection that had been bequeathed to it by a Miss Adelaide Milton deGroot. Among the paintings that the Met acquired from her, and which it chose to get rid of, was Henri Rousseau's *The Tropics*. At the same time, the museum disposed of a van Gogh called *The Olive Pickers* to a New York dealer. The *New York Times* got wind of this and raised a hue and cry that still echoes. There might very well have been no fuss if there had not been some obfuscation on the part of the director of the Metropolitan, who did not come clean when the disposal of the paintings was first rumored. The effect of the publicity was a general impression that the museum was irresponsible in its duty to the public, and especially in its disregard of the wishes of the late Miss deGroot. She evidently expected, though she had no guarantee, that her bequest was in perpetuity. *The Tropics* was sold to a New York dealer for $800,000 and bought from the dealer by a Japanese investor for several times that. The Met has other van Goghs that it considers superior to *The Olive Pickers*, but, as a

172

member of the museum's staff said to me recently, "The Rousseau was a mistake. We shouldn't have let it go. I assume we did so because we needed money for purchases of works thought to be more important to the collection."

That is all water over the dam, and its spilling may well have had a very salutary effect. The problem of deaccessioning was aired, and, to some degree, this long-established museum and library practice became better understood. It also has put museums on their mettle, I believe, and has caused them to think, not just twice, but a dozen times, before they jettison any of their holdings. As tax-free institutions, they properly come under public scrutiny and in some cases can deaccession only with the approval of the attorney general of the state.

I have talked with a number of museum officials about this problem. I asked Perry Rathbone, the retired director of the Museum of Fine Arts in Boston, when it was that he first encountered deaccessioning. "I remember," he said, "when I was a young assistant at the Detroit museum, studying a catalogue of porcelains being disposed of by a museum in Berlin." Obviously the Berlin museum had more porcelains than were needed in its collection. It can be assumed that the ones they wished to dispose of were duplicates of ones they kept or were kinds of which they had finer examples. Another museum man, a curator, said that only very rarely did his museum deaccession any item in the collection over which he presides, and then it is likely to be an exchange with another museum: "If we have six pictures by X and none by Y and another museum is in the reverse situation, we will sometimes make an exchange. It enriches both collections. It's one way of filling the gaps in a collection. You could call it 'spreading the wealth.' "

Recently the Wadsworth Atheneum, in Hartford, Connecticut, a splendid small museum, sold a set of valuable books given to it in its early days by J. P. Morgan. Only twice in the museum's long history, which goes back to the mid-nineteenth century, had the books been displayed. The trustees—wisely, I think—decided to sell the books at auction in order to purchase paintings and sculpture that could be constantly on public view. The books brought $400,000. During the 1979–80 season, New York's Metropolitan sold more than half a million dollars' worth of paintings through one Manhattan auction house. Some had once borne the names of great masters; time and connoisseurship had reattributed them to less important artists. Last June and September, the New York Society Library sold a large number of Audubon prints of birds from a set that had been stolen and recovered partially pillaged. To the astonished delight of the library's trustees, the sale fetched more than one million dollars, which will be used for much-needed construction of more stack space and reading rooms.

On the other side of Central Park, the New-York Historical Society sold at auction a number of early Italian and Flemish paintings, which were part of a collection that had been left to the society in the mid-nineteenth century. It had obtained the permission of the attorney general to sell, on the grounds that the pictures were in no way related to its function as one of the great custodians of American, and especially New York, historical materials. The society has retained the best of it—called the Thomas Jefferson Bryan Collection—as an example of sophisticated collecting in New York in the 1830s and 1840s, and has lent several especially distinguished pictures from it to the Metropolitan, where they are on display in its old masters galleries.

Who can quarrel with that kind of deaccessioning? You'd be surprised. Many scholars shudder at the very word. Understandably they like things "kept together for study purposes." Many donors are alarmed by the prospect that their tax-deductible generosity may not assure them of perpetual fame. Civic pride can raise its head when works of art threaten to leave town, as two beautiful wooden sculptures by William Rush recently threatened to leave Philadelphia, and Gilbert Stuart's portraits of George and Martha Washington threatened to leave Boston.

Just as there are good and bad acquisitions, so there are good and bad deaccessions, and it is time that usually decides which is which. On balance, though, isn't it better that works of art leave the collections where they have worn out their welcome and find their way to homes where they are loved? Eventually the distinguished ones will almost certainly turn up in important museums, where they will enhance a collection and delight a new public.

Architectural Digest, 1981

Shaping Popular Tastes

*P*ressures on the public taste are more acute today, more persuasive, and more carefully contrived and organized than they have ever been, and in some ways they are more subtle. The shaping of taste is essentially the science of merchandising, whether of detergents or cars or books or objects of fine and decorative art. Museums with their blockbuster exhibitions are every bit as involved in merchandising taste as the Chrysler Corporation is involved in publicizing this year's models. (The launching of King Tut and the new Plymouth Horizon have much in common.) The basis of tastemaking is, and always has been, snob appeal—the appeal to our instincts to want to be better than our equals or aspire to our betters, for even in the most democratic societies there are inevitably those who in some respects are our betters—intellectually, financially, physically, morally, or socially.

There are two theories of shaping popular taste that complement each other: the trickle-down theory, which is as old as civilization, and the trickle-up theory, which seems to be a recent manifestation. Both have demonstrable validity today.

A music critic said to me recently, "The influence of Schönberg and the twelve-tone scale has ruined modern composition [the trickle-down theory]. The only positive contribution to music in our century has been jazz and its influence [the trickle-up theory]."

The same rules can be applied in obvious ways to fashions in clothes—"copying down" from Paris haute couture by the Seventh Avenue rag trade for the mass market, and the rise of blue jeans from work pants to high-fashion fanny flaunters. The same can be said of the popularity of peasant cooking, folk art, and the compact car. The convention may not be so obvious when it comes to cars or furniture or architecture as it is to clothes, but analogies are not hard to find. The Finnish architect Alvar Aalto's "cottage furniture"

175

quickly became chic in the 1930s for the avant-garde and is now prized by collectors. Trickle-up had much to do with the rise of the compact car from the Volkswagen to the current popular taste for European and Japanese imports. It was not only economy that made them popular, it was a kind of reverse snobbery aimed at those who disported themselves in palatial rolling stock. It was not only the gas shortage that reduced the status of the big car, it was a massive trickle-up of taste.

If the popular taste cannot be precisely defined, there are those who think that it can be measured. The networks measure it with ratings, publishers with best-seller lists, and movie producers with the take at the box office. Manufacturers of soft and hard goods and the merchants who sell them measure popular taste with sales charts and computers. Critics throw their hats at it, but they do not think of the popular taste as low (or anyway not the lowest) and certainly not as high or elite.

The popular taste cannot be pinned to a particular place or area (though there are geographical differences) or to any economic or social class. Nor is taste definable by any measure of educational accomplishment or professional classification. So attempts to capture the popular taste are games played by many different sets of rules, which depend on what those who make the rules think of as popular and how they set about to capture their particular markets. (At one end of the scale there are popular and unpopular recordings of Bach's *Goldberg Variations,* just as at the other there are popular and unpopular takes of rock tunes.) Perhaps the popular taste can be inadequately, and certainly inexactly, defined as what the majority of people at any given time like or dislike or are indifferent to. However it is defined, the shaping of taste is a mysterious exercise in intuition and guesswork with some of the risk tempered by the relatively new "science" of market research. More commonly, as television demonstrates with its pilot shows, popular taste is determined by trial and error.

Tastemakers have been busy in America since the early years of the nineteenth century trying to manipulate the popular taste, often, as they insisted, to improve it. Up to about 1830 taste had been regarded as the province of the rich and aristocratic, who looked to Europe, and most particularly to England, for their models of architecture and decoration and manners. But when in 1829 Andrew Jackson was elected to the presidency and "the ruffians," as the established families called them, invaded the White House, taste suddenly became a concern to a great many women (particularly) who had not given it much thought before. In this first age of the common man many men and women wanted to be as uncommon as possible and to adopt what were considered to be proper refinements of behavior and dress and surroundings. At about this same time factories began to turn out decorative textiles and carpets by the thousands of yards and furniture at a prodigious rate that weavers and cabinet makers had never before dreamed of. Almost everyone could afford to have taste, and the profusion of choices created a confusion that a new breed of tastemakers helped as much to confound as to correct. Publishers produced books of etiquette and household advice by the dozens, and soon magazines on parlor tables were filled with suggestions on how to dress and decorate in the latest styles. Since their editors and authors had little confidence in what they might originate, they borrowed the standards of the gentry of Europe who, to judge from the character of Victorian interiors, were somewhat confused about matters of taste themselves.

Tastemaking grew into a substantial industry in the nineteenth century, but the means at hand were limited largely to the printed word, to illustrated papers, and to the lecture platforms. Advertising became gradually more sophisticated, and press agentry, of which P. T. Barnum was the magnificent exemplar, grew into a profession that later became known as public relations and was called by one lordly practitioner "the engineering of consent." In the mid-century, magazines like *Godey's Lady's Book* and *Harper's New Monthly Magazine* provided readers not only with fashion plates of the latest styles from London and Paris and Berlin but with articles on the design of "villas and cottages" for a population that was largely rural. The most ambitious assaults on the popular taste in the nineteenth century were the Centennial Exhibition in Philadelphia in 1876 and the World's Columbian Exposition ("The White City") in Chicago in 1893. Such world's fairs as these (and at the time they were the most imposing ever held anywhere) were substitutes for international travel. They brought the taste of the far and near corners of the world to Americans, who flocked to them by the millions and took the world home with them. The Centennial changed the taste in both domestic and official architecture, and gingerbread triumphed. The White City implanted a new neoclassicism on America and established Beaux-Arts architecture as de rigueur for banks and railroad stations, state capitals, and every other sort of public edifice from Portland, Maine, to Portland, Oregon.

Technology in the last years of the nineteenth century and the early years of this one radically changed the means by which tastemakers could influence the public appetites and season their tastes. The phonograph, which Edison invented by accident in the 1870s, was a full-fledged musical instrument by 1900. It brought symphonies and operas to many thousands who had never heard an orchestra (except the band concert on the village green) or had never listened to an operatic tenor or soprano. The voices of Enrico Caruso and Nellie Melba reverberated in parlors in remote towns as well as in cities, along with peppy tunes from music halls and jazz from New Orleans and Chicago. High-speed presses for the first time turned out color illustrations in magazines like *The Ladies' Home Journal*, which had reached a circulation of a million readers. Fashions that in the 1860s took ten years to be adopted in the West were now available, if not accepted, in days. The word from Paris, France, arrived in Paris, Arkansas, as quickly as ships could get the news to New York and magazines could get the pictures into print. In 1920 Westinghouse in Pittsburgh began to broadcast music, and it was not long before listeners could choose from a smorgasbord of kinds and qualities of performance. Also in the 1920s the movies were giving Americans a taste of how other people in other places with other incomes dressed and decorated their houses. And in cities they sat in palaces of oriental splendor to watch the heroes and heroines of the silver screen disport themselves. It was not until 1927 that they could hear as well as see them.

Television, the most pervasive instrument ever to assault the popular taste, got its feeble start after World War II, when a few people watched black-and-white pictures on tiny screens, many of them wearing dark glasses to protect their eyes against the glare. For all its variety, from the refined and sometimes rarefied offerings of public television to the brassy level of game shows and sit-coms, the medium seems to me to operate neither on the trickle-down nor the trickle-up principles of shaping the public taste. It seems only to trickle-along, confirming the best and worst of our taste or, if that sounds elitist, what is the easiest for some and the hardest for others to accept. Like gelatin in salmon mousse, it sets taste in molds, something for almost every existing appetite from pornography to poetry, from vacuity to violence, from morning to night—

and all night, too. For all its flexibility, television is more a mirror of taste than a shaper of it. Barnum, however, would have loved it. It is the pitchman's dream.

The Phenomenon of Change,
Cooper-Hewitt Museum, 1984

Magnet for Americans

As a people, it sometimes seems, we have an insatiable nostalgia for what never was. We flock to Disney World as we flock to Williamsburg, not just by the hundreds of thousands but by the millions. It is illusion we seek rather more than we seek history, because history, if it is interesting at all, is usually not pleasant—at least not pleasant by modern standards of comfort or, of course, sanitation. The illusion of history makes us feel good as history itself would not. It makes us feel as though we had progressed from a primitive to a sophisticated state of being. This is nonsense, of course, but it is nonsense we scarcely seem able to do without.

Less than a century ago an Englishman, James Bryce (he later became Lord Bryce), wrote a book about America that is a landmark in its genre. After a series of visits to this country which took him into a great many of our continental corners, and after having talked with all manner of people from chambermaids to presidents, he produced a three-volume work called *The American Commonwealth*. In a chapter titled "The Uniformity of America" (something we complain of today when we talk about taste but which we diligently promote with every mass-produced object from cars to curtains to canned goods) he said: "It is the absence in nearly all the American cities of anything that speaks of the past that makes their external aspect so unsuggestive. In pacing their busy streets and admiring their handsome city halls and churches, one's heart sinks at the feeling that nothing historically interesting ever has happened here."

What this suggests, among other things, is that our forebears had no interest in what were the old days, probably the bad old days to them. This suggests that Americans have come lately to nostalgia, that it is only recently that they have made not only a fetish but an industry of it.

180

There are no better examples of this than the two I have mentioned, the frivolous creations of Walt Disney Productions, one for each coast (Disneyland and Disney World) and the serious archeological creation (or more accurately re-creation) of Williamsburg in Virginia, built, one might say, on the stumps of a once important town. They have more in common than either of them, I believe, would be likely to admit. At Disneyland and Disney World two teams are at work, "the imagineers" and "the illusioneers." In Williamsburg it is the historians and the archeologists who are at work on nostalgia. As I understand it, the Disney imagineers dream up the fantasies that ably and amiably misrepresent the past, and the illusioneers are the practical chaps who convert imagination into false fronts. At Williamsburg, where seriousness is all important and the beauty is three dimensional (and a great deal more than skin deep), the historians and the archeologists work hand in hand to produce a facsimile as accurate as possible of what a provincial capital town must have been in the days before the Revolution. Their purpose is primarily educational, whereas the purpose of the Disney fantasies is primarily escapist.

Disney World, which is fresh in my mind as Disneyland is not, looked to me recently like a town designed by a Landmarks Preservation Commission in a moment of euphoria. No late nineteenth-century town in America was ever so spic-and-span, its surfaces so crisply painted, its shops so engaging or its public buildings so little abused by political hangers-on or so unstained by tobacco juice. Here was a spotless, odorless town made by pastry cooks, not by architects and carpenters, too good to be true, as fantasy should be, and filled with anachronisms that would drive a Williamsburg archeologist up the wall: Horsecars and motor buses head to tail, the "Old West" rubbing elbows with a "Crystal Palace," a remote country cousin of the first world's fair building ever built in 1851 in London. There is nothing feckless about the management of Disney World, and yet there is nothing that so denies the past as to represent it as clean and sweet smelling. Williamsburg in this regard no more tells the truth than Disneyland or Disney World. You can't expect archeologists to reproduce the stink of open drains in the street or unrefrigerated meat or unbathed patriots, now can you?

Daniel Webster once said, "The past, at least, is secure," a statement which, if he were now alive, he would find necessary to qualify in a dozen ways. It is unlikely that there has ever been a nation more reckless with its past than ours, so quick to tear down its monuments for the sake of a better real-estate deal, so careless with the genius of its architects and artists if they happened to stand in the way of what we call progress when what we mean is profit.

What Disney's fantasy towns and Williamsburg represent is a revolt against progress and an escape from what we are encouraged to believe are economic realities. There is an interesting contradiction in the fact that at the same time we are ruthless about tearing down perfectly useful and occasionally beautiful buildings because we say they are uneconomic, we spend millions upon millions to construct inaccurate imitations of what we destroy. We do this in order to create an illusion of a world that never was and to kid ourselves into believing that there were times and places in the not very distant past where we might have escaped the pressures of time and place, of speed and congestion.

Lord Bryce was righter than he knew when he said, "One's heart sinks at the feeling that nothing historically interesting ever has happened here, perhaps ever will happen." But he would not have envisioned the day when nostalgia for an American past that never was would be something that millions of Americans would pay through the nose for, as they do at Disney's billion-dollar escape hatches. He could not have guessed that, in this nation that urgently claims the future for its own, nostalgia based on fantasy, not fact, would draw us like bees to honeysuckle.

Architectural Digest, 1975

Our Fortunes in the Cards

L et us not be solemn about postcards, which have always been designed to be at least casual and usually frivolous, but let us not underrate them as far more reliable instruments of fortune-telling than, say, tarot cards. If you like to read the American character from its artifacts, a preoccupation of mine, look at its postcards. You will find not just an entertaining and instructive measure of its taste but also of its moral and social values and aspirations and, of course, its pratfalls.

Just a few years ago anyone could stop at a flea market or rummage sale and pick up handfuls of old postcards for a few cents apiece. I used them, as many people do, to save myself the trouble of writing letters when all I had to say could be said politely in twenty-five or thirty words on the back of a picture whose charm was its inappropriateness—the dining room of an Edwardian hotel, for example; a Ferris wheel against hand-tinted clouds; a moonlit nocturne of the Bay of Naples; or a free-floating bunch of violets with a purple ribbon.

Now the deltiologists have stepped in with their sharp eyes, as avid as a lot of ferrets and as competitive as any dedicated band of collectors, and consequently these happy nonsequiturs of correspondence are increasingly hard to find. A deltiologist, you might possibly not know (I have recently found out and am showing off), is a postcard and postal card collector, and the name comes from the Greek word *deltion*, meaning "a small tablet for writing." There are thousands of deltiologists, and in general they are looking for rarities or sets (series on a given topic drawn by the same artists—the stages of a romance, from meeting to flirtation to spooning to marriage, for example), or they specialize in certain subject matters—hotels, flying machines, balloons, dirigibles, airplanes—or catastrophes real and imagined—erupting volcanoes, earthquakes, train

183

wrecks, city fires, and so on and on. Some collect only postal cards, which are those on which the postage is printed by the government. They were the original type of mailing card. The first American illustrated postal cards with pictures in color were of the Chicago World's Fair (Columbian Exposition) in 1893. This distinction is something deltiologists care about, even if the rest of the world does not.

For those of us who are interested in taste and its vagaries, the distinction does not matter. Postcards and illustrated postal cards are as precious as lamp catalogues, early Sears Roebuck catalogues, or plumbing and furniture and clothing catalogues, which are all documents of the history of taste and of social mores of the first importance and often of the greatest amusement. Postcards, of course, do not get revived, as lamps and furniture do, but they tell a far more comprehensive social and moral story, not just of taste but of political and sentimental values, of causes to be fought for or to be ridiculed, places to be proud of, travels to be recorded or envied, sentiments to be treasured for their gentleness or detested for their obtuseness.

Postcards are, and always have been, printed to be sold by the thousands—if possible, by the millions—to masses of people, and the last thing their manufacturers have worried about is good taste. Most cards required no basic issue, just basic instincts, though issues, if they were hot enough, produced millions of cards. If they preached the virtues of women's suffrage, which they did, you may be sure there were cards poking vicious fun at women in politics. When temperance was an issue (as it was at the height of the golden age of postcards, between 1890 and World War I), you may be sure that the Lady with the Hatchet (Carry Nation) got equal time with Old John Barleycorn on cards, quite probably printed by the same company. All that was needed was a popular issue to produce paper fodder for the flames of opinion.

Issues, however, were least among the concerns of card publishers and their public. Sin was big. Indeed, you will find all of the Seven Deadly Sins celebrated on cards: *pride* (Texas cowboys riding on gigantic jackrabbits), *envy* (little boys watching big boys eat watermelon), *gluttony* (interiors of restaurants with tables heaped with rich foods), *sloth* (men lolling in hammocks, women lying flat on beaches), *avarice* (often indistinguishable from *envy* but especially seen in cards showing the homes of the very rich and of movie stars), and finally, *lust*, which comes in all sorts of variants, though what was considered risqué (like the French cards of wispy women in the embraces of wispy men) half a century ago looks tame enough to decorate a nursery wall today.

This is the merest hint of what one can read in cards about our foibles and fortunes, our humor and habitats, and our delights. If the deltiologists are saving these most ephemeral artifacts from extinction, they should be classified with other and better-known preservationists as welcome champions of endangered species.

Architectural Digest, 1977

IV

Do You Speak Architecture?

*T*here is something to be said for architecture as an international language, a sort of Esperanto or lingua franca that speaks with a vocabulary understood almost everywhere. In our day architectural styles, which change more rapidly than they did a couple of centuries ago, are no sooner off the drafting board in London or New York or Milan than they turn up in Paris or Mexico City.

Architects these days are peripatetic. I. M. Pei of New York currently has his hand in the refurbishing of the Louvre in Paris. Robert Venturi of Philadelphia is designing the extension of the National Gallery in London. James Stirling of London (via Scotland) has completed a new building for the Harvard art museums in Cambridge, and Arata Isozaki of Tokyo is the architect of the new Museum of Contemporary Art in Los Angeles. In Paris the Pompidou Center was designed by a Briton, Richard Rogers, and an Italian, Renzo Piano. Its founding director was Pontus Hulten, a Swede, who subsequently went to Los Angeles to help get the Museum of Contemporary Art on its way and is currently director of Venice's Palazzo Grassi. They all speak the Esperanto of architecture, though they speak it with different accents and use different clichés and colloquialisms. Whether we like what they are saying or not, we get the pitch.

You will recall that what we now call "modernism" in architecture was first known as the International Style. It emerged after the First World War and was associated most particularly with Gropius and the Bauhaus, with Le Corbusier and Mies van der Rohe, and with J. J. Oud of Holland and a few others whose work was introduced to the American public by an exhibition at the Museum of Modern Art in New York in 1932. The show, which subsequently traveled in a smaller version around the country, was called "Modern Architecture: International Exhibition."

It was organized by three young men: Alfred H. Barr, Jr., the museum's director; Philip Johnson, a serious dilettante of architecture who wouldn't become an architect for another dozen or more years; and Henry-Russell Hitchcock, Jr., the undisputed dean of American architectural historians. It was they who are thought to have coined the phrase "the International Style," partly, I have been told, because they did not know what else to call it. There are those who say that it was Mrs. Barr who, listening to them puzzle over what to call what they were about to display, suggested the phrase that has become part of architecture's jargon.

But styles of architecture have been international for millennia, and if the vocabulary has gradually expanded as new methods of building (primarily of holding up roofs) have been invented, the basic language has not. Look around you in any city in America or Europe, and you will find the ancient Greeks and variations on their temples. We call it classical, but in its early days it was an international style that was first a Greek trademark and with alterations a Roman one or, more accurately, a way of making the empire builders of Greece and Rome feel at home wherever they conquered and settled down. They held up their roofs with posts and lintels, a technique at least as ancient as the enormous vertical stones that supported massive horizontal stones at Stonehenge.

The post-and-lintel technique was used for centuries before the arch took over as the identifying cliché of officialdom for Romans. It was a round arch used for sports palaces like the Colosseum, for sporting places like the Baths of Caracalla, and for aqueducts where solid masonry would have been wasteful of stone. The round arch became an international cliché, a familiar part of the architectural vocabulary, when the church took it up and built basilicas and cathedrals in a style we now call Romanesque and the English called Norman. The round arch has never been wholly out of fashion since it was invented. In the nineteenth century there was a revival of interest in Romanesque architecture. The Cathedral of St. John the Divine in New York, for example, started out to be Romanesque in the 1890s, but the trustees changed their minds and with a new architect turned it into Gothic, or tried to. It is now some of both.

There are all sorts of Gothic, to be sure, but its appeal initially lay in the fact that with pointed arches, flying buttresses, and a new style of piers and vaulting it was possible to build higher and wider—

span greater areas—than before. Bigger was better, then as now. Gothic caught on all over Western Europe in the late twelfth century and stuck. It became the new international style for ecclesiastical buildings and seats of learning. There have been several Gothic Revivals, one in the eighteenth century and another in the nineteenth century, when the pointed arch became fashionable for country houses, churches, and public buildings in America as well as in England. Early in our own century, Collegiate Gothic became de rigueur for colleges from Yale and Princeton to the University of Chicago. There is a story, probably apocryphal, that someone at the University of Chicago wrote his counterpart at Oxford asking how to design a science building in the Gothic manner. The reply came back, "Sorry. We can't help you. We haven't built a Gothic building in six hundred years."

This frivolous once-over-lightly of architectural styles is merely to suggest that while the vocabulary of buildings necessarily changes with time, place, circumstance, and engineering inventiveness, the language that makes architecture international has roots common to all ages and places. Architecture is the art of shelter or, to put it another way, the art of making shelter interesting, convenient, and at its best, beautiful. It may shelter people or gods or cattle, but it is essentially walls and roofs embellished in various ways for various purposes. It is a language with many regional dialects. You don't find many Oriental pagoda roofs in New England or Byzantine onion domes in Iowa, or at least I don't, though I've seen onion domes on houses in small Texas towns. It is also a language in which visual clichés have a way of recurring, sometimes after they have disappeared for years. The round arch is back in postmodern architecture, for instance, and ornament, which was considered sinful by the modernists, is creeping back. Classical elements as they were used by Palladio in the late Renaissance are becoming fashionable again. No one, except a few old-fashioned functionalists, is outraged.

But it is not only architects who are peripatetic—so, it seems, are buildings. They move from century to century by standing still and from place to place by imitation or inspiration. Today's innovations have a way of becoming tomorrow's clichés; the good ones become part of architecture's language. Buildings may speak with a variety of tongues and sometimes speak in riddles, but "Buildings," as a traveler in the nineteenth century wrote, "are the books that everybody unconsciously reads." Nobody needs a trot to read them for, as Walt Whitman observed, "All architecture is what you do to it when you look upon it."

Architectural Digest, 1987

Philosopher of the Country House

*T*here are not many roads in the Berkshires that stretch for a mile or so on level ground without turning and twisting to adapt themselves to the hills or to what were once cow paths. But early in the spring I was driving along one such road during the late afternoon when the shadows were growing long.

On either side, set well back, were houses surrounded by daffodils and narcissus and flowering shrubs and fruit trees and wide, neatly mowed lawns. There were several white houses and an occasional gray or moss-green or mustard-yellow one sheltered by tall maples. Some of the houses had been built within the last fifty years, but more of them were older than that, and a few were older than the century, some by a long shot.

There was an orderliness and pride and quiet dignity about them. Some were backed by conventional red barns and green fields stretching away, though none was a working farm any longer. They were country houses, and I had the conviction that they would not have looked as they did, been as tidy and welcoming and suitable and attractive as they were, if it had not been for a gentleman who died in 1852. He was surely responsible for the pleasant aspect and spirit that pervaded them, though it is unlikely that any of their occupants have ever heard of him.

This gentleman (and there is no question that he was a gentleman) was Andrew Jackson Downing, a landscape architect as half his profession and a writer and editor of *The Horticulturalist* as the other half. His was a very popular magazine in the days when 80 percent of Americans lived in the country, most of them on farms. They read his advice, much of it of the most practical sort, and his admonitions, some of them of a moral tone, with eagerness and respect. It has been accurately told of Downing, a modest and moderate man, that he was the most influential tastemaker of his time.

A writer in *Harper's New Monthly Magazine* said of him twenty years
after he died at the age of thirty-seven, "No American has built for
himself a more permanent monument than Downing the landscape
gardener."

Downing was an acute observer and prolific writer about those
aspects of American life that were dear to him, and none was dearer
than his determination to raise the standards of rural life. "So long
as men are forced to live in log huts and follow the hunter's life,"
he wrote, "we must not be surprised at lynch law and the use of
the bowie knife. But, when smiling lawns and tasteful cottages be-
gin to embellish a country, we know that order and culture are
established."

Metaphorically, Andrew Jackson Downing was born in a garden, in the town of Newburgh on the west bank of the Hudson,
where his father was a nurseryman. Downing was only seven years
old when his father died, and as a boy he worked, when he was
not attending school, with his older brother, who took over their
father's business. There was not enough money to send him to college, but he was a diligent boy with a taste for agricultural science,
and by the time he was twenty-one he had become a recognized
horticultural authority in the Hudson Valley and looked upon by
the owners of the great estates of that region as "a gentleman, a
scholar, and . . . a most practical man."

But his taste and interests extended beyond gardens to the houses
they were designed to embellish. When he was a young man, the
most usual kind of house being built, not just in the East but by
families as they moved west, was a modified Greek temple adapted
to the uses of a country family. We now call these houses Greek
Revival, and they came in all sizes, from very modest to very grand.
They were so prevalent that they were thought proper to include
in our national hymn which celebrated our "rocks and rills . . .
and templed hills." Downing thought it was ridiculous for American farmers to be living in temples with wooden columns and por-
ticoes on the facades and incongruous chimneys sticking out of the
low-pitched roofs. He inveighed against them in his magazine, and
in 1850 he published a book of essays entitled *The Architecture of
Country Houses*.

His preface to this volume, which is illustrated with engravings
of houses he approved of and plans for them, starts with the declaration: "There are three excellent reasons why my countrymen

should have good houses. The first is, because a good house (and by this I mean a fitting, tasteful, and significant dwelling) is a powerful means of civilization. . . . The second reason is, because the *individual home* has a great social value for a people. . . . The third reason is, because there is a moral influence in a country home—when, among an educated, truthful, and refined people, it is an echo of their character—which is more powerful than any mere oral teachings of virtue and morality." Downing elaborated at length on his three reasons; indeed the volume is essentially a treatise on proper taste in architecture and decoration and its moral and social importance.

It was time, Downing preached, for a new approach to domestic dwellings, especially country houses, and one of the clichés he wanted to be rid of was the white paint that universally covered the temples and clapboard houses. "Some of our freshly painted villages, seen on a bright summer day, might give a man with weak eyes a fit of ophthalmia," he wrote; the only reason he saw for painting houses white was ostentation, to attract attention. "We think, in the beginning," he said, "that the color of all buildings in the country should be of those *soft and quiet shades* called neutral tints, such as fawn, drab, gray, brown, etc., and that all positive colors, such as white, yellow, red, blue, black, etc., should always be avoided." Houses should, he contended, blend into the colors of the landscape, not stand out against them.

The houses he recommended to replace the temples were mostly what we now call Gothic Revival, fashionable then in England as "the pointed style," though he insisted that "a dwelling house should look like a dwelling house." Delightful as Downing's Gothic cottages and villas appear today, it is hard for us to believe that an essentially ecclesiastical or collegiate style of building was any more suitable to an American country family than a temple. Though some of his contemporaries quibbled with Downing's taste, no one could deny his passionate dedication to improving the conditions under which country houses served the families who occupied them, planted them with gardens and trees, and embellished their lawns.

Downing was not an architect; he was a civilizer. He relied on his remarkable friend A. J. Davis, who designed some of America's most handsome country houses, to turn his sketches into illustrations for his books. Such was Downing's reputation that President Millard Fillmore commissioned him to landscape not only the Capitol but also the grounds of that splendid country house once known as the President's Palace and now called the White House.

A tragedy ended Downing's life early. A Hudson River steamer that was racing downstream to New York against a rival ship caught fire, and Downing was last seen throwing deck chairs from a burning deck into the water to serve as life rafts for those who had jumped overboard. His wife was one of those thus saved. If Downing's life was short, the influence of this all-but-forgotten man persists wherever there are tasteful cottages set in smiling lawns, like those I saw one spring evening on a straight stretch of road in the Berkshires.

Architectural Digest, 1987

Eastlake, Prophet with Honor

*I*n these days of aesthetic pacifism, when it seems almost impossible to pick a fight over what is art and what is not, what is good taste and what is bad, revivals are parlor games. The functionalists are no longer fighting the romantics, as they did with such glee and vituperation thirty years ago, for we are enjoying (if that is the word) a live-and-let-live era of taste. The outlandish is no longer considered lunatic; it is merely experimental. The fur-lined teacup, which, in the 1930s, evoked cries of blasphemy when it was solemnly displayed at the Museum of Modern Art, would today be looked on by even the most conservative as mild satire. We have come to a time when, in the splendid words of the late great actress Mrs. Patrick Campbell, "I don't care what you do, so long as you don't do it in the streets and frighten the horses."

So we often turn our amusements and some piquancy of style and taste to the days when there were, indeed, horses in the streets to frighten, a time when a small book on taste could change the interiors of American houses from coast to coast. Very little is remembered about that book, modestly called *Hints on Household Taste* and published in 1872, or about its author, an Englishman named Charles Lock Eastlake. Eastlake is having a revival—not the man or his book, but the furniture for which he is held responsible; indeed, not the furniture he liked or designed but the furniture—superficially based on his principles—that factories turned out and sold through mail-order houses and department stores.

Eastlake was more than a writer and designer. He was a revivalist in two senses: He not only found his inspiration in earlier styles but he also proclaimed their virtues with the conviction of a revivalist preacher. He looked for inspiration to what he regarded as the more "honest" days of design and craftsmanship, for he was eager to reverse the trend toward machine-made tawdriness that he saw all about him. His furniture was characterized by a somewhat foursquare character with echoes of Jacobean and earlier monkish pieces, and his designs, though not rigidly geometric, seem to have been made with a ruler and T-square rather than with a French curve. They were sturdy in structure, and above all, they were "honest."

In the preface to the American edition of *Hints*, its editor said of Eastlake, "He rightly thinks that the public taste is corrupt, and he does not scruple to declare it so. . . . He sees that fashion rules, and that few are shocked by sham and pretension, and he proclaims it."

Evidently this kind of tough talk was just what Americans had been waiting to hear, and they did not scruple to gobble it up. Eastlake spoke with the authority of both profession and nationality. He was a designer and a connoisseur of impeccable credentials, and he was also an Englishman; it was to England that genteel Americans looked in the 1870s for the rules of polite manners as well as the formulas of proper taste.

Eastlake was the nephew of Sir Charles Eastlake, the president of the Royal Academy and as famous as any English artist of his day. In his own right, Charles Lock Eastlake was elected secretary of the Royal Institute of Architects, and a few years after the publication of *Hints on Household Taste*, the prime minister, Lord Beaconsfield (Disraeli), appointed him keeper of the National Gallery in London. It was Eastlake who, for the first time, tried to make historical sense of that remarkable collection and to give it proper care. He arranged the paintings by "schools," a new concept, and moreover put them under glass to protect them from London's penetrating smog.

It seems to have been the morality of Eastlake's argument that captivated his readers and those who read about him in magazines or heard of his ideas from upholsterers—as interior designers were then called. His paragraphs were peppered with words like "purity," "honesty," "sincerity," "character," and "stability." He fussed at what he called "shabby gentility" and the "detestable practice" of facades that were "shams" and "structural deceits." He railed at furniture manufacturers and said, "This branch of artistic manufacture has been entrusted to those whose taste, if it can be called taste at all, can be no more referred to correct principles of design than the gimcrack decorations of a wedding cake could be tested by any standard of sculpturesque beauty."

In 1881, *Harper's Bazaar,* describing the Eastlake furor, declared: "Suddenly the voice of the prophet Eastlake was heard crying in the wilderness, 'Repent ye, for the Kingdom of the Tasteful is at hand!' . . . We began to talk about 'harmonies' and 'gradations,' about the 'sincere' in joinery and decoration, as if we knew what we meant . . . and if our earlier state was grim and tasteless our later development is too often jumbled and grotesque."

Americans loved the sermon of the prophet, but they evidently went home and sinned in the same confused ways. True converts are rare to any revivalist, and if Eastlake's sermons did not fall on deaf ears, they evidently went in one eager ear and out the other, pausing only long enough to give their hearers a delicious sense of sin.

But who is to say what the sins of taste are today? There is a great deal that passes for good taste that I find abominable, and some of what the good taste people think is bad, I find beautiful. I suspect that what we need is a Charles Lock Eastlake in our midst again so that we might choose up sides and have a wingding rhubarb rather than the polite, aesthetic pacifist tea party that now benumbs our sensibilities and sedates our convictions. There's nothing like a good row to keep taste from becoming smug and to start the creative juices flowing.

Architectural Digest, 1978

The Urbane Mr. Hunt

*R*ichard Morris Hunt must have been one of the most amiable of men; he was certainly the most popular American architect of his day and very probably the most famous. New Yorkers thought so highly of him, indeed, that they erected a statue of him in Central Park—"In recognition of his services to the cause of art in America." This honor, which was paid him in 1898, three years after he died, has been accorded no other architect and almost no one but politicians. New Yorkers do not think much of or about him today. Youngsters disfigure his likeness with graffiti, and, one by one, real estate investors have torn down his buildings—not all of them, but nearly all. The facade of the Metropolitan Museum and its Great Hall and marble staircase (saved only by a howl from preservationists a few years ago) are his principal New York memorials.

Many good and some excellent architects are forgotten, but those who are innovators—who set their individual style on their art-cum-business—are likely not to be. Hunt was not one of those; his reputation suffered a decline soon after he died, and it slept uneasily in histories of architecture. It is now being refurbished. The most recent refurbishment is an excellent biography, *Richard Morris Hunt,* by Professor Paul R. Baker of New York University—a book I recommend to those whose interest in American architecture is more than just casual. It is the first comprehensive biography of Hunt and chronicle of his work, and as such, it is a very useful and instructive history of American architecture for most of the nineteenth century. Hunt knew everybody who was anybody in his profession, and taught or worked with a great many of them. He also knew everybody who was anybody among the vastly rich of the eastern seaboard (the Vanderbilts, Astors, and Goelets, for instance) in the last half of his century, and they vied for his friendship and the skill of

his pencil as though he provided passports to immortality. He became in his later years the "dean of American architecture," the
sort of epithet reserved for the revered as they grow old and have
been overtaken by events or by fashion.

Hunt was wellborn, as his contemporaries would have said, in
Brattleboro, Vermont, in 1828, to a father who was a congressman
and a mother who, early widowed, was a woman of determined
character and intelligence, and "noted for her beauty and her artistic talent." Richard was the fourth of five children, and if he became the most famous of them, he was not, in my judgment, the
most gifted. His older brother William was a very considerable artist. And it was because William developed a persistent cough that
Mrs. Hunt decided, on the advice of a physician, to take her children to a warmer clime. She chose the south of France. But for
William's cough, we might never have heard of Richard Morris Hunt
as an architect. He had planned to go to West Point.

Hunt owes his reputation to what he brought back from Europe, and especially from France. His most important weapons were
his energy, his newly acquired architectural skill, and an intelligent
eye—all weapons that had been fired in the furnace of the École
des Beaux-Arts in Paris. He was the first American to go through
the rigors of Beaux-Arts architectural training—the first of many.
He so distinguished himself as a hardworking and clever designer
that Hector Martin Lefuel, in whose atelier he worked as a student
in the 1840s, hired him to assist him as *inspecteur des travaux* on the
new structures then being built to connect the Louvre and the Tuileries. When Hunt said he was determined to return to America,
Lefuel "offered him any government position within his control if
he would stay in Paris."

But the young architect, his head filled with images of European
châteaux and palaces, churches and public monuments (he had
traveled extensively), decided that his native land needed to be
awakened to the beauties of the arts, which meant, of course, the
arts of Europe. There were few architects in America then; most
people who needed houses or business blocks relied on carpenter-
builders, who in turn relied on the designs in "plan books" and
building magazines. No school of architecture even existed. Such
architects as there were had learned, as did lawyers, by working as
assistants or apprentices to practitioners.

Soon after his arrival in New York, Hunt established an atelier of young aspirants. He was a natural teacher—"inspiring," "vehement," and "strenuous." It was one of Hunt's young men, William R. Ware, who, while practicing in Boston and running an atelier like Hunt's, was asked by the Massachusetts Institute of Technology in 1866 to organize the first school of architecture in America.

In many respects Hunt was more interesting for what he was than for what he designed and built. He had an important impact on the taste of the rich, which filtered down to the merely well-to-do, who in turn took to building little châteaux in imitation of Hunt's big ones. He understood the client-architect relationship thoroughly. He once said to his son, "The first thing you've got to remember is that it's your client's money you are spending. Your business is to get the best results you can, following their wishes. If they want you to build a house upside down, standing on its chimney, it's up to you to do it, and to get the best possible results." No wonder his clients loved him! He was an expert problem solver, whether the problem called for a simple practical solution or an outrageously elaborate one like The Breakers or Marble House at Newport. His Tenth Street Studios in New York were the haunts of our most distinguished nineteenth-century artists, and his French flats were America's first apartment houses. (They were looked on as immoral, partly because everything French had overtones of sin, and partly because it was thought indecent to have people living above and below one's private dwelling.) He designed tombs, pedestals for statues (including the one on which stands the Statue of Liberty in New York Harbor), and he was the Grand Old Man of the Chicago World's Fair of 1893. His Administration Building at the head of the Lagoon was the fair's most conspicuous structure.

The reasons Hunt's reputation went into a decline after his death are better than the ones for a Hunt revival. He was a pastiche maker in an era when all the culture that social status demanded came from abroad. He arrived from Paris at the right time and in the right places for gratifying tycoons and their heirs who wanted to emulate in grandeur the princes of the Renaissance, and he was thoroughly versed in the architectural vocabulary to satisfy them. He was in no sense an innovator, except as a tastemaker; he was a gentleman's gentleman, with expansive charm, a spry wit, an eye for style, and a great capacity for enjoyment and for inspiring it in others. His business was not unlike that of Ben Sonnenberg, the late publicist and collector, who said, "My job is to put little men on big pedestals." Hunt's pedestals were magnificent, and if his tongue was in his cheek, he did not let it show.

Architectural Digest, 1981

A Sculptor's Celebration of Heroes

*A*ugustus Saint-Gaudens, who may or may not have been the greatest sculptor America had produced (I do not want to provoke an argument about this, as you see), was a vigorous man, an enthusiast by nature, and he believed in the times and the world he lived in. Whatever he undertook he went at with panache, a panache coupled with subtlety and a profound sense of human dignity free from sentimentality but not from humor.

I paid a call on him in Cornish, New Hampshire, not long ago— or so it almost seems; he died in 1907. His house and his studio, his gardens and pools, have been sensibly designated a National Historic Site and are taken care of by the National Park Service. It was quite clear not only from the pieces of sculpture excellently displayed indoors and out but also from the house and its gardens that he was a man who celebrated life. Moreover, he was not afraid to celebrate public heroes and events (as most sculptors are today) and private friends, and he looked upon his profession as a craft that he was fortunate enough to be able to elevate to the level of art. He worked hard to help others do the same thing.

The house at Cornish, called Aspet (the name of the town in France where Saint-Gaudens's father was born), is not a grand one but it is what New Englanders would call "substantial." It was red brick when Saint-Gaudens discovered it in 1885, and as it looked gloomy to him, he painted it white. The sculptor tacked a wide porch supported by Ionic columns on the south side of the pleasant foursquare house, prompting a friend to say that the house looked like an "upright New England farmer with a new set of false teeth." The "teeth" are now nearly obscured by vines, but the view to Mt. Ascutney is not.

I approached Aspet with some suspicion. I have always been suspicious of shrines, and that is what Aspet most certainly is. Shrines are memorials, and by definition memorials are dead. In some respects my misgivings were justified. A sculptor's studio in Saint-Gaudens's day was a confusion of bent wire and pipe, of tools scattered on tables, of half-done pieces covered with wet cloths to keep the clay from hardening, of discarded sketches of hands and noses gathering dust in corners. (Today the material is often not clay but metal; the tools are shears and welding equipment.) But Aspet is as tidy as a bandbox and as hushed as a chapel. If the delicate portraits in low relief of his friends like Robert Louis Stevenson seem to speak in hushed tones of his mastery of that extremely difficult medium, and the monumental works like the *Diana* that topped the original Madison Square Garden speak boldly of his unconventional and vigorous stance in a time of tiresome realism and timid gentility, one gets no idea of how Saint-Gaudens worked at Aspet or what it looked or sounded like when he was in his studio. However, shrine or no shrine the place is not dead but alive.

It takes very little imagination to see the dapper sculptor with his Vandyke beard, who loved to ski and play hockey and take part in charades, looking at his garden sculpture of satyrs and laughing at you for taking them seriously. On the other hand, one can see him looking critically, but not without satisfaction, at the replica of the somber memorial to Henry Adams's wife (the original is in Rock Creek Cemetery in Washington), and saying, as the record shows, "He wanted a figure to symbolize 'the acceptance, intellectually, of the inevitable.' " And he might have added, "Poor Mrs. Adams committed suicide, you know." In front of the full-scale replica of the Robert Gould Shaw Memorial in Boston, possibly his greatest piece, he might have recalled the correspondence with a friend who had criticized the piece. Saint-Gaudens wrote him, "It's the way the thing's done that makes it right or wrong, that's about the only creed I have in art."

I came away wondering what had happened to sculpture that celebrated people and events; what, in other words, had happened to public sculpture that once was concerned with heroes and heroic occasions. I could think of just one, Eero Saarinen's lofty graceful arch in St. Louis, and he was not a sculptor, but an architect. I decided that the only heroes sculptors recognize these days are themselves. Public sculpture exists now almost entirely to relieve deadly open spaces left by architects—plateaus of concrete or terrazzo that have to be "broken up" or "relieved" by monumental abstractions—monuments, that is, to sculpture itself and its makers. It becomes exterior decoration made out of introspection and "self-expression," intellectually contrived sculpture in an emotional void to fill a physical void.

Which is not to say, of course, that if Saint-Gaudens were alive today he wouldn't be pushing the edges of his art into new forms, just as Calder did with such joy and Henry Moore with such solemnity. Like every great artist, Saint-Gaudens was not one step, but two, ahead of that perennial Keystone Kop—popular taste.

Architectural Digest, 1978

The Moving Spirits of Ringwood

A bout ninety minutes by car out of New York is what was once a summer house and is now a public monument called Ringwood Manor. It is in the town of Ringwood in northern New Jersey, just a cannon shot over the New York state line from Tuxedo Park, home of the original dinner jacket. Ringwood at one time had a great deal to do with cannon shot; it was the site of various iron foundries, and cannonballs were among its products. Ringwood was the country place of three generations of Coopers and Hewitts, families that made their fortunes in iron, and it does not let you forget it. Its grounds are decorated with objects made from the fruit of its forges.

The house is in a style that could well be called Nineteenth-Century American Higgledy-Piggledy. It is a little bit of almost every architectural revival from the beginning of the century until its very end, from Classical through Gothic to Queen Anne and finally to Beaux-Arts Neoclassicism. (The columned porte cochere was designed by Stanford White around 1900.) It is a long house that seems to stretch along the ground as though two giants had used it for a tug-of-war. The original house was built circa 1810 by industrialist Martin Ryerson. Its subsequent owner, Peter Cooper, extended it by attaching other nearby buildings. This, of course, made for a very uneven roofline, as if a country village had been squished together. So Cooper had a continuous roof placed over the lot and at a subsequent date had the entire miscellaneous exterior, except for the roof, covered with white stucco to give the house a look of unity, which its interior belies to this day.

Peter Cooper was the founder of Cooper Union, a free school of the arts and sciences in New York intended to provide indigent young people with the kind of education he as a poor boy could not afford. His fortune was made in the iron business, but by avocation he was an inspired tinkerer and inventor who, among other things, designed America's first working steam locomotive, called "Tom Thumb."

But Ringwood today owes more to Cooper's son-in-law and to his granddaughters than it does to Cooper. The son-in-law was Abram S. Hewitt, and two of his daughters, Sarah and Eleanor Hewitt, were the moving spirits and founders of what is now the Cooper-Hewitt Museum in New York. The brownstone mansion in which the Hewitts lived on lower Lexington Avenue has been torn down, so the only standing domestic evidence of the tastes of the eccentric Misses Hewitt is to be found intact at Ringwood.

Ringwood is not a beautiful house, but it is a very personal one filled with echoes of curiously interesting persons. Abram Hewitt was a successful businessman (Cooper's younger partner), a congressman, and for one term a reform mayor of New York. His hand is heavy in the house, especially in the oak staircase into which his and his wife's initials are carved as ornament. Yet the prevailing character of the house is, or so it seems to me, the imprint left on it by the Hewitt sisters.

There were three of them. The second oldest was Sarah, the most commanding, eccentric, and brilliant of the three. The youngest was Eleanor—energetic, athletic, a wizard with a needle, level-headed, hard-working, and humorous. Only Amelia, the oldest, married; if she left an imprint anywhere, it was elsewhere. Both Sarah and Eleanor were acquisitive, but not in any scatterbrained way. They were nothing if not purposeful.

They decided when they were quite young to be collectors of things. It seems not to have mattered what kinds of things as long as they were of rare quality and design. When they were still teenagers, they spent their accumulated allowances to purchase a collection of ancient textiles. As they grew a little older, it became their ambition to start a museum on the fourth floor of their grandfather's Cooper Union. It was in his original plans to have a museum there that would demonstrate "the true philosophy of life," by which he meant a museum of natural wonders; he went so far as to buy a stuffed white whale. The two sisters had a different vision—a collection for the edification of the Union's art students and a source of inspiration and example for commercial designers.

Ringwood was a summer place for the Hewitts, summer often starting in May and lasting until December. In midsummer, year after year, Sarah and Eleanor sailed to Europe to haunt museums, especially those of the decorative arts, and to search among dealers for drawings and prints, textiles, ceramics, and all manner of other treasures for their museum. Sarah, who was a very large woman and grew larger as she grew older, was propelled through museums in a wheelchair guided by her butler, whom she took everywhere with her. Eleanor was always with her, a buffer for her sister's imperious behavior.

At Ringwood Sarah would have no electric bells since she was afraid of short circuits, so she kept a hunting horn by her bed with which to let out a blast when she wanted her breakfast. She would not have a telephone in the house either, and so she had a cement booth built for one outside. When she wanted her carriage—she would not allow an automobile on the property—her butler stood at the front door and summoned it with a bugle. By her bed she kept a policeman's truncheon in case an intrepid male should violate her privacy.

Eleanor, on the other hand, though she had her own foibles (it is said that when she sailed to Europe, she wore two padded Chinese costumes so that if there were a catastrophe and she found herself in the icy waters of the Atlantic, they would keep her warm), was something of a sportswoman. She claimed to have brought lawn tennis to America. She was an expert with a fly rod, a skill she learned from her brother, who was a national champion. She loved to skate and ride and climb mountains and dance. She was never, even when sedentary in her carriage, without a piece of embroidery in her hands, and a friend once said, "Nothing disturbed her calm or upset her cheerful equanimity." She was said to have had the largest collection of erotica in New York, which after her death her brother is thought to have disposed of by throwing it into the East River.

Ringwood, as it is now decorated, reflects the Hewitts' belief that good taste fell apart at the end of the eighteenth century, for this is a Victorian house with an overcast of the kind of "French taste" that Edith Wharton wrote about. The French drawing room, for example, is ornamented with sizable copies of paintings by Fragonard set into pale green walls; the music room is surrounded by European wallpaper printed with a nautical scene. For a house of the period there is a minimum of clutter. Instead there are large Chinese vases and almost-full-size marble copies of familiar French sculptures. If the outside is higgledy-piggledy architecture, the interior is what might be called controlled higgledy-piggledy decoration, as eccentric and personal as the ladies who put their mark on it.

Ringwood is rare among old houses open to the public. It is not trying to instruct us in anything, give us a history lesson, improve our taste, astonish us with rarities or overpower us with extravagance. It merely says, Here is an interesting place lived in by interesting people who enjoyed themselves in rather unconventional ways. They knew what they liked, and they knew what they thought others ought to like. I like it. It lives and breathes.

Architectural Digest, 1987

On Knowing Wright from Wrong

*T*wice it has been my privilege, and more particularly my pleasure, to spend the weekend with friends in Frank Lloyd Wright houses: a large and famous one (indeed the most famous of all) and a modest, early, and, except to Wright buffs, relatively obscure one. The first visit was about a dozen years ago to Fallingwater, the house over the waterfall at Bear Run, Pennsylvania. The second one was made a few months ago to the Barton House, as it is called after its first occupant, in Buffalo, New York.

Fallingwater, when I visited it, was still lived in on weekends by Edgar Kaufmann, Jr., whose father, a department store magnate, had commissioned Wright to build it. As a very young man, Edgar (to distinguish him from his father, Mr. K., Sr.) had been a member of the "Fellowship" at Wright's establishment in Wisconsin, called Taliesin, where Wright took into his rambling dwelling and drafting rooms "apprentices in residence." It was he who persuaded his father to ask Wright to build the house and persuaded Wright to accept the commission, offering as inducement a thousand acres of woodland and meadows and streams and leaving the selection of the site to the architect.

Wright and Mr. K., Sr., a couple of freewheeling spirits with vigorous and adventurous temperaments, evidently got along famously, and the result of their cooperation was completed in 1936. Wayne Andrews, the architectural historian, has called it "the most famous modern house in the world, and not undeservedly, for no other architect in modern times has wooed and won a site so spectacular."

The Barton House, on the other hand, is on a site so little spectacular that it hardly seems a site at all. The house sits on a quiet street in Buffalo, not far from the university. It is certainly unlike any other house on the street in style, but it does not lord it over

211

its neighbors—most of which are in the customary manner of the first decade of this century, variations on bungalows or watery versions of Queen Anne. They are divided from one another by narrow driveways and each has its small napkin of front lawn. The Barton House was Wright's first building of half a dozen he erected in the first years of the century in Buffalo, and it was completed in 1903, a two-story structure with wide eaves, unmistakably "early Wright" and impossible to overlook.

It was commissioned by Darwin Martin of the Larkin Company, a mail-order and wholesale grocery and soap business. Wright had built a house for Darwin's brother, W. E. Martin, in Oak Park, Illinois (that Martin was president of the firm that made E.Z.-brand stove polish), and the Buffalo Martin was impressed. He commissioned a grand house for himself and a small house for his brother-in-law, and they were connected by a low wall and an elegant pergola, an L-shaped affair at the right angle of which was a conservatory. The small house was built before the large one, now the alumni office of Buffalo University and something of a wreck. The pergola was torn down some years ago by a real estate speculator, and the Barton House now stands free and independent and dignified. Its present owners, Eleanor and Eric Larrabee, bought the house next to it a few years ago and tore it down so that their house is on a double lot with some elbow room.

A Frank Lloyd Wright house has to be stayed in to be believed, and it has to be believed in by its occupants to remain a Frank Lloyd Wright house. It is possible to reduce a Wright house to a shambles by tinkering with the work of "the Master," but it is not easy. The flow of its open spaces can be cut off by partitions. Its walls can be painted in gaudy colors and pictures hung on them, though Wright did not like pictures to distract from his design and left little space for them. Its stained-glass windows can be replaced with something that lets in more light, and its built-in furniture can be ripped out. Wright once said, "I have been black and blue in some spot, somewhere, almost all my life from too intimate contact with my own furniture." But short of desecration of this sort, a Wright house is in charge of whoever lives in it. The house, not the occupant, sets the style.

It was very soon after I had the pleasure of staying at Fallingwater that Edgar K., Jr., gave it and its experimental forest to the Pennsylvania Conservancy. He reasoned that people who were primarily interested in the forests and streams were the people to protect the character of the house, for without the waterfall over which it extends, the marriage of house and water would vanish and with it much of its magic. Fallingwater has this in common with the Grand Canyon: nobody has ever been able to give a true sense of its dimensions and character with a camera. Sound and depth are as much a part of the house as its physical structure which, as one critic put it, is "a matchless fusion of fantasy and engineering." I know of no other building into which an architect has built sound as an essential, almost structural element. Water pounding and splashing on stones is always there, and though the sound is not obtrusive—quite the contrary—it takes a bit of getting used to. I woke in the middle of the first night I was there to what I thought was a summer storm; I went to the wide wall of window only to find the sky filled with stars. The sound of running water has another, more common effect, to be sure, on one half awake.

Edgar K., Jr., lived *with* his house as much as he lived *in* it, for the house itself was a presence that demanded respect; indeed, it demanded a degree of loving subservience. Now that he is no longer there, it must suffer from his absence, although Mr. Larrabee says that he understands that the Conservancy and the Kaufmann Foundation between them are now "doing a superb job maintaining it and making it accessible to a carefully controlled flow of visitors." Edgar enjoyed it and humored it and tended it and was justly proud of it as the work of imagination and skill and defiance that it was—as a work of art. And, indeed, it still is.

Instead of starting from scratch the Larrabees took on a house that had suffered from distaste. It had been lived in by several families who bought or rented it because, I gather, no one else wanted it and because it was cheap for the amount of space it provided. They had done what they could to tame the house (one might almost say domesticate it) by painting it in what Mrs. Larrabee called *gelati* colors with chintz at the windows and other devices for concealing Mr. Wright's presence. Mrs. Larrabee, who is an architect, told me that Wright once visited the house, looked about, and said to the then occupant, "You don't deserve to live in a Frank Lloyd Wright house." To which the occupant replied, "I don't know what sin I have committed to deserve such a fate."

Obviously the Larrabees *do* deserve to live in a Wright house, and they have had a lovely time making the house speak for itself again. The walls are now as spare as Wright meant them to be, and the furniture, though not of Wright's own design, speaks to the condition of the house in its comfortable simplicity. The curtains are gone from the windows, which Wright designed with iridescent opalescent glass discreetly used to provide color without keeping out light.

Since Wright apparently had as little interest in providing space for books as for pictures, Mrs. Larrabee designed tall, freestanding revolving bookcases using Wright's uprights for the stair banister as their basic pattern. Mr. Larrabee, until recently executive director of the New York State Council on the Arts, is a writer on many subjects and therefore, to put it mildly, bookish. The essential quality of the house is not in its details, though they are thoroughly Wrightian, but in the beautiful spaces that flow into other spaces. Here is the open plan by the man who gave it to the twentieth century, which slowly took it to its bosom.

The Larrabees, as the Kaufmanns did at Fallingwater, are living in style, and what that means depends on where you put the accent. "*Living* in style" implies that how one acts is the important thing and style means luxury. "Living in *style*," on the other hand, means living fashionably or keeping up with your particular breed of Joneses. But "*living in style*" means surrounded, encompassed by style, not necessarily either fashionable or luxurious, but satisfying in ways that neither fashion nor luxury can be.

Architectural Digest, 1975

The Zeus of Oak Park

A few months ago I spent a drizzling Sunday afternoon in Oak
Park, a suburb of Chicago that regards itself with justification
as the center of a particular world—indeed, the epicenter of an architectural disturbance. From it have emanated more waves of influence than from any suburb I can think of. The Oak Park waves
were set in motion by a one-man earthquake: an inspired man; in
many respects an arrogant, touchy, sometimes unscrupulous man;
a romantic, a visionary, a pain in the neck.

This, of course, was Frank Lloyd Wright, a bonded and certified
architectural genius, one of our nation's very few. Wright's personal flag flies over Oak Park and casts its lively shadow next door
over the town of River Forest. In these two suburbs, filled with all
manner of what we called villas in the nineteenth century, there
are thirty Frank Lloyd Wright structures—twenty-eight houses, a
tennis club, and a Unitarian church. The shadow, to be sure, does
not stop there. It, or its semblance in the works of other architects,
occurs with great frequency in and about Chicago too.

Wright's noblest house in what might be called the Oak Park
Style, but is commonly called the Prairie Style, is on the other side
of Chicago, near the university. It is the Robie House, built in 1909
for a businessman who made his fortune in bicycles and sewing
machines, and whose name will be long remembered in the annals
of architecture as an adventurous patron. The Robie House is the
epitome of the Prairie Style, with its long ground-hugging horizontal look—like a ship loaded to its Plimsoll line, low and belonging
to the elements for which it was built.

Except that it is flat, the home of the Prairie Style could scarcely
be less like a prairie. Wright lived and worked at the corner of
Forest and Chicago avenues in Oak Park from 1889 until 1909,
when he left his wife and six children and eloped with the wife of

215

a client. The place he built to live in, and the studio he later attached to it, are in the process of being restored by the Frank Lloyd Wright Home and Studio Foundation. This labor of love is being performed with the care and precision of a surgical procedure—partly by paid professionals, partly by unpaid professionals, and partly by eager volunteers, converts to the increasingly popular practice of architectural restoration and reclamation.

Carla Lind, executive director of the foundation—who might or might not have been relieved to spend this dismal afternoon not watching a soccer game in which her son was playing—showed a few of us the house and the studio. The house is a small one, in which small rooms imply spaciousness, spaces flowing into other spaces, early indications of the open plan Wright is said to have introduced to domestic architecture, and which is so essential a signature of his Prairie houses. The small dining room—with its tall-backed and rigidly upright chairs, its delicately leaded bay windows, its cupboards that are fully a part of the architecture, its intricately patterned light screen above the table—could almost have been a practice exercise for a much larger dining room. The living room was a far cry from the similar kind of room the Metropolitan Museum in New York has recently installed, a large and elegant room of breathtaking proportions and subtleties of detail, rescued from a house Wright built from 1912 to 1914 for the Francis W. Little family in Wayzata, Minnesota. (A ruckus has erupted in Minneapolis, I have heard, because this room was allowed to slip through local fingers, along with other treasures in the house.)

Wright's own living room is, I think it fair to say, spacious looking, though small, with a round-arched fireplace recessed in an alcove. Set into the four corners of the ceiling are rectangles of plaster ornament similar to those in Louis Sullivan's Chicago Auditorium, on which Wright worked with his first master, the only architect he admitted had any influence on his style. Wright was adamant in his refusal to acknowledge any influences on his work, even those of the Japanese houses he had seen, influences so apparent to the most casual observer. He wanted it thought that his inspiration sprang, like Athena, full-fledged from the brow of this architectural Zeus.

Wright's house and studio grew in response to a necessity for more living and working space. He kept adding to the original modest structure, and as he did, his style evolved a vocabulary of design more and more characteristic of what commonly identifies his work. What started as a simple Shingle Style dwelling, with a sharply peaked roof, soon acquired the strong horizontals of the Prairie houses. It was, in his metaphor, an "organic house," the exterior of which grew from the needs inside. Physical needs, that is, not sentimental needs; Wright had no use for nostalgia. His inventiveness and the fertility of his drafting pencil are in evidence wherever the eye alights—in every detail, as in every concept of space; in the intricacy of the screens that hide sources of light in the ceilings; in the eloquence of a barrel-vaulted playroom for his children. This was a room meant to be romped in, and it says so.

The drafting room, attached by a covered passageway to the house, is two stories high, with clerestory windows and an octagonal balcony hung on a chain harness that looks down from all eight sides. A small octagonal library repeats the motif. There was still a great deal of shoring up and refinishing to be done when I was there, but as it was a Sunday, the only laborers in evidence were two young volunteer architects digging in the mud to plant a willow tree where Wright originally found one growing and incorporated it into his plan.

Our group walked in the rain to look at nearby Wright houses— there are guided tours for those who want them, and 35,000 visitors came last year. We then drove around Oak Park and River Forest with Carla Lind as our guide. She said and, in saying it, pronounced a double truth about Wright and his clients and their successors: "It was an interesting, independent breed who commissioned these houses, and so are the people who live in them now and love them and restore them."

Architectural Digest, 1984

Architecture and Illusion

*M*iami Beach is a strip of sand more readily associated with beach umbrellas and bikinis than with cultural history, especially architectural history. To a conscientious, civic-minded, and nostalgic group of Miamians, however, it comprises "the finest collection of Art Deco buildings in the United States and perhaps the world." This collection has had a good deal of publicity in the last two or three years for several good reasons.

Not the least of these is the revival of interest in a style of the 1920s and 1930s that retired into the shadows of disrepute after World War II, and among sophisticates of the arts, before that. The revival is said to be partly a nostalgia for the Jazz Age of the 1920s, which spawned Art Deco—an age social critics today are inclined to insist was more simple-minded than our present frenetic one and more secure. I am not sure it was. It ended, after all, in a depression followed by a war. Many thought that civilization was going to the dogs then, just as there are those who think so now, and for the same reason—failing morality.

But the Art Deco revival is also a sensible concern with not wanting the past to slip away because of neglect or greed, an attitude evidenced by the recent spread of Landmarks Preservation Commissions to hundreds of communities and by the need of cultural historians to have something new to explore and of dealers to have new/old wares with which to beguile.

The name of the style, like the names of many styles—Gothic, Baroque, and the new one, Luminist, for American landscape painting of the nineteenth century—was an afterthought. It derives from what dominated an exposition in Paris in 1925 that was called *L'Exposition internationale des arts décoratifs et industriels modernes*. It was essentially a "machine art" in looks, if not necessarily in manufacture, and it supplanted the turn-of-the-century fashion for Art

Nouveau, which, to oversimplify it, was an art of floral forms as practiced by such masters as Hector Guimard—who designed the entrances to the Paris Métro—and America's Louis Comfort Tiffany.

Those of us who espoused, sometimes skeptically and halfheartedly, the doctrines of the Bauhaus and Le Corbusier's "machine for living" and defended "functionalism" thought of the Style Moderne—as Art Deco was then called—as "modernistic," and dismissed it as an aberration. Much of it was "streamlined," a word adopted from the design of locomotives and other vehicles in which wind resistance is a factor to be reckoned with. It produced wind-resistant teapots, toasters, bookcases, coffee tables, and steam irons that weren't going anywhere. They are now much admired as period pieces—but not for their streamlining.

Art Deco, as it first flowered and is now being refurbished in Miami Beach, is Pop architecture. It was not for highbrows, as Bauhaus modern and the International Style were. Art Deco was an architecture that had a clean, up-to-date look and was not afraid to use ornament and bright colors for their own sakes. It had a chic simplicity with an element of luxury built in, modern and sybaritic at the same time. At its best, it was very rich indeed—as in the lobby of the Chrysler Building in New York, with its vibrating combinations of metal and inlaid woods, or in the interiors of Radio City Music Hall, designed by Donald Deskey and recently refurbished. Murals of garlanded, floating, sinuous nudes ornamented grand staircases in hotels in those days, and etched-glass panels of stylized flowers enclosed telephone booths. It was—to use a cliché of the thirties—rich but not gaudy. And there was gaiety in its fantasy.

After World War II, Art Deco was forgotten for about twenty-five years. Examples of it began to turn up in dealers' galleries some years after Art Nouveau was enjoying a revival. It was in the late 1960s that it reemerged as something interesting to collectors, and the first American exhibition devoted to it was held at Finch College in New York in 1970 and subsequently traveled to Minneapolis. It has not, so far as I know, been seriously revived as a style of interior design, though pieces of it—tables, chairs, mirrors, rugs, textiles, and lamps, some of splendid craftsmanship and design—have found themselves welcome and at home, just as Art Nouveau objects have.

As I suggested in an essay on the *Queen Elizabeth 2*, there seems to have been a new ephemeral style that displaced Art Deco; I called it "Art Disco." (The names of styles are usually afterthoughts, invented, like this one, when the style is dead or dying.) Disco dancing is on the way out, it is said, and so perhaps is Art Disco. Small loss, but not uninteresting.

It is a style of illusions—illusions outside space and time, illusions of frenetic motion. It is there, but it is not there, like the colors that spatter around a dance floor and on the dancers from a revolving mirrored ball in the ceiling. It is a conjuring trick: the light is quicker than the eye. Now you see it, now you don't. *Psychedelic* is a word in its vocabulary. The flashing of strobe lights, which destroy space and time, are part of its structureless nature. It is more than a style of comforting fantasy; at its extreme it is a style of frantic escape.

It seems to me likely that Morris Lapidus, the architect of the Fontainebleau Hotel in Miami, was the father of Art Disco. He was frankly interested in making illusions of luxury and of providing a setting in which hotel guests might live a fantasy existence. Things were not what they seemed; they were what they seemed to have been in the movie sets of the 1930s. Grand staircases were not for walking up, but for walking halfway up and, like a princess or a movie queen, sweeping down. There were steps up to a platform at the entrance of a dining room so that one could look down on those who were there (and be looked up to by them) as one came down a few steps to the level of the tables—a trick also used in the *QE2*. Stylistically it was a happy hodgepodge, a theatrical concept by a man who had trained at the Beaux-Arts and planned to be a set designer. Obviously Las Vegas took Lapidus's ideas of fantasy and pushed them to the edge of hysteria, both in the dark caverns inside and the gigantic electric signs outside.

Motion with lights and reflections and sound is an important element of Art Disco. Think of the early Wurlitzer jukeboxes (primitive Disco) and the pinball machines that buzz, ring, and imitate fireworks. Think of the background of the Academy Awards last April—multicolored whirling and flashing elements in an illusion of unlimited space.

If Art Disco is a style at all, it reflects this particular moment in our national restlessness. Mobility, both physical and social, has always been an American characteristic, but the jitters has not. Art-historically, one could say that it is a stylistic by-blow of Op Art and kinetic sculpture. One might also say that Pop Art is a parody of Art Disco. In science-fiction films Art Disco reaches its peak, as in *Star Wars,* where illusion with the saving grace of humor is carried beyond the brink of belief. Like much Art Disco, *Star Wars* kids itself.

A friend of mine, an art historian and collector of Art Nouveau, with whom I talked about Art Disco, said, "I see what you mean. It has to do with ambiguity of space." After a moment, he added, "What's more, you can't collect it any more than you can collect conceptual art."

That, we agreed, was quite probably the best thing about it.

Architectural Digest, 1980

Junk

*T*here is more than a tendency, there is a concerted movement, among architectural pundits these days to solemnize "junk architecture"—motels with their monstrous signs like frozen fireworks, strips like those in Las Vegas and Los Angeles, fast-food joints, theme parks, and other teats on the roadside sow at which Americans, perpetually in a hurry, feed their bellies, their cars, and their imaginations. Junk, we are told, is quintessentially American and must be taken seriously as vernacular art. It is populist art, the art of the people.

To some purists, junk is outrageous; to some, it is amusing, an attitude its defenders regard as patronizing. To others, like sociologists and cultural historians, it is "significant" as artifacts of civilization. To the perpetually breathless seekers after the latest aesthetic gimmick, it is beautiful. To say that junk architecture is "in" is to use an epithet that is "out," but it is currently chic in those circles where fashion is more important than style.

The social importance and engaging qualities of junk architecture are an old and familiar story to historians of American taste. What is now called junk has played a lively role in the shaping and sometimes the distortion of American life. It dates at least from the gimcrackery of more than a century ago: the floating Gothic palaces that paraded inland waters propelled by lacily encased side wheels and topped with fringed chimneys; the early "palace hotels," as flossy as Marie Antoinette's boudoir; and the lapidary eye-boggling resort hotels of Miami. Much of the American character can be read in those flights of fancy—its readiness to be taken in by intimations (and imitations) of luxury, by false fronts and parodies of elegance. It is theme parks like Disney World that have brought such harmless and engaging dupery to new peaks of ingeniousness. This is the part of the American dream that has been illusion for its own sake, and if moralists have railed against it, it seems to have had as many virtues of good clean fun as it had vices.

But there is a wave of solemnity toward junk architecture in the choppy seas of criticism. Junk that was built for frivolity's sake, much of it packaging, not architecture, is now being probed and analyzed for deeper significance, a turnabout that was inevitable. Critics being what they are, they are always in search of a fresh point of assault, always looking for a "new meaning."

It is frequently said that the Pop artists of the 1960s made the sophisticated public—and the critics too, of course—look at junk with new eyes, who revealed half seriously and half ironically that in every can of soup lurks a soul and a social reprimand, that the artifacts of junk are "meaningful" and significant, as manifestations of our time, our place, and our circumstances. This would seem to be the art of *circumstantialism*. (Don't look in your dictionary for this word. I just made it up.)

Junk is to architecture as slang is to cultivated speech. Just as slang can be vivid and appropriate and enrich the language, so junk can enrich architecture, but, like slang, junk gets limp from overuse, boring when it is a substitute for thought, and offensive when it is used in the wrong circumstances. It is cliché architecture, a sort of greeting-card architecture—jokey, sentimental, flashy, mindless.

This interest in the slang of architecture and the architecture of circumstantialism—circumstances largely beyond our control, it seems—has inspired an art of its own. Painters photograph gas stations and buses and diners in color, and from the photographs make immaculate paintings that are displays of formidable technique. Put in perspective, this is merely the obverse of the nineteenth-century trick of making photographs look like paintings, and just as sentimental. Indeed, the concern about modern junk architecture is paralleled and was preceded by a similar concern about Victorian junk architecture. Much of the same spirit pervades them both, much of the same disregard of the appropriateness of the sites they occupy: little gingerbread palaces set in rows six feet apart; wooden boxes with gewgaws applied to make them look like better architecture. They are echoed today by the ubiquitous shingle mansards that are clipped on supermarkets and fast-food outlets.

One of the virtues of junk is that most of it has a way of consuming itself; the public quickly gets tired of it and wants a new kind of junk. This is as true of junk architecture as it is of junk music and literature. The junk architecture of the nineteenth century had its counterpart in penny dreadfuls, as today's has its counterpart in comic books. It is interesting as ephemera, but it is about as reliable an index of American culture as penny dreadfuls are of the culture of our great great grandparents.

It is, however, an index of self-consciousness. Has there ever been a society so intent on collecting itself, on staring in the mirror at its public face, on searching for virtues in its faults, and faults in its virtues, as this? I doubt it.

Architectural Digest, 1979

Eccentric Circles

*O*nce in a great while I come on a restoration of a building that overcomes my natural suspicion that what is being told by it is only a half-truth at best. If you are as suspicious as I am of the cosmetics that are so frequently applied to old buildings to make them look the way our generation thinks they ought to have looked, rather than the way the people who lived and worked in them meant them to look, I commend to you the Shaker Village, in Hancock, Massachusetts, and particularly to a circular stone barn. The barn is, I say without reservation, one of the glories of New England architecture. The Shaker Village—now a historical museum complex—is a lesson in restoring the past in a way that makes it plausible.

The Shakers ardently believed in heavenly intercourse, but seemed determined—because they flatly ruled out sexual intercourse as sinful—to do themselves in. They perpetuated their communities by conversion and by adopting orphans. If they were eccentric in their beliefs, they were hardheaded and practical, ingenious and inventive, when it came to farming, making furniture, weaving, and building in a manner so direct and simple that it almost seems to do it a disfavor to call it by so fancy a name as *architecture*. They were functionalists in design, who make twentieth-century functionalists look like fuzzy-headed romantics, and they had, it appears, a sense of style, order, and simple elegance that few designers and craftsmen of any age have surpassed.

But about the barn. I saw it first a good many years ago when it was full of cows and had the warm, sweet-sour smell of a working dairy. A few Shakers were still farming the land then, acreage as neat as Shaker furniture and buildings, in a wide flat valley in the Berkshires on the road from Pittsfield to Albany. I walked up the ramp to the third level of this circular structure, the ramp that hay and silage wagons once drove up, to a very wide balcony that circles the interior. On the tier below were the cows in their wooden stanchions, facing the center, about four dozen of them. The slightly sloped, conical roof had a cupola at its center through which light came, much as it does from the hole in the dome of the Pantheon in Rome. From this hole, wooden beams like the spokes of a wheel fanned out to the rims of the circular roof, every second beam split about fifteen feet before it reached the rim, like a slender graceful Y. The effect was both delicate and strong, and it reminded me of the way Alvar Aalto, the great Finnish architect, used bent-wood members. Aalto's intention, however, was, to a considerable degree, aesthetic; the Shaker design was entirely practical. It served God's purpose and man's.

The reason for the three-tiered circular design, supported within by vertical and horizontal unfinished timbers, was that one man could feed the cattle. He moved around the circle throwing fodder from the balcony—but this is not a discourse on the management of cows.

Not quite. Cows determined the shape of the circular barn, and they kept it from falling apart. Sanitation laws in Massachusetts forced the cows out; the commonwealth decreed that cows could not be permitted to live on wooden floors. So when I next visited the barn, about ten years ago, it was empty and its splendid masonry was cracking apart. It seems that the body heat of the cows kept the stored winter crop and the walls themselves from freezing (its gets to thirty degrees below in Hancock once in a while), and the beautiful structure threatened to collapse. There was no way to repair it, so it was completely reconstructed. The original cost of the masonry in the mid-nineteenth century was five hundred dollars plus the board of the masons. Herman Melville, who was then living in Pittsfield, noted in his copy of *A History of Berkshire County* that this was "Amazing!"—amazingly expensive, amazing that the Shakers should have squandered all that money on such a foolish building. Nobody, it is believed, had ever built a circular dairy barn before.

Many have been built since, but I very much doubt if there is any that for quality of interior space or for delicacy and yet firmness of construction comes close to the Shaker Barn at Hancock, much less surpasses it.

Circular buildings are as old as architecture and farming. In

Neolithic times, about 10,000 B.C., those who are said to have invented farming lived in circular dwellings. Some Eskimos still build circular igloos, but the circular buildings with which we are most familiar are likely to have been ceremonial rather than practical: the Temple of Vesta, for example; the Pantheon, the Castel Sant'Angelo (Tomb of the emperor Hadrian) in Rome; the great baptistries in Florence and Pisa; the Temple of Heaven in Peking. (I am including sports arenas like one by Luigi Nervi in Rome, among ceremonial buildings, and why not? They also are modern temples, places of idolatry and fanaticism, some of which I too share.)

Attempts to put modern people in round houses or nearly round houses have not been successful enough to be generally adopted. After World War II, Buckminster Fuller designed a round house of aluminum that stood on a central column and could be rotated to accommodate the sun. It was called the Dymaxion House, and it was meant to be a solution to the postwar demand for inexpensive prefabricated housing. In the middle of the nineteenth century a phrenologist named O. S. Fowler published a little book called *A Home for All*, with plans for an octagonal house and a moral doctrine to justify it. It started a short-lived fad. If it wasn't a circle, it was an approach to one. Ten years or so ago I had lunch in an Oklahoma house that was based on circles and included a circular living room with a circular "conversation pit" and a circular swimming pool.

Where the cows lived in Hancock is a great deal handsomer. Now that the cows are gone, the round barn has become a temple of a sort, a temple of a dead religious sect that any gods could be proud of.

Architectural Digest, 1979

False Fronts

*H*ave you seen what they're doing to the old Commodore?" my friend Avery said, as we walked through Grand Central on our way to lunch. We had passed a hundred or so construction men in hard hats killing the end of their lunch hour. "They're covering it with mirrors."

The Commodore, on Forty-second Street, abuts the station. It was one of the rush of hotels built in New York in the first decades of the century, sumptuous buildings with vast glittering ballrooms, lobbies several stories high with ornate balconies and mezzanines and chandeliers, great expanses of marble, gilded woodwork, and a sense of spacious luxury and comfort. "Palaces for the people," they were called. In those days redcaps—not hard hats—lolled in the station waiting for work. They carried the travelers' luggage from Pullman cars to the hotel and were tipped with nickels and dimes. Grand Central's great concourse was not plastered with enormous illuminated advertisements, and the sun, which is now blocked by skyscrapers on three sides, streamed in long shafts through enormously tall windows.

A few days after Avery made his comment, I walked by the Commodore on the opposite side of Forty-second Street. For six stories or so, partly hidden by scaffolding, was the old stone facade, somewhat skinned down, and above it a sheet of glass rose toward the sky like the mirror Avery said it was. It looked rather beautiful with the tower of the Chrysler Building to its east and the dignified sculptured facade of Grant Central to its west—a patently false front bounded by two authentic and imaginative buildings, masterpieces in their different ways, expressions of power from different eras, the ages of the automobile and of the railroad.

The application of false fronts has a long and respectable, if not exactly noble, tradition in America. When it was no longer necessary to build dwellings that were merely basic shelter, we started to put false fronts on many of our houses. In the early 1800s we built temples of wood in a style we now call Greek Revival, with columns—also of wood—on their fronts in imitation of places where ancient pagans worshiped but would not have dreamed of living. Gods lived in temples, to be sure, and what was good enough for gods was good enough (or none too good) for the citizens of our young republic. Houses that were grand in front petered out into "cold cupboards" and woodsheds behind. Temples were so common they were celebrated in our early national anthem, "America," which sings of "rocks and rills . . . and templed hills."

Some years after the temple had gone out of fashion (it was followed briefly by the "Gothick" style) and "Queen Anne" had then become the thing, an architect named William M. Woollett published a small book in 1878 called *Old Homes Made New*. In it he explained with drawings how—by stripping off the columns and adding porches, peaked roofs, balconies, and "Elizabethan" chimneys—a temple could become as up-to-date as the fringed shawl, the Empress Eugénie hat, and the bustle.

The Chicago World's Fair in 1893 brought columns back into fashion. Subsequently they became all but mandatory for banks. There was something about them that bespoke solidity and conservatism. Banks that could not afford to rebuild or build anew simply added columns, which made those old buildings look like enterprises of unquestioned probity.

The American love affair with false fronts seems to be built into our character. When I was a boy living in a New York suburb, there was a fashion for "Tudor," which reduced to its minimum cliché (and it usually was) meant half-timbered exteriors—dark-brown beams, at what looked like structural angles, surrounded by rough cream-colored stucco. The beams bore no relation to what held the building up; they had an "olde English" look, which was their only functional purpose. Some suburban houses and apartment buildings were built in this manner, but there was a contractor in our suburb (and there must have been many like him elsewhere) who made a comfortable fortune stripping off Queen Anne porches and balconies and putting on Tudor slipcovers in their place. The Elizabethan chimneys were, of course, quite in keeping. By some eccentricity of taste, the Tudor rage was contemporary with the "Early American" craze for spinning wheels and cobbler's benches and corner cupboards. To be sure, they were both attempts to create the illusion of what have recently become popularized as "roots."

Merchants have long made a practice of using false fronts to attract trade. In the frontier towns it took the form of raising the front to make a one-story building look as though it were two stories. It didn't fool anybody, of course, but it made a building stand out from others near it.

Now the practice has been reversed. "Modern" storefronts are plastered on the street floor (sometimes the first two or three floors) of distinguished old buildings in order to seem up-to-date and on the usually accurate assumption that city folk do not look up. Only travelers look up. So, for example, the building that used to be Tiffany's splendid store, before it moved a few blocks up Fifth Avenue, now houses a discount store with a brand new bottom of shiny pressed metal of some sort and the same old top. The only store I can think of on Fifth Avenue that has retained its original elegance is the Scribner Book Store. It is now a designated city landmark.

Several years ago I drove from New York to Los Angeles and back, and wherever I looked there were new mansard roofs of shingles being applied—like false eyebrows or wigs—to supermarkets, fast-food restaurants, service stations, rural and urban shops, and motels. Here were hundreds of examples of how to be up-to-the-minute by turning back the clock.

While I can think of no civilization that has not set great store by cosmetic embellishment, I can think of none more devoted than America to what might be referred to as "Grecian formula" architecture.

Architectural Digest, 1980

The Architecture of Make-Believe

*I*t was a very long way around, and it took a very long time, but I went from New York to Asolo, an ancient hill town northwest of Venice, by way of Sarasota, Florida. Some years ago I had lectured in a small "Venetian" theater that is attached to the Ringling Museum in Sarasota. The theater dates from 1798, I have since learned, and had originally been built into a castle in Asolo. It was dismantled in the 1930s to make way for a movie theater, and an antiques dealer rescued it and put the pieces in storage. In the 1950s, A. Everett Austin, Jr., then the director of the Ringling, negotiated its purchase for about ten thousand dollars and, with state funds, reassembled and erected it. The museum's trustees acted wisely. The elegant little theater, a faint echo of the Fenice in Venice, has three tiers of tiny boxes and is ornamented with delightful Rococo details and painted in sympathetic colors. It is so intimate in scale that it seemed to me possible from its stage to shake hands with anyone in the audience.

My pleasant recollection of the Asolo theater, where Eleonora Duse performed as a child and to which she frequently returned during her career, was a reason—or at least an excuse—not merely to see the town from which it came, but to visit three of the theater's progenitors in that part of Italy. Asolo is a pretty, seductive town, loftily situated above fertile plains; architecturally, its most interesting attraction is the coming to it and the going from it. It is in Andrea Palladio country, no great distance from the magnificent villas he built in the sixteenth century as farmhouses for noble families in styles that have been imitated for country seats ever since. This is the district of the Villa Barbaro at Maser, with its trompe l'oeil frescoes by Veronese; the Villa Emo, with its wide, shallow steps up which horsemen could ride; the magnificent, though non-

Palladian, Villa Pisani; the Villa Rotunda, inspiration for Thomas
Jefferson's Monticello, and so on.

But this trip was not for villas; it was for the great theaters in
Vicenza, Sabbioneta, and Mantua. It is comparisons that lend spice
to travel.

Palladio's Teatro Olimpico in Vicenza, about an hour from Asolo,
is enfolded in a brick building that in no manner betrays the architectural magnificence it conceals. The entrance is through a garden
set about with Renaissance statues, now much the worse for wear
but no less handsome for that. In 1580 the Olympic Academy, a
group of humanists, most of them nobles, commissioned Palladio,
who was one of the group's founders, to design a theater for the
performance of ancient tragedies. The theater he subsequently created was based on what was known of Roman theaters. It is a lofty
space, filled with light and presided over by dozens of sculptured
members of the Academy in Roman dress.

The stage Palladio envisioned is as unlike a modern stage as the
accommodations for the audience are unlike the cushioned rows of
modern theaters. There is no proscenium, and the backdrop—it seems
a demeaning word for such a noble structure—is a permanent architectural facade penetrated by a central arch flanked by two large
portals. Through each of these are vistas of streets constructed in
false perspectives to give a deceptive sense of depth. The facade is
columned and ornamented with statues in niches and topped by a
series of reliefs depicting the labors of Hercules. If this sounds miscellaneous, it is not, but it is delightfully mischievous.

The Teatro Olimpico was still under construction when Palladio
died, and his assistant, Vicenzo Scamozzi, who designed the trompe
l'oeil street architecture, completed it in 1586.

A few years later Scamozzi was commissioned by the duke Ves-
pasiano Gonzaga to create a theater near his palace in Sabbioneta,
a town twenty miles south of Mantua. It bears a family resemblance to Palladio's theater, most particularly in the fringe of sculptured figures that stand in an arc above the loggia, which is embellished with frescoes depicting life at Gonzaga's court. The theater,
which can seat about 175 persons (fewer than the Sarasota theater), had only a brief active life. The duke died a few years after it
was finished, and his court slowly dissolved. For a while in this
century it was used as a movie house without suffering any essen-

tial damage, and it has now been restored to what must be close to its original splendor.

The Antonio Bibiena Theater in Mantua, built in 1767, epitomizes an entirely different sort of fantasy, the consequence of nearly two centuries of experiment and of the Baroque explosion of theatricality. Four generations of the Bibiena family added the dynamite of their imaginations to this explosion, which reverberated in all the major theaters of Europe, and its echoes were still to be heard in the American movie palaces of the 1930s. It is an ornate bell-shaped auditorium with four tiers of boxes—better for gossiping than for observance of a performance—and a stage faintly reminiscent of Palladio's. A custodian let me tiptoe in and sit in the back as the dress rehearsal of a ballet was in progress—a ballet of children, the oldest just in their teens, all dressed up as princes and princesses, slightly wobbly on their slippered feet and all deadly serious. It was an enchanting spectacle but not, surely, as enchanting as the first recital given there in 1770 by a boy the age of some of the dancers: Wolfgang Amadeus Mozart, then fourteen years old.

The three venerable theaters I visited from Asolo are all alive once more, but none is livelier than the Asolo in Sarasota. December and January constitute the opera season there. Autumn belongs to the Asolo State Theatre Company, and all year long the little theater proffers lectures on the arts, "fine" films (Monday nights), and chamber music. Mr. Austin, who found the theater and brought it to Sarasota, was an expert amateur magician. He never waved his wand more brilliantly than when he whisked to Florida the gem that Asolo had rejected.

Architectural Digest, 1983

Architecture as Photography

*O*ne of the obvious hazards of an architectural exhibition such as "Transformations in Modern Architecture," which originated at the Museum of Modern Art a few months ago, is that the photographers often come off as more interesting artists than the architects. If that does not seem like a fair statement, let me put it another way: Buildings thus seen are only as interesting as photographers make them, and many of them, one suspects, are not nearly as interesting in fact as in photo. Architecture on sensitized paper is only skin-deep so, in fact, "Transformations" is a photography show, not an architectural exhibition.

In very few of the buildings (there are about four hundred of them) that are pictured in the exhibition does one see photographs of what goes on within the external skin. In other words this is a "skin show," and its seductions, such as they are, are titillating but unreal. Of all the arts, architecture is the one that lends itself least to being judged out of its context and from the outside. To judge a building, one must get into it, or failing that, be shown—somehow—what is behind its outer walls.

That is not to say that "Transformations" is not an interesting and revealing exhibition. It is extremely interesting. It is not intended to display the "best" architecture of the two decades; in the words of Arthur Drexler, the director of the museum's Department of Architecture and Design, the exhibition illustrates "that the history of modern architecture during the last two decades involves ideas first propounded thirty or forty years ago."

This exhibition, then, is in a sense a postscript to another, a very revealing one, that took place at the museum in 1932, or forty-seven years ago. It was the museum's first architectural show; indeed, at that time no other museum in America had an architectural department. The show was called "Modern Architecture,

International Exhibition," and it was the crusade and brainchild of Alfred H. Barr, Jr., Henry-Russell Hitchcock, Jr., and Philip Johnson, who was not yet an architect. It was this exhibition that gave the International Style its name. It is difficult today to summon up the anger and spite that the exhibition evoked. It seemed to be a denial of everything the noble art of architecture stood for. It was anti-Christ to the Beaux-Arts religion, a religion to which the faithful had flocked for so long.

To some, "modern" architecture seemed excessively doctrinaire in its pronouncements, overburdened with theory and intellectual justification, if spare in everything else. Its slogans were too pat: "Less is more." "The machine for modern living." "Form follows function." It seemed antihuman, though the doctrine was loaded with generalizations about social reform. It was also antistyle, because style was identified with the eclecticism of the Beaux-Arts and was considered by the new mentors, Gropius, Mies van der Rohe, Oud, and Le Corbusier, as a dirty word. But if we mistrusted the doctrine, we were fascinated by the spare elegance and inventiveness of the buildings. Their unconventionality and their promise of new life did, indeed, hold our attention.

If the social doctrines seem to have been swamped by experience, the structural and, yes, "stylistic" ideas of the old masters of modern architecture dominate the buildings of the current exhibition. Here are the International Style trademarks. Here are the long horizontal stripes of Gropius pulled out to what seems a mile. Here are his and Mies's glass wall turned into vertical reflecting pools in which the occupants swim behind undulating towers of glass. Here is Le Corbusier's "brutalism" contorted into a newer, more accusing kind of public hair shirt in the Hayward Gallery in London and in Paul Rudolph's Art and Architecture Building at Yale. Here is what used to be the skin and bones of Mies's severe and refined building, now all skin and no bones, buildings that seem to exist only as reflections of the sky or of other buildings, that glisten with the sun, and whose surfaces move with the passing clouds—the photographer's dream.

That is not all, of course. There are buildings that look as though their architects had used the catalogue of another Museum of Modern Art exhibition, in 1964, "Architecture without Architects" by Bernard Rudofsky, as their textbook. These are buildings put together of units, like towns of single-room dwellings piled on hillsides. The result is a kind of instant vernacular suitable to an exhibition of photographs, for the buildings have much of the accidental quality often associated with tourists' snapshots and candid photographs.

If there are what seem to be caricatures of architecture in the exhibition, they are not the fault of the photographers. They have done their best with what they had to work with. If there are buildings that look better than they are, it is most assuredly the photographer's art that has made them so. Photographers have taken the place of the old-fashioned renderers who used pencil and brush and watercolor to create illusions of glorious buildings in beautiful surroundings from architects' rough sketches. I had the uneasy feeling that many of the buildings were designed more with an eye to how well they could be photographed than to how they would look to the naked eye—that it was illusion that mattered, not structure. Cosmetic architecture, you might call it, in which all that matters is the skin and its artificial blushes.

Architectural Digest, 1979

A Major Resurgence of Gothic

*S*omething is about to happen to a very old architectural friend of mine, my oldest such friend, that could not have happened ten years ago. My friend, which I have known intimately from the time I was nine, has grown in the interval, as friends will, and changed its looks, though the familiar features are still there. The friend—you will see why I call it that—is the Episcopal Cathedral of Saint John the Divine on Morningside Heights in New York, the biggest cathedral in Christendom. (Saint Peter's is twice as big, but strictly speaking, it is a basilica, not a cathedral.)

If I have an uncommon nostalgia about this great anachronistic pile of granite and limestone, I have good reason for it. I was a resident choirboy at Saint John's from the time I was nine until my voice changed in 1925 when I was fourteen. In other words, I worked there. This is not, however, about personal nostalgia; this is a Lazarus story—the revival of a revival that I thought had died.

Saint John the Divine has a curious history, though it is probably no more curious than that of any other great ecclesiastical pile. It has been built in spurts, sometimes headed in one stylistic direction, sometimes in another. The original plan was by the architects Heins & LaFarge, who won a competition for the design in 1883. The competition drawings, which have been preserved, ranged from gilded mosques to every variation of Gothic and Byzantine and Romanesque. By comparison, the Heins-LaFarge scheme was rather forthright: it was essentially Romanesque with rounded arches partially slip-covered in the "pointed style," or Gothic.

Work on the cathedral began in 1892 at a time when its towers above Morningside Heights could have been expected to dominate the city, for it was surrounded largely by open land. But the building ran into trouble before a stone was laid. Streams and quicksand beneath the surface took the architects by surprise, and a great deal of money vanished into the hole deep enough to reach bedrock. Finally, the choir, the ambulatory, and the apse were built—Gothic on the outside, Romanesque inside—and four massive granite arches were constructed for the crossing. They were intended to support a tremendous "lantern" and spire, but structurally they could not. For complex personal and technical reasons, there was a falling-out between the architects and the Cathedral's committee.

Enter fashion: Romanesque was out; Gothic was back in, so the committee lit on Ralph Adams Cram, a Boston architect who had built a number of successful churches in the Gothic manner. He was a designer with a secure knowledge of everything that had been built in the Middle Ages—the great centuries of Gothic cathedrals—and a master of refined detail. If Gothic had nothing to do with the twentieth century and modern technologies of construction and materials, that was no matter to him or the committee. What had been good enough for the city of Salisbury in England in 1220 was considered good enough for Morningside Heights in 1920. So Cram set about to conceal or undo as best he could the Romanesque of his predecessors and to impose his Gothic imagination on a building for the ages.

To the Romanesque choir and crossing he planned to add a very tall and very long five-aisle nave. When I first knew the cathedral in 1920, LaFarge's crossing was covered by a "temporary" tile dome, under which there was a very large wire netting, lest tiles should fall on the congregation more than 125 feet below. (None ever did. The dome is still there and the netting is gone.) One side of the crossing opened into the choir then, and the other three sides were walled up with concrete pierced with windows. The foundations of Cram's nave had been built, but none of its walls yet stood. We used to play soccer on what is now the floor of the nave; it was 250 feet long and 146 feet wide. The walls of the nave have long since been built, the west front partly completed, and the choir "Gothicized." Pearl Harbor put a stop to the work.

Now construction is about to be resumed. The second Gothic Revival in America is about to be re-revived.

This may not seem surprising until one considers that ten years or so ago the very idea of modern Gothic was a laughing matter. To contemporary architects and critics, the cathedral was an enormous expensive joke. The very idea of building a medieval monument at vast expense in a twentieth-century city was preposterous.

But within a few years, such has been the effect of landmarks preservation, architectural conservation, and the national preoccupation with the past that it is possible not only to embark on finishing Saint John's according to Cram's plan but to have it greeted with enthusiasm. The city fathers, local planning board, Morningside Heights community, and local architectural pundits are delighted.

And why not? This is the third Gothic Revival in America, following the one sponsored by the eloquent Andrew Jackson Downing in the 1840s and the boom in Collegiate Gothic in the 1890s, which lasted until about 1930 and covered campuses from New Haven to Chicago and points west with pointed arches and pinnacles, keeps, and imitation moats. I doubt if the revivification of Saint John's will spawn a crop of little Gothic churches across the nation, though it might. But as we enter what is being hailed as "a new era of architectural eclecticism," or so Philip Johnson insists, it is likely that its effects will inspire the searching pencils of young architects.

One of the rediscovered heroes of the new eclecticism is Raymond Hood, the designer from the 1920s of the Chicago Tribune Tower. And what style is it? Gothic, of course.

Architectural Digest, 1979

A *Matter of Scale*

*S*everal months ago I was at a benefit for the American Academy in Rome given in New York at the new AT&T building designed by Philip Johnson—a magnet for much disparagement and, in my opinion, much justified praise. The party began with cocktails in the main lobby, which opens onto Madison Avenue through magnificent arches of ecclesiastical dimensions. In the center of the lobby on a tall plinth sheathed in black marble stands a colossal (I use the word in its traditional, not its Hollywood, sense) statue by Evelyn Beatrice Longham, twenty-four feet tall and commonly known as the "Golden Boy." It once embellished the top of the old AT&T building in downtown New York where it was a sort of equivalent of *Freedom* by Thomas Crawford, which is the spike on the top of the Capitol in Washington. In the new building, in a great stone cage, perches this gilded, muscular, and winged male nude, symbolically grasping a handful of lightning and draped in cable somewhat in the way the Laocoön is draped in serpents. The sculpture is called *Spirit of Communication.*

Around the base of this giant, moving about and chattering amiably with drinks in their hands, were roughly two hundred men and women in evening dress. I said to architect Michael Graves, a trustee of the academy and once a Rome Prize Fellow there, "Have you noticed that everyone here looks about four feet tall?" "So they do," he said. It was Golden Boy that had shrunk us, he and the towering space needed to accommodate him. Perhaps only the depiction of a human figure could have done it; an equivalently big Calder stabile would not have had the same miniaturizing effect on this festive congregation of art benefactors.

Scale, I thought, can make Pygmies of us all, just as it can make us taller than we are. Scale is a matter of how the human body is measured by the space that contains it, indoors and out.

240

The basic measure of scale is man, and in architectural renderings and models it is customarily a six-foot figure. It is scale, of course, that determines to a great degree our pleasure or our dismay in our surroundings. Scale can be comforting or forbidding. It can strike us with awe or with fear. Because of its implications it can enliven or elevate our spirits, or disgust us. Philip Johnson, I'm sure, was trying to impress us (and his client), not demean us, and he was using a device as ancient as the temples of Greece where a colossal figure of a god all but filled the temple that housed it—"a goddess in a closet," as John McAndrew, the architectural historian, wrote about how the gold-and-ivory figure of Athena in the Parthenon must have looked.

Most of us give little thought to scale when we consider whether we are pleased by our surroundings or disturbed by them, but think of it or not, we feel it. Architects always have it in mind, even when they are considering it only in terms of the dollar value of rentable square feet. Ideally, they would like to give us all the room we could want in which to feel both free and protected, space that assures ease and dignity and self-respect, space that is scaled to our convenience and measured to fit our sense of propriety as well as our social aspirations and our cultural comfort.

There was a time not very long ago when, by contrast with most of today's public buildings and some private ones, space was used lavishly for purposes we no longer consider suitable—or, if they are suitable, no longer economical. In the great days of the railroads, for example, stations had an exuberant spaciousness that made passengers feel they were important participants in an exciting adventure. They were treated as essential elements in an expanding world made available to them by steel and steam. They were surrounded by marble walls (free of advertising), grand staircases, vaulted waiting rooms and soaring concourses. In the Grand Central Terminal in New York, they looked up with wonder at a heaven pierced with electric stars that picked out the constellations. In the Union Station in Washington, Daniel Burnham, the presiding architect of Chicago's Columbian Exposition of 1893, provided waiting passengers with a great hall to prepare them for great adventures. It was Daniel Burnham who said to his fellow architects of the exposition, "Make no little plans; they have no magic to stir men's blood."

How few public buildings today are built to stir men's blood!

Terminals have become compression chambers, especially air terminals, designed as though to freeze the blood for packaging in the capsules we will fly in with our elbows scrunched to our sides and our knees tucked under our chins. Office buildings, as soaring as they may be on the outside, with huge glass walls that reflect clouds and become part of the sky, are hives within, layers of low-ceilinged floor space rearrangeable at whim by partitions. Banks, once dignified, becolumned structures, are squashed into the bottoms of skyscrapers, and their customers are fed to the tellers' wickets in queues, between ropes, like sheep to the shearing.

I exaggerate the facts but not the spirit of the scale we so often have to live with. Bigness is not the measure of civilized scale; its elements are appropriateness and proportion. A cathedral or a temple can afford to be vast, and man seems very small within it—a relation between man and divinity that the spirit recognizes and by which we are awed and sometimes comforted. It is possible to be as entirely private in an immense man-made space like Saint Peter's in Rome as it is in a walled garden. On the other hand, anyone who has stood on the rim of the Grand Canyon has felt the mystery of a scale so great that man cannot be a measure of it.

Bigger is, obviously, by no means better. Even the greatest palaces—the Escorial or Versailles or Windsor—are made humane with little, person-size rooms like libraries and studies and boudoirs. Bigness for the sake of ostentation quickly grows tiresome or oppressive—elevating to the ego of its creator or owner, but diminishing to the rest of us. It is not the size of space that matters; it is the civilizing relationship between ourselves and space that we are pleased to call human scale and by which, in fact, we mean scale that is humane.

Architectural Digest, 1985

Revivals—What Next?

*N*ot so many years ago the climate of the arts was such that an artist hoped to be discovered before he died; now he hopes to be revived before he dies.

We live in an age of revivals, not just of individual artists but of entire schools. Ours is a time when we are constantly looking for something out of the past that will both temper and embellish the present, something that will give the effect of slowing the pace of change by which our lives are hustled from sensation to sensation. We seek to mollify the "onward and upward!" urge with the quieter gratifications of remembering the pleasures of the past, especially if they were ones we did not know first-hand, recalling what we assume to be concepts of the good life that inspired our forebears. Hence revivals.

We are likely to think of revivals less in terms of the fine arts than of architecture or the decorative arts, though they often go hand in hand. Some revivals we choose to live with are matters of adopted style, some are matters of mood. The ones that are stylish are usually intended to impress others, the ones of mood to satisfy ourselves. This is not to say that style and mood are separable; they are not. It is when style dominates mood that personality disappears and individuality along with it.

The revival of Early American in the 1920s became a chronic national nostalgia that needs no description. In the next decade the beginning of a Victorian revival followed but did not displace the barn-and-attic plundering of the Early American craze and preceded the fascination in the 1950s with turn-of-the-century Art Nouveau and its sensuous colors and curves. And in the 1970s, when Modern seemed to grow tiresome, Art Deco, which had been the bête noire of those who accepted the Bauhaus gospel of good design, exerted a new fascination on collectors, designers, and decorators. Now, once again, the Bauhaus, apple of the Museum of Modern Art's eye in the thirties and forties, is coming back into fashion, along with the furniture of the great Finnish architect Alvar Aalto, much of which had gone to the attic. At the moment there is a revival of crafts of all sorts—ceramics, textiles, glass, metalwork—which echoes the crafts movement of the late nineteenth century when William Morris was the prophet and guru of the "Artistic Craze." There is even a revival of interest today in the so-called Craftsman homes of Morris's American disciple Gustav Stickley and in the limp leather books and limp philosophical aphorisms of Elbert Hubbard, "the sage of East Aurora," New York. We look back not in anger but in whimsy.

The revival of artists, painters particularly, has followed a similar if not quite parallel path. It took until the 1960s for a revival of the long-despised Hudson River School of landscape painters (Cole, Durand, Church, and Kensett among them) to happen, for the bright sun of approbation again to light their broad, romantic depictions of wild real estate. The prices they brought rose to six figures and recently to seven. Their reclamation was followed by the revival of American Impressionists like Childe Hassam and Maurice Prendergast, who, to be sure, had not been forgotten but were way out of fashion, like faded debutantes. More recently, the painters of the Ashcan School, who had shocked art lovers in the early years of this century by their forthright depiction of the seamy side of city life, have become "important" again to dealers, museums, and collectors. And so it goes. Just now artists who worked for a bare livelihood on the New Deal's WPA art projects are coming back into favor, and American Abstractionists of the first rank, like Stuart Davis, and somewhat lesser-known ones, like George L. K. Morris and Ralston Crawford, are emerging as talents of authority. They had been overshadowed by the post–World War II artists of the New York School—Jackson Pollock, Robert Motherwell, Bradley Walker Tomlin, and other formidable talents.

But if we live in an age of revivals, we also live in a time of popgun reputations, of sharp reports followed by streams of empty air. Ours is an era when celebrity or notoriety—too often the same thing—happens quickly, but fame arrives at its usual ambling pace. An artist, visual or literary, of any appreciable talent can scarcely go unrecognized, such is the hunger of the media to find news where there is even the scantiest wink of interest or productive eccentricity, and such is the public appetite for new sensations. The ignored genius, a popular romantic figure made believable by such rare and idiosyncratic giants as van Gogh, is more myth than man, more phantom than woman. Even the most resolute recluse, for the very reason that he flees the limelight, is good copy.

Not, to be sure, that artists want to go undiscovered. As a rule they do not work just for themselves; they work to persuade, to please, to inform, perhaps to inspire, sometimes to jolt, to have their worth recognized (popularity is not the artist's measure of success; it is the approval of his peers), and to make a living—an often elusive by-product of recognition. The artist who is revived is not the one who hares off after a new style in order to attract attention but the one who pursues his private convictions because he believes he knows best.

Twenty-odd years ago I was the moderator of a symposium at which, for an audience of a few hundred, the novelist and poet Robert Penn Warren, the painter Ben Shahn, and the critic and composer Virgil Thomson were asked to discuss the question "Who does the artist work for?" The symposium took place at the MacDowell Colony, a New Hampshire institution that provides artists and writers, composers and filmmakers, with a quiet place to pursue their muses. Warren, who has a vast following of readers, said that he worked only for himself. Shahn, as famous as any American artist of his day, said that he had in mind a handful of friends whose judgment he respected. Thomson, now a grand old man of music, said: "It's like Spanish boys playing bullfight. It takes three of them: one to be the bull, one to be the matador, and one to stand by and shout *'Olé!'* "

The artist's or writer's hopes go beyond finding someone to shout "Olé!" That is merely being discovered. Olé's have a way of dwindling to murmurs of approbation and finally to silence. But happily for many of today's artists they live in a time when revivals not only are fashionable but come so quickly that they trip on each other's heels. Being shunted aside by new talents does not mean permanent obscurity. Those who speak eloquently and authentically for the spirit of their times will be heard from again, often a good deal sooner than they may expect.

Architectural Digest, 1985

Yesterday's World of Tomorrow

*M*ore than any man-contrived events I can think of, world's fairs leave a residue of nostalgia long after the crowds who have gazed at them and been awed by their wonders have departed. We keep celebrating the ones long gone. They are (or used to be—I do not know that there is a world's fair anywhere on the drawing boards today, though I may be wrong) like clouds of brightly colored balloons set free in the air with a separate imagination tied to each string. Whatever the practical purposes of these world's fairs (and they were often municipal promotion schemes at heart), they produced flights of fancy and ingenuity that were survived by concepts and products that affected everyone's future—everyone, that is, within the reach of science and the arts. They have also been responsible for a lot that is tawdry, meaningless, and silly, but so has every such megaton detonation of the popular imagination.

I am reminded of this by a small exhibition, at which I recently spent an hour, at the New-York Historical Society, one of the truly remarkable New York museums and libraries, to which New Yorkers and visitors to the city pay far less heed than they should. It is, as they say, "packed with goodies" delightfully displayed—a remarkable collection of nineteenth-century American painting, a portrait collection more impressive than that of the National Portrait Gallery in Washington, collections of handsome American silver, toys, fire engines, furniture, and many other distinguished or decorative or nostalgic objects. I admit to a certain bias, but not to exaggeration; I am a member of the society's board. The show was a room filled with memorabilia of the 1939 World's Fair, held on Flushing Meadow in New York City—the first fair I ever saw. It was called "The World of Tomorrow." It both was and wasn't.

Like all such fairs, it was in some respects not of this world at all—a never-never land, a fantasy made visible and tangible—a world of architectural spun sugar, of the smell of frying fat and roasting coffee, of formal gardens planted for a single season, of bands and calliopes and the splashing of fountains, of thousands upon thousands of delighted and often bewildered people. This world's fair, like nearly all fairs, was built primarily to vanish (though it hasn't entirely), its ephemeral magic to be blown away at the end of a summer like dandelion feathers. It opened for a second year, I remember, but the bloom was gone—wilted like a "son of" movie.

The World of Tomorrow looked at today was a world of architectural transition. It was not as purely Art Deco as the Chicago "Century of Progress" fair of 1933, and yet it was not the architecture of glass-curtain walls that began to turn cities into reflections of the sky after World War II. It had scale, there is no doubt of that. The big buildings were very big indeed, and they were filled with visions of man at his most mobile and, lest we forget, most "streamlined." Streamlining in 1939 was as fashionable in the design of a toaster or a telephone as of a railroad engine or an airplane. Functionalism was also big, sometimes only visually. The National Cash Register building, for example, was shaped like a tremendous white cash register, and every time another visitor came through one of the turnstiles at an entrance to the fair, the number at the top of the giant register jumped up by one; that number reached the millions before the summer was long gone. The Ford Motor Company building had a spiral ramp that looks now in photographs as though it were the grandfather of the modern parking garage, on the one hand, and of the ubiquitous traffic cloverleaf on the other. It was designed, incidentally, not by an architect but by the industrial designer Walter Dorwin Teague.

What remains of the fair is a solid building (now used largely for municipal offices), a spacious park, and Billy Rose's famous Aquacade where shows are still given each summer. More important, however, are the highways, which were initially constructed to handle the fair traffic and are now the principal access roads to the city's airports. Fantasy has left its useful and not unintentional residue.

If, however, you should ask anyone who had been to that fair or any member of the legion of world's fair buffs what pops first into his head when reminded of it, he would be likely to say the "Trylon and Perisphere," a towering white three-sided spike with a tremendous ball next to its base. It dominated the fair as the

Washington Monument dominates the Mall in Washington, D.C. It was the fair's "trademark," and it was adapted in miniature to all sorts of gadgets that were sold or given away as souvenirs. The New-York Historical Society's exhibition showed dozens of them. This streamlined symbol was made into salt and pepper shakers, into penholders for desks, into soap, thermos bottles, and belt buckles. It was used to ornament coasters and dishes and teapots, change purses, earrings, key cases, flashlights, bookends, and pocket mirrors. It was made into a game of ringtoss, and in one instance it embellished a small radio. The one I liked best was a tray on which the Trylon and Perisphere was set side by side with the facade of the Hall of Communications against a sky made of exotic butterfly wings.

The Trylon and Perisphere was designed by Harrison and Fouilhoux, one of the firms that worked on the plans of Rockefeller Center. How it took the shape it did is a story I believe has not been published before. The fair's unforgettable symbol was primarily the work of a young architect, Max Abramovitz, who later became Harrison's partner. He is an old friend of mine, and I once asked him how he arrived at the solution that became so famous.

"It was meant to represent the finite and the infinite," he said. "At first we thought that the Perisphere should be half below the ground so that what showed was a dome, but the engineers found out that there was a lot of water under that ground, and we could no more keep the ball down than you could keep a Ping-Pong ball half under water. Then we had the idea that we would have two square towers, one on either side of the ball, but the engineers said that that wouldn't work either because of the instability of the foundations in the wet ground; the towers might tip. It was they who suggested a triangular structure. If it tipped a little, the tilt would scarcely show. Nobody would notice it. That's how the Trylon happened. In the office we called it 'the ball and spike.' It was the fair's public relations boys who dreamed up 'Trylon and Perisphere.' "

What a nice example this is of the nature of world's fair architecture—the marriage of fact and fantasy, with fantasy yielding to practical considerations but undoubtedly remaining fantasy. I never think of the World of Tomorrow without the image of the Ping-Pong ball that wouldn't stay down. Tomorrows are like that.

Architectural Digest, 1980

Growing Old Gracefully

*H*ow tall is New York City's Chrysler Building? I was recently investigating the history of early skyscrapers, and I wanted to know. I remembered that for a few months in the late twenties or early thirties the Chrysler was the tallest structure in the world. Its spire, like a shimmering hatpin, towered above everything around it, rising from waves of silvery wedges of metal above gargoyles in the winged shapes of Chrysler radiator caps. In what seemed no time the Empire State Building had topped it with a tower that was supposed to be a mooring mast for dirigibles, a fantasy only a little less unreal, given the updrafts, than its use as King Kong's perch.

You would think—or, anyway, I thought—that modern histories of architecture would answer my question about the Chrysler Building in a jiffy. The building was not just a record-breaking structure of rather uncommon design; it is now one of the most respected, indeed lavishly praised, buildings of its time. But no. My architectural library is not extensive, but it is not skimpy, either. I went through volumes devoted to modern architecture, and I did not find even so much as a disparaging reference to the Chrysler. It might never have existed.

It was not ignored in the thirties by critics; it was figuratively spat upon. Any sprightly, forward-looking architectural pundit of the time was steeped in the doctrines of the Bauhaus as they were preached to Americans by the brand-new Museum of Modern Art. Philip Johnson, in his twenties and still years away from becoming an architect, Henry-Russell Hitchcock, Jr., now properly regarded as the dean of architectural historians in America, and Alfred Barr, then the thirty-year-old founding director of the museum, were the principal bearers of "the word" as it had been promulgated by Walter Gropius, first in Weimar then in Dessau, in the 1920s.

The Chrysler Building fit none of the Bauhaus standards of frankly

249

expressed functionalism but fell rather into what Barr called "the trivial bad taste of Paris 'modernistic.' " This, in his view, was worse than bad taste—it was vulgar; and its extravagant ornament was cheap rhinestones thrown in the public's face.

I believed it; so did my friends. We thought the Chrysler Building was pure "kitsch," a word we felt rather sophisticated to know at all in those days. There was no doubt that it was "modernistic," a disparaging epithet we applied freely and smugly to what is now so treasured by so many as Art Deco.

Our blind spot!

A few years ago Philip Johnson spoke on the architecture of the thirties. This once ardent disciple of the Bauhaus, and still its warm admirer, said in effect: "We were so passionately concerned with the doctrine of the new architecture that opposed the traditions of the Beaux-Arts and its silly classic-romantic teachings that we were wearing blinders. Anything that did not fit our concept of honest architecture was contemptible." (I do neither his eloquence nor his wit justice. Incidentally, can you think of any building more eloquent in its statement of principle, or more witty, than Johnson's "glass house"?)

Quite recently I came upon an article about Minoru Yamasaki's design for the World Trade Center in New York, whose twin towers, like the Chrysler Building, were momentarily the tallest structures anywhere. The author says of Yamasaki's rectangular, unbroken soaring structures: "With bearing wall construction there can be no graceful setbacks and spires that distinguish such old-time New York skyscrapers as the Empire State Building and the Chrysler Building." And he quotes another critic, who called Yamasaki "a popular architectural kitsch-monger."

It is obvious that what is kitsch to one generation is often sublime to the next. It never would have occurred to my generation to think there was anything graceful about what we regarded as the ponderous and pompous Empire State Building or the claptrap Chrysler confection.

How blind we were! How dogmatic! How condescending! How like our successors!

I would not have it otherwise. We were convinced of the morality of our cause, the clarity of our vision, and the infallibility of our logic. We knew where the social responsibilities of architecture lay and what physical shapes they should take. We knew good from bad and right from wrong. We knew the Chrysler Building was bad and wrong and kitsch, just as our successors know it is good and right and beautiful. Agreement on principles and utter disagreement on forms (or, if you prefer, the constancy of belief and the mobility of taste) are what keep architecture from stagnation.

In case you care, the answer to the question I first posed is 1,046 feet. The Empire State is 1,250; the World Trade Center, 1,350; and the Sears Tower in Chicago 1,454—a gain of about ten feet a year for forty-odd years. I should have looked in the *World Almanac* in the first place.

Architectural Digest, 1977

Exploring Inner Space

*O*uter space, a preoccupation of our time (and perhaps of time from now on), belongs to astronomers, as it has at least since Ptolemy, and to a special brand of mechanics called astronauts and their dispatchers. It also belongs to theologians, in a manner of speaking, to cartoonists, special-effects men and women and other dissemblers of the silver screen, to science fiction writers, and, of course, to children and the people who create their battery-driven toys. It does not belong to artists, except to illustrators who make an attempt at explaining what scientists see in their mind's eyes; call them technical draftsmen.

Artists have quite enough on their hands with inner space—more than enough. And so, it seems, do most of the rest of us. Indeed, three dimensions—the space we live and move in—are complexities we often take comfort in reducing to two manageable dimensions. We like the great outdoors and distant views of vast landscapes and cityscapes, and we think of ourselves as an exceedingly mobile people, always on the road or in the air, on the go, moving through one space on our way to another. And yet we spend most of our lives living two-dimensional existences out of preference. We take in the world, both physical and intellectual, on the flat, because we like it that way and can make sense of it.

The history of art since the Cro-Magnons painted bison on the walls of the caves of Altamira in northern Spain, probably fifteen thousand years ago (and who knows how long before that?), has been the conversion of the round to the flat, of three dimensions to two. But it has also been the continual process of turning observations, ideas, beliefs, and flights of imagination into comprehensible, though often mysterious, flat pictures. (It is fashionable today to call them images.) This is not just so they can be understood by others but so they can be trapped and made permanent—the fleeting beast made to stop in its leap, the passing thought reduced to a symbol, sometimes elaborate, sometimes simple, sometimes a pictograph, a diagram, or words on paper.

Cartographers have made the real world flat and therefore comprehensible and possible to get around in. When it was proved to most people's satisfaction in the fifteenth century that the world was round, it then had to be made flat again. Globes were reduced to two dimensions by devices such as Gerardus Mercator's projection, a flat symbol for a spherical world. Globes are inconvenient, if ornamental; they don't lie flat in a drawer or hang on a wall or fit in a glove compartment. For everyday purposes, the fact that the world is round is a nuisance. So it is logical that we should live in a two-dimensional world a great deal of the time, and it is the arts—fine, crude, and merely practical—that make this possible. More than that, they determine what we think our two-dimensional world looks like.

Very little of what the artist presents to us in two dimensions bears more than a symbolic resemblance to reality, and yet we not only understand it at once but accept it as valid. Each generation has its own set of lenses, its own way, for example, of seeing what a face looks like or what makes an acceptable rendering of a landscape or a textile, a tree or a cloud. It would be easy to call this interpretation rather than observation, but the history of art demonstrates that observation changes radically from one time to another in the same way that what is important to a given time and particular people changes.

There are styles of seeing just as there are styles of dressing, of makeup, of hairdos. An eighteenth-century portrait, for example, has eyes and nose and mouth that are characteristically eighteenth century because that is the way they looked to eighteenth-century eyes, what people then wanted them to look like and what artists taught them to expect. Nineteenth-century faces have a very different look, not because faces change but because the way artists see and reduce them to flat surfaces change. The two-dimensional world of the nineteenth century was as different from the eighteenth century two-dimensional world as it is from our world, as a glance at landscapes painted in each century attests. Inner space is no more predictable than outer space, perhaps less predictable.

Not all, but nearly all, of our impressions of what I have chosen to call inner space are illusions on flat surfaces—photographs, television tubes, movie screens, pictures on walls and in books and magazines. Though technical ingenuity has made possible the projection of three-dimensional images on the screen, it is flat pictures that have prevailed. While occasionally 3-D is fun, mostly it is gimmicky and tiring—even when inner space moves, we like it to keep its place on a flat surface. This is illusion enough for us. When movies were first shown in nickelodeons at the beginning of the century, a picture of a train rushing toward the audience caused panic in the theater. Even now, when a batter hits a line drive directly at the television camera, I duck. If it were in 3-D, I'd dive.

The fact is that we can experience inner space constantly without anxiety because we know it is not going to engulf us. It is going to stay right where the artist or camera has put it for our instruction, to stimulate but not overwhelm our emotions and sometimes to challenge our wits. We do not have to don a space suit and climb into a capsule to explore. We don't even have to dicker with a travel agent or suffer the indifference of a room clerk. Inner space comes to us, and we can accept it or leave it as the whim of the moment takes us.

Architectural Digest, 1986

ABOUT THE AUTHOR

RUSSELL LYNES was born in Great Barrington, Massachusetts, in 1910, graduated from Yale in 1932, and twelve years later joined the editorial staff of *Harper's Magazine,* of which he was managing editor from 1948 to 1968. He is the author of twelve books, including this one, of which *The Tastemakers, Confessions of a Dilettante, The Art-Makers of Nineteenth Century America, Good Old Modern,* and *More Than Meets the Eye* are concerned primarily with the arts and American society. His articles and essays have appeared in many magazines and journals, and he has lectured in many universities and museums. He has written regular columns for *Harper's* ("After Hours"), *Art in America* ("The State of Taste"), and *Architectural Digest,* where "Russell Lynes Observes" appeared from 1974 to 1987. He has served on the Landmarks Preservation and Arts commissions of New York, been president of the Archives of American Art, the MacDowell Colony, and the Century Association, and served on the boards of the American Academy in Rome, the New-York Historical Society, and the Council of Cooper-Hewitt Museum. He is a Fellow of the Society of American Historians.